BLITZ SPIRIT

Dear Matey J,

You are
a good egg. O ← you

Love
from
your big best
sister

X

BLITZ SPIRIT

*Voices of Britain
Living Through Crisis,
1939–1945*

— Becky Brown
with the Mass Observation Archive

H
HODDER &
STOUGHTON

First published in Great Britain in 2020 by Hodder & Stoughton
An Hachette UK company

1

Copyright © Becky Brown 2020

Mass Observation material © The Trustees of the Mass Observation Archive

The right of Becky Brown to be identified as the Author of the Work has been
asserted by her in accordance with the Copyright, Designs and Patents Act 1988.

A CIP catalogue record for this title is available from the British Library

Hardback ISBN 9781529347050
eBook ISBN 9781529347043

Typeset in Sabon MT by Hewer Text UK Ltd, Edinburgh
Printed and bound in Great Britain by Clays Ltd, Elcograf S.p.A.

Hodder & Stoughton policy is to use papers that are natural, renewable
and recyclable products and made from wood grown in sustainable
forests. The logging and manufacturing processes are expected to
conform to the environmental regulations of the country of origin.

Hodder & Stoughton Ltd
Carmelite House
50 Victoria Embankment
London EC4Y 0DZ

www.hodder.co.uk

For Tom

CONTENTS

INTRODUCTION

'Today I feel crisis-blasé. I am unmoved by what the beastly press says. I don't believe a word of their reportage'
30 August 1939, four days before the outbreak of the Second
World War.

At the start of 2020, I was deeply immersed in the Mass-Observation Archive. This extraordinary repository of ordinary people's diaries, written for the most part during the Second World War, contains over a million pages' worth of writing. These pieces of paper, whether pencil-scribbled scrap or meticulously typed letterhead, document every conceivable response to crisis, from bravery to cowardice, stoicism to panic, selfishness to selflessness. These accounts, merely academically interesting to me the year before, provoked in 2020 a new and mysterious feeling. I examined it for a while before reaching my verdict: déjà vu.

'The modern world does not seem to care about lives being lost' (1939)

'It does seem that the Govt. do not take enough action in actually <u>preventing</u> the population from doing unnecessary travelling' (1941)

'Events are moving at an astonishing rate. I feel as if I am poised on a precipice, waiting for the signal to start off on the giddy plunge into "after the war".' (1945)

There, in words written over three-quarters of a century ago, were the same questions, pontifications, hopes and invectives that were crowding my social media feeds and pouring plaintively down my phone. They were utterly relatable, and in stark contrast to everything I thought I understood about life during the Second World War. Those years, which live on for many as the stuff of legend – rich pickings for novels and films, fridge magnets and motivational posters – are traditionally bathed in the golden glow of 'Blitz Spirit'. This alleged wartime phenomenon has little space for twenty-first-century human frailties such as succumbing to unnecessary trips to the shops, or hugging your grandmother. We are used to hearing about 'Blitz Spirit' as a psychological bunting that festooned the national mind, a one-size-fits-all utility suit that the nation donned for The Duration, allowing every person to dig their way to victory with a song and a smile.

The diaries of Mass-Observation's participants affirm what we should already know – that few people can indefinitely repress their thoughts, hopes and desires for a greater cause. Each of the voices preserved in the Archive offers resounding proof that the home front was a tableau of 46 million human beings. In reading their accounts we are reminded that, before August 1939, these were normal people living normal lives. They bought what they could afford and ate what they fancied. They planned careers and raised families. Most were free to go where they pleased, when they pleased.

The declaration of war in September 1939 heralded the beginning of six years of dizzying disruption. Once-tight-knit families found themselves at opposite ends of the country, and those who remained at home gave over lovingly tended lawns to vegetable patches and bomb shelters. Hopes and habits held for decades vanished as thousands ended their studies or cut short promising careers. Others put dreams of having a family or pursuing a quiet retirement on hold. The sacrifices they were asked to make were extraordinary in their breadth and variety, and came with absolutely no guarantee of winning.

The credibility of the grin-and-bear-it nature of Blitz Spirit is predicated on foreknowledge of an inevitable victory. This is what makes the testimonies held in the Mass-Observation Archive so valuable and so poignant – they are riddled with fear of defeat. These are lives experienced by the minute and the day, not the week or the year. The rawness of their stories challenges the potent forces of nostalgia and hindsight, both of which have conspired to distort our view of our national ability to deal with crisis.

Mass-Observation (or 'MO' as it was affectionately termed by its participants) was founded in 1937 with exactly that idea in mind – to tell a truer, fuller version of events than was available in the newspapers or recorded in the history books. The three men behind it were anthropologist and polymath Tom Harrisson, painter and film-maker Humphrey Jennings and poet and journalist Charles Madge. Their aim, which they laid out in a letter published in the *New Statesman*, was to create an 'anthropology of ourselves' – a study of the everyday lives of ordinary British people. From MO's inception until the early 1950s, a variety of first- and second-hand observation schemes were carried out. Key among these was a volunteer group of around 500 people called the 'National Panel of Diarists'. They came from all walks of life and almost every part of the UK, and submitted their personal diaries on a monthly basis from August 1939 onwards. Others replied to regular questionnaires called 'Directives', which elicited their opinions on the burning issues of the day, and the smouldering mundanities of their day-to-day lives.

Harrisson, who incidentally wore 'ornithologist' as one of his many hats, saw MO as 'the study of Britons rather as if they were birds'. I have approached the diaries in that same spirit – not as a historian or anthropologist (for I have no claim to either title) but instead as an enthusiastic watcher of people and their behaviour. Just as there is often more pleasure to be found in watching blackbirds in the garden than parrots at the zoo, I have delighted in spotting the familiar. These moments, these frissons of connection between who we are now and who we were then, took on almost magical significance. As if bringing each person briefly back to life.

Reading someone else's diary feels like a powerful gesture of solidarity, an affirmation that says: 'I hear you, I recognise that you lived.' The MO diaries are a window into hundreds of existences, each distinct, all valuable. Participation was optional and diarists were welcome to commit whatever amount of time they wished. Some wrote faithfully and continuously throughout the war (and occasionally for long after), others wrote in bursts that fell years apart. Some wrote once and never again. Some ignored the war and were preoccupied by the personal intricacies of their immediate circle. Others ignored their own lives entirely, seeing them, perhaps, as unimportant in the face of the grand sweep of the political or military landscape. Most, however, fall somewhere in between and chose to interweave accounts of their day-to-day lives with their thoughts and responses to the national and international situation.

In all of their voices, preserved by MO's magnificent act of scholarly foresight, we hear a vibrant, discordant humanity and see the ordinary lives that must necessarily continue behind an extraordinary event. I hope it brings comfort to others, as it has to me, to realise that the idea of one 'Blitz Spirit' is as untruthful as it is patronising. In the face of chaos and tragedy we all do what we can to 'get by' – we are all dually significant and insignificant in the eyes of history.

A note on diarists

In constructing *Blitz Spirit* I've preserved the anonymity under which the Mass-Observation participants chose to write, and have duly reproduced each entry under the diarist's assigned four-digit MO Archive number, adding – for the benefit of context – a note of their gender, profession and location.

That said, this book joins a long line of publications that have drawn from the Mass-Observation Archive, and I've inevitably stumbled upon voices I recognised from earlier books. This has been one of the great joys of the compilation process, akin to bumping into old friends in the street.

For those who are curious to explore beyond this book, I've included a list of these previously published diarists and the books in which their voices may be found in 'Further Reading'.

A note on occupations and locations

It was not unusual for people to change jobs on multiple occasions throughout the war. This was due, in large part, to either necessity or increased opportunity. When an Observer changed occupation I have amended their title accordingly.

Some villages, towns and cities have changed counties since the 1940s. Where an Observer clearly stated their county throughout their diary I have preserved their labelling, even if it is now technically erroneous. Where their county went unstated by the Observer, I have employed my own labelling based on current designations.

1. IT'S A PITY THE WAR HAS COME JUST NOW

August to December 1939

<pre>
Monday September 11

        How long will it last ? Three clients have
asked me today. I say three years, the official
estimate; it's easier than speculating. Really I don't
think it will last so long. Germany will crack under
the strain.
        I saw B. who is in the balloon barrage. He
complains of ' lack of sleep and not enough time
to myself, and the work is bloody hard.
        The landlady's sister is distressed. Her son
has been called up for overseas service. ' They are
sending him out there without enough experience to be
killed. I have brought him up to this age (19) just
for nothing it seems. If only we mothers could get
together and let the world know we don't want to
go to war with any country.
        If only Chamberlain had been honest. He could
have delivered a speech on the 3rd, beginning something
like this ; ' I am afraid my policy has led this
country into a hell of a mess. If I am to maintain my
prestige, and of course the prestige of my country, then
we must go to war. No I am not a Christian. If I was
I should be ready to answer evil with good. Sorry and
all that. '
        A girl, nineteen, typist, sophisticated, said,
' its a pity the war has come just now, to spoil the
best years of my life, jsut when I want to have a good
time. '

Tuesday.September 12.

        The prospect of three years of this war-contolled
life is awful. The wish to escape grows stronger.
</pre>

'A girl, nineteen, typist, sophisticated, said "It's a pity the war has come just now, to spoil the best years of my life, just when I want to have a good time." '

In August's Directive, Mass-Observation sends out a request for people to keep and submit personal diaries of what is then termed 'The Crisis'. Within days 'The Crisis' had mutated into 'The War', and the voluntary Observers find themselves documenting the opening salvos of a global conflict – one that will last for six years and impact each and every person in an unprecedented number of ways.

On 3 September 1939, Britain declares war on Germany. Across the country sweeping measures are put in place to avoid loss of life: nightly blackouts are instituted, cinemas and theatres closed, hospitals cleared to make room for civilian casualties that are anticipated to reach into the tens of thousands. Almost a million vulnerable people are evacuated from cities into 'safe areas', where they are joined by hordes of 'private' evacuees, those with the financial means to relocate of their own accord. However, by the end of the year this all seems to be a fuss about nothing. No bombs have fallen, no invading armies have arrived, and the conflict has been largely confined to naval battles.

For those on the home front, the early months are defined by exceptionally rapid change and accompanying panic. Pre-emptive stockpiling (and the ensuing shortages) drive panic-buying. Many are relocated hundreds of miles from home – separated from parents, children, friends and family – and feel terribly displaced. For others the unfamiliarity of the situation is invigorating, with the war a welcome change from the months and years of uneasy peace that preceded it. But as 1939 hurries to a close with no sign of the promised dangers, many find themselves trying to get back to (or perhaps just drifting towards) normal life again. The public are at odds over what is the 'correct' behaviour and the right level of caution. Their scrutiny of each other is close and often merciless. For every person angered by a mother recalling her children from the countryside there is another irritated by being ordered to bring their gas mask to the theatre or livid at the thought of digging up a prize lawn for potatoes. The longer-term risks – Death by gas attack! Starvation! – feel perhaps too distant, or too terrible, to contemplate. Humour and stoicism are typical, thriving on the benign novelty of what will later be called 'The Phoney War'.

*   *   *

Diarist 5228, M, Textile Warehouseman, Birmingham, 27/08/39
A young fellow, apparently oblivious of the sea and sunshine is reading a Sunday paper, an article entitled, 'What War Would Mean to You.' Fool. I am on holiday. I try to dismiss the crisis. It breaks in on my thoughts. The landlord of the local inn has put up a large notice: DON'T GET THE JITTERS. DRINK MY BITTERS.

Diarist 5342, F, Housewife, London, 28/08/39
Situation seemed so critical this morning that I decided to dash up to town & get my hair done – it was overdue last week & I was pretty woolly. Told H. & he said 'Why worry – can't you go locally if there is a war?' Know I shall which was why I determined to have one more decent cut & set.

Diarist 5228, M, Textile Warehouseman, Birmingham, 30/08/39
Human nature can't play up to large-scale tension like this for an indefinite period. Mass feelings, like individual ones, reach a limit. Today I feel crisis-blasé. I am unmoved by what the beastly press says. I don't believe a word of their reportage, that is how I

feel. I bought a News Chronicle this morning, read the serial, and threw it away. The feeling that Hitler's got to talk seems more general. 'If he had been intent on war,' said a middle-aged woman, 'he would have struck last weekend. But you know what I think, there'll be a revolution in Germany. They won't stand him. They aren't all behind him.' Several have voiced this opinion without suggesting how such a revolution would begin or who will start it. It seems a wish-fulfilment thought to me.

Diarist 5402, F, Retired Teacher, Kingsbury, London, 31/08/39
Aug 31 finds me in a sister's bungalow in Bucks. News in the morning's paper all seemed stale, 6 o'clock news, that evacuation is to start tomorrow, brings realisation of what this means tonight to parents, teachers & hostesses. For the first time (I am a semi-invalid) begin to wonder what I could do to help – think it just possible that I could mind or perhaps teach some children a few hours daily, & so relieve someone else.

Diarist 5399, F, Retired Nurse, Steyning, West Sussex, 31/08/39
Have had a letter from a woman in Luxembourg who has worked over here for five years. The woman for whom she has worked for years, has written to tell her that she is having two refugees in her house and will not want her. The woman had gone home on holiday. Her employer let her buy a return ticket and has given her no notice. My friend is coming back and has asked if she may come and stay until she can get another post. I said 'Of course.' Her employer, a man and wife, not old, and in good health (both of them) live in Angmering and have done all they can to get out of taking any children from evacuation areas. It is likely they are taking refugee women so as to be able to say they are full up, and

incidentally they will get the housework done cheaply. There is a good deal of this selfishness among the middle class of retired people.

Diarist 5011, M, Clerk, London, 31/08/39
On leaving the cinema, we find that three newspaper sellers are doing a very brisk business, though their papers contain no further news than those their customers bought 3 hours before. But somehow it seems as though anything might have happened in the interval, it seems so long.

Diarist 5228, M, Textile Warehouseman, Birmingham, 31/08/39
Hope existed until the moment we heard that tomorrow children are to be sent into the country. Evacuation; another word which has suddenly entered the plain man's vocabulary. I had the feeling that such a step would not be taken unless 'they were expecting it'. For the third time I had the feeling of last Sept, that queer mixture of fear and vague excitement, and a general inability to accept the wide consequences.

Diarist 5390, F, Shipping Firm Secretary, Glasgow, 01/09/39
At lunchtime I bought two small bottles of sal volatile.

This morning Mr. Mitchell said 'Hoarding is now illegal. This will put an end to your little game.' I said, 'After war is declared I shall buy nothing, believing that the goods in the shops should go to those who are too poor to have laid in stocks already. Just at the moment I am hanging between two decisions, one that buying is patriotic foresight, and the other that it is a dirty form of hoarding.'

Diarist 5055, M, Teacher, Llandovery, Caernarvonshire, 01/09/39

Sermons in the school Chapel on Sundays last term always had a few remarks about the 'terrible times' in which we were living. This term started in the same way but for the last three Sundays we have had no mention of the war; sermons have reverted to type and deal with 'temptations', 'animal lusts' and the observance of the Church's biddings for Lent. Oddly enough there has been no mention of rationing!

Diarist 5390, F, Shipping Firm Secretary, Glasgow, 02/09/39

Wireless on all the evening. If the youth of fifty years hence should ask me how I reacted to the tremendous events of today, I expect I shall 'remember' hanging on the announcer's words. But the truth is I only listened with half an ear. I am desperately anxious to get our house arranged in such a way that we can best handle whatever may arise. For some time past I have been collecting big tins with tight-fitting lids, and I have been begging Mother to put all the groceries at present in cardboard boxes into tins, partly as a protection against mice, partly as a protection against damp, and partly as a protection against gas. Mother, who is a 'Sunshine Susie' does not expect any of these troubles.

Diarist 5340, F, Landed Gentry, Hatfield Peverel, Essex, 03/09/39

When [the evacuees] had gone I enjoyed the 'silence singing softly backward' until 11.15 when I had been told by the gardener an important announcement would be given out on the wireless. It would either be peace or war & anxiety increased as the time drew near. Then it was the latter. I stood up for God save the King & my little dog got out of her basket & stood beside me.

At eleven o'clock this morning, Mr. Chamberlain announced that we were at war with Germany. Almost immediately after came an air-raid warning, which, although it was later proved to have been a false alarm, was disturbing by its suddenness. All that beautiful Sunday, we were practically confined indoors. Although over half a million persons have been evacuated from London by the government, quite as many have evacuated themselves, so that where I was looked amazingly empty. About the only persons remaining seem to be those concerned with A.R.P. A host of barrage balloons hovered overhead. Looking up one road, lined by trees on both sides, I counted thirty-two. Another alarm in the middle of the night, had us hurriedly downstairs in what clothes we could slip on. There we sat, quiet and half asleep, for fifteen minutes, until the all-clear sounded. As my family were going to the South coast, and I to the East, it was a sad farewell, for we could not tell when we would be together again.

Waited anxiously in morning for news. Heard that Govt had proclaimed State of War. Awful feeling of hopelessness so great that suggestion that we could help families from Fulham stranded in house next door came as a relief. Householders being away, 6 Mothers and 17 children (under 5 years) were parked there late last night as 8000 children landed in Woking with insufficient billets. Last night women had slept on the floor. My sister and I ransacked locked bedrooms, dragged out more mattresses and made more beds. Went for a walk on the common, a most beautiful, calm, peaceful day, impossible to believe horrors are taking place somewhere, a mood of incredulity, anxiety and yet light-heartedness for the beauty of the day filled us, and we speculated on everything that might happen and what the future would bring. In ordinary life one can be more or less certain of the inevitability of one day's routine following another, but now . . .

Diarist 5228, M, Textile Warehouseman, Birmingham, 03/09/39
Clearly the motive for citizens to join ARP posts was not prompted entirely by love of country. (I have done no ARP work myself, and I don't want to belittle those who have sincerely given their time to do it). But an air-raid warden walking in one of our parks heard the news at eleven. At once he compelled all the children to go home at once if they hadn't a gas mask. A misuse of power. Does he realise that the very thing we are about to fight is that misuse of power on a broader scale?

Diarist 5390, F, Shipping Firm Secretary, Glasgow, 03/09/39
Today is just like an 'ordinary' Sunday but somehow it is not an 'ordinary' Sunday. We have had our meals at the same time. I have finished clearing out the periodicals and spent quite a time on Mass-Observation. Then there has been the usual Sunday ironing and mending for tomorrow. It has been just like an 'ordinary' Sunday, but all the time there is the thought 'This is the last of the ordinary Sundays.'

Diarist 5199, M, Railway Draughtsman, Wilmslow, Cheshire, 03/09/39

In Sale, women residents were angry at evacuated children being insufficient to go round! Along a certain road, the residents had agreed to take certain numbers of children. Half the road had been provided with their quotas, and then, alas, the flow of children ceased, and then – disappointment and anger!

Diarist 5228, M, Textile Warehouseman, Birmingham, 05/09/39

Mrs B—, a medium, says she has been in touch with the spirit of Napoleon, who informed her that the war would last for sixty-one years. If I live I shall be eighty-six when peace comes. A leaden thought.

Diarist 5262, F, Artist, London, 09/09/39

Coming down we stopped at the village of Clee St. Margaret and asked a kind-looking woman for tea. It was really a small farm, – an ancient stone cottage with a byre and garden, and two sheepdogs lying on the lawn. While we waited for the kettle to boil on the wood fire, two children, 2 and 3 ½ came in. They were Londoners, speaking real Cockney without dental consonants, and were staying without their parents. The little boy was very pert and confiding, and sat on R's knee and asked for what he wanted. The woman picked him up and kissed him absent-mindedly while she talked to us. He threw his arms around her neck, and she said placidly 'Oh yes, he's taken a fancy to me.'

Diarist 5228, M, Textile Warehouseman, Birmingham, 11/09/39
A girl, nineteen, typist, sophisticated, said 'it's a pity the war has come just now, to spoil the best years of my life, just when I want to have a good time.'

Diarist 5007, M, Journalist, Horley, Surrey, 14/09/39
The nation seems to be divided into 2 camps. Those who lust for blood & glory & are joining up, and those who are carrying on as usual (or would if they hadn't been sacked from their jobs by the thousand). The former seem to be no better than lowest animals, whereas the latter seem to be largely – tho' not by any means entirely – apathetic. As someone said, the other day 'sell the bloody Poles – the whole lot of them, who cares. And next year, sell the Rumanians. They're no better than the Nazis, neither is the d— British Empire!'

Diarist 5434, F, Psychiatric Nurse, Gosforth, Newcastle-upon-Tyne, 14/09/39
[I am keeping this diary] in order that in this war that began on Sept 3rd 1939 I might find some relief for the feelings I have about this terrible calamity & those I have about being in [Newcastle-upon-Tyne City Mental Hospital] at such a time (& also at any time).

Diarist 5402, F, Retired Teacher, Kingsbury, London, 19/09/39
My ten-year-old niece departed for Boarding school – after many tears. Wonder what effect the widespread break-up of family life will have on next generation?

<u>Diarist 5376, F, Teacher, Burwash Weald, East Sussex, 26/09/39</u>
We feel we have drawn a lucky one in the evacuee lottery, with nice parents, & we are really fond of her. Should be sorry to lose her & hate to risk possible new one.

<u>Diarist 5315, F, Teacher, Taunton, Somerset</u>
<u>(evacuated from London), 30/09/39</u>
I ought to say that my <u>physical</u> reaction to the war was a light-headedness that made even ordinary duties accompanying evac-uation, billeting, visiting foster-parents, keeping my own in reasonably good spirits a strain. I was continually afraid my head would fall forward, or that the ground wouldn't be there at my next step. This still recurs.

That was probably partly responsible for a great feeling of unreality & an incapacity to coordinate the various parts of my life. I therefore felt I was a most unreliable observer.

<u>Diarist 5163, M, Park Keeper, Eltham, London, 01/10/39</u>
Churchill on the radio at 9-15 sums up the first month of the war. A fine cheering talk – Churchill at his best. His opinion of the Russian intervention: that she has scotched Germany's drive to the Baltic and the Balkans; that Britain, France and herself have identical interests in keeping Germany out of South-East Europe seems to me logical and reasonable. He pats Italy on the back for remaining neutral and refers rather encouragingly to Italy's defection and subsequent alliance with us in the last war. Winston is an orator. He's worth all of 'em put together.

Diarist 5096, M, Retired Insurance Actuary, Edinburgh, 03/10/39

A letter from a friend living ten miles out of town describes the trials of those who have been burdened with evacuees. One lady went out for half an hour, on her return found that every drawer in the house had been emptied out on the floor and stirred about, another found a party of young men sitting round her polished dining room table careless of any marks they might make. The writer had a stormy interview with the Receiver as, owing to heart trouble she refused to take any children herself, a medical certificate had to be procured before she was exempted, happily the extreme quietness of country life and the absence of 'the pictures' caused the most turbulent to go home after a few days.

Diarist 5228, M, Textile Warehouseman, Birmingham, 04/10/39

In bed. Try to imagine what I should do if there was an air raid. Should I stay in bed and risk a bomb coming through the ceiling or get up and risk catching a fresh chill? Eventually decided to stay in bed with head under the clothes of course. Do a crossword. One clue says; Hitler doesn't like them. Four letters, the second letter E. I fill in 'Reds', but of course it's wrong it should be 'Jews'.

Diarist 5250, F, Actress, London, 05/10/39

Took a joint and a few groceries to an old man I met while I was doing social work last spring. He is a pensioner and does not draw it till Fridays so Thursday was a good day. He told me his son was forced to close his animal shop as he was not selling anything but bird seed. They had to get rid of budgerigars for about 2/- a pair.

Diarist 5242, F, Housewife, Swansea, Glamorgan, 06/10/39
The [A.R.P] lecturer-tester arrived expecting to have (no more than) 25 to test & there was between 50 and 60. The civilian response here is really marvellous <u>and</u> genuine. Among those taking the course of lectures, same time as myself were:- Head of grammar school, Head & teachers of other schools, secretary of secondary school, bank clerks, business Men, one young parson, several ladies who (like myself) wanted to do their bit & were getting down to it seriously. <u>All</u> were <u>proud</u> to wear their badge.

Diarist 5324, F, Garage Assistant, Snettisham, Norfolk, 07/10/39
I have slept in room with Mother since Father died & Mother has been threatening to move me into the spare bedroom all the summer owing to face powder being spilt on the carpet. Today she moved me because she said if a bomb hit her end of the house I might be saved up the other end. She says if we are spread out there might be one survivor to have the money left behind.

Diarist 5118, M, Surveyor's Pupil, Trowbridge, Wiltshire, 10/10/39
Our neighbour has told us today that she will not keep her evacuee boys after she starts lighting fires & when it becomes too cold for them to stay out of the dining room. So much for her!

Diarist 5173, M, Chief Electrician, Blackburn, Lancashire, 13/10/39
What a tremendous effort the B.B.C has to make to keep the war alive. In the 9pm news the announcer asked the listeners to listen

very carefully for a very important announcement and after a dramatic pause stated that Friday the 13th had proved an unlucky day for German U-boats as three had been reported sunk that day. I was in a room with six other adults and their only reaction was an audible intake of breath as though the tension had been relieved.

Diarist 5216, M, Research Chemist, Broxbourne, Hertfordshire, 14/10/39

On a sudden impulse I went to visit a friend who lives in Highbury, and had coffee with him after his lunch. His wife is a doctor, her practice has faded so she has agreed with another doctor to hand it over temporarily, and she has gone to a fresh practice in South Wales. Her husband, who was London agent for a New York publisher, has lost that job and is a L.C.C. Ambulance driver on the night shift. Their child, nearly a year old, is staying in Anglesey with her nurse and some cousins. A tragically scattered family, very closely knit as a rule.

Diarist 5366, F, Housewife, Little Wilbraham, Cambridgeshire (evacuated from London), 17/10/39

To Rectory afternoon for bandaging practice. The Rector's wife amuses me rather. She speaks as if the village were going to be strewn with casualties in the near future.

Diarist 5278, F, Civil Servant, London, 19/10/39

We had a welcome hot meal and took tea up to my sitting room to listen to the German news in English; strongly worded attack on Churchill included. I have listened about a dozen times since the outbreak to this station; they sound mostly quite as reasonable and convincing as the BBC, so that I am more than ever wondering where TRUTH lies.

Diarist 5073, M, Printer, Durrington, West Sussex, 26/10/39
I have placed a copy of 'Mein Kampf' in a fairly prominent position on my shelves. The reactions of friends are rather interesting. Before the war broke out all who observed it expressed a mild interest, and suggested that perhaps they would borrow it some time. Since the war however I have had, from the same people such suggestions as 'burn it', 'chuck it in the dustbin' and the question 'do you realise that you are assisting Hitler by contributing to royalties?'

Diarist 5035, M, Power Loom Turner, Huddersfield, West Yorkshire, 04/11/39
Across the way a door kept opening and letting out a flood of light, when all the assistants would chorus – 'Shut that door!'

They seemed to be getting a lot of fun out of this. Walking past the poulteress, a voice in the dark was calling out, 'nice rabbits', which sounded very forlorn, and caused people to titter.

Diarist 5102, M, Student, Armagh, County Armagh, 06/11/39
A very quiet day. I worked at French all morning and afternoon. Flo received a letter from Eire from an old boyfriend. It was a pointless letter and it didn't seem worth writing. I suggested to look under the stamp and see if it said 'We are starving.' We got quite hilarious over this and decided to put 'We are starving' under the stamp of our next letter to Helen.

Diarist 5312, F, Nursing Sister and Hospital Tutor, Chester, Cheshire, 11/11/39

This morning at lunch I was reminded that it is armistice-day. I said that I thought the whole ceremony was sheer mockery, for here we are at war again. I have thought for years that it should be dropped. If the ceremonies were not so military I should not mind so much. I spent a normal day on duty and a quiet evening knitting, reading etc. I heard the Queen's speech and thought it quite good. The programme was good all the evening not too blatantly national. I think we should all try to think internationally, and there will be no real peace until we do.

Diarist 5420, F, Housewife, Birmingham, 13/11/39

Our shelter. This is us, now smile, it so expresses us that when I saw it, I burst out laughing.

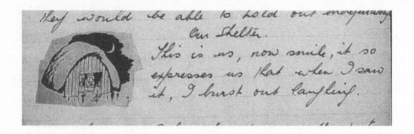

Diarist 5306, F, Housewife, Burnley, Lancashire, 13/11/39

Went to Cinema (film – The Four Feathers). The place was packed. Remember how popular the book was in the last war. This war feels more and more like a continuation of the last one. I think we felt more grief then at the loss of life. The modern world does not seem to care about lives being lost (3000 lost on the roads in two months).

Diarist 5228, M, Textile Warehouseman, Birmingham, 14/11/39

I have had a letter from my friend G in Derby. He tells me about the way the declaration of war affected one of his pals, V.

V rang him up and said he was clearing out, it wasn't his war and what was there for him in London now that the bright lights had been removed. With 25/- on him and the parting words to his boss 'I'm going out and may not be back for some time,' (like Captain Oates) he just disappeared. G has heard nothing of him since. G thinks he has killed himself.

I think, ironically, there should be an official list of these, headed Killed in Inaction. However it is very easy to sneer at V and say he couldn't take it. But it was his life.

Diarist 5396, F, Writer and Artist, Port Isaac, Cornwall (evacuated from London), 25/11/39

The Red Cross activities continue though they have now reached the stage when feuds are likely to develop and some petty jealousy has already been exhibited because one person was allowed to do all the cutting out.

And so it goes on dead and dull day after day, and from what I hear the B.E.F. feel nothing better at the Western Front — one mother reporting that her son was simply bored to death with being over in France with nothing to do. A war of ennui – as Hamburg so aptly put it.

Diarist 5269, F, Sanatorium Patient, Lymington, Hampshire, 26/11/39

I skim the paper & refrain from listening to any one of the News Bulletins. I know I'm playing ostrich & trying to forget the war is on. I stopped taking the Daily Worker because its 'Stop the

War' policy only made me more doubtful than ever about the 'rights & wrongs' of our policy. I've thought over the pros & cons until I'm tired of it, & come to no decision, so now I try to shut my ears & eyes to news of the war.

Diarist 5396, F, Writer and Artist, Port Isaac, Cornwall (evacuated from London), 26/11/39

A wet windy day confined to the house when one curses from the bottom of one's heart the war and its makers for exiling one far from one's friends and interests. The only effect of the war that can be noticed today is the absence of the maid, whose marriage did come off a fortnight ago in spite of the bridegroom's delinquencies, who has gone over to Saltash for the day to see her husband and incidentally to discuss the getting together of a small home.

Diarist 5054, M, Tea Merchant, Walton-on-the-Naze, Essex, 26/11/39

After nearly three months since the outbreak of war, the unanimous opinion seems to be, 'This is a funny war.' The contrast between these almost boringly uneventful days and the catastrophe which was expected to come swiftly and without warning, no doubt accounts for this. Except for some slight inconvenience, mainly to do with daily food requirements, the war has not come home to most people. In fact, some dealers in foodstuffs, and I am one, almost wish that it would come nearer home to some. I specialise in tea, and before the war supplied a better tea at the price than any in the district. Now, teas are drawn by ballot, and I have to take what I can get. For this 'Service' the government charges what amounts to 1¾d per lb. Consequently, my tea costs more and is not so good, and unfortunately many of my customers don't appreciate the situation. I don't altogether blame them.

Diarist 5205, M, Shop Assistant, Great Baddow, Essex, 29/11/39
Bought ten Christmas cards; my sister had already bought five. The cards are the conventional kind. I think they ought to have some bearing on the special circumstances in which we are living.

Diarist 5399, F, Retired Nurse, Steyning, West Sussex, 04/12/39
Terrible storm of rain and wind here last night. I felt very sorrowful thinking of the men at sea. WE grumble at the 'blackout' but what of the blackout at sea, with all the other war dangers to face? Saw the searchlights on around here on Friday. A wonderful sight. Must have been forty or fifty long white fingers stretching across the sky from all round the horizon. I don't see how any plane could dodge them. Received an appeal for donation to Royal Alfred Seaman's Home for disabled merchant seamen. Had to send what I could; we owe those men so much.

Diarist 5240, F, Teacher, Watford, Hertfordshire, 04/12/39
In the cinema showing 'Confessions of a Nazi Spy', children boo-ed heartily at a picture of Hitler.

Diarist 5396, F, Writer and Artist, Port Isaac, Cornwall, 05/12/39
In the light of what has happened it appears to me that it would have been a sound idea if people had had all the possibilities put before them before they were rushed into registering to have their children evacuated. Of course it is always easier to be wise after the event, but I think that parents should have been summoned

to meetings presenting the case for evacuation to them – pointing out that it might be for no end, on the other hand that it might mean the difference between life and death for the children – also it should have been pointed out to them that the time the children would be away would be indefinite and that family life in the ordinary sense would be completely broken up for the time being – maybe even for years. Then after parents had been given the opportunity to consider the pros and cons of the case – it should have been put to the vote – and if evacuation had been decided against – and I'm not absolutely sure if it's been a good thing myself, for it seems to me that the psychological disruption of evacuation may well be equal to the evils of living under war-conditions – then all the money that was spent on evacuation could quite well have been devoted to making schools safe and the building of adequate air-raid shelters.

Diarist 5121, M, Schoolboy, Manchester, 05/12/39

The relaxing of the rule about taking gas masks to entertainments is generally welcomed. 'When you have other parcels, it's such a bother' was one comment I heard on the rule (from a domestic servant, female, about 25). People still don't carry the mask because of a possible raid – the only motive is because it is impossible to do things without it. We are not war-conscious yet – which is I think on the whole good. But I was surprised when a relative (age 72, approx.) in the USA suggested in a letter received today that she might come over – it seems to me a crazy thing to do, but the Americans are even less conscious of the war than we are, I suppose.

Diarist 5262, F, Artist, London, 06/12/39

We were in a big pub in Chelsea, London's Greenwich village, drinking with an artist friend of ours who has just got a commission to paint a maharajah. It was soon after opening time. The barmaid was reading about the invasion of Finland in the evening paper. The barman came in, putting on his white coat, and a large tabby cat immediately jumped off the counter, and ran up to him, mewing.

'He wants lobster,' said the barmaid, looking up, 'but he'll only get prawns tonight.'

'But that's not his regular food, is it?' I asked, rather surprised.

'Oh no,' she said, also rather surprised. 'He gets liver and steak and things like that. But he likes to have a bit of lobster in the bar. Fourteen years old, he is. Nice old cat.'

She went on reading about the refugees, fleeing in sledges in the snow. I felt glad that the old cat was too young to remember about the last war, and hoped they would go on being able to keep it from him about this one.

Diarist 5228, M, Textile Warehouseman, Birmingham, 09/12/39

I had a letter from Norman who is stationed near Peterborough in the Air Force. He writes; 'I never realised in peacetime how lucky we were, we only seem to be half living these days.'

Diarist 5054, M, Tea Merchant, Walton-on-the-Naze, Essex, 09/12/39

Coming out of Tottenham Ct. Rd. Underground station at 7.30 p.m. in the black-out, the country cousins found themselves in difficulties, guidance having to be sought to find out which of the four cross roads was Charing X Rd. Funnily enough, our guide was an Indian who spoke very broken English. I don't suppose I should have asked him had I been able to see what he looked like.

Diarist 5240, F, Teacher, Watford, Hertfordshire, 09/12/39

Women have so insulted shop assistants that the rule – that assistants may not be rude to customers or 'answer back' – has been relaxed, by the manager of a big store here. The girls are often in tears, & the men greatly upset, by selfish customers who blame assistants when they can't get what butter or sugar they think they want. A shop assistant's lot is none too easy in these days when it was a rarity to get one's shopping list complete. There is always some item which has not come from the warehouse, or has been delayed on the way.

Diarist 5312, F, Nursing Sister and Hospital Tutor, Chester, Cheshire, 11/12/39

We are to have a party on Thursday to enliven the blackout. Three of the nurses have made all the arrangements, and all are to go dressed as evacuees. The party is to be given by Lord and Lady Haw-Haw, specially come from Berlin to make secret investigations on social conditions in England. There will be a feature broadcast from the party. (fake!) Sister B. and I are to represent them.

Diarist 5054, M, Tea Merchant, Walton-on-the-Naze, Essex, 11/12/39

With the coming of fogs, the striving to be home before dark is becoming desperate. There, one can take up what might be described as 'wartime' hobbies. On the advice and direction of a broadcaster on 'Knitting for men'. I have reached half way on my first 'creation' – a vest, and am very proud of it.

Diarist 5276, F, Masseuse, Redhill, Surrey, 14/12/39

Woman – 50 – upper prof. class – says they are saving their petrol for a grand Christmas tour to all their friends, after which they have to lay up the car for the duration; says they are having as much festivity as possible, as they feel after this that, with rationing & increasing prices, there won't be any more chance to be extravagant.

Diarist 5382, F, Social Worker, London, 16/12/39

One small [evacuee] boy suddenly lets out a howl, just as the D.T.O. [District Transportation Officer] is coming into the carriage. He has been standing on the seat, leaning through the window, and his cap has blown off onto the line. We explain that we cannot stop the train to look for it, and that it was his own fault for hanging out of the window, etc. He calms down, but presently begins to howl again. This time he has swallowed a sweet, and thinks it is stuck in his throat. We look down his throat, but nothing can be seen, but he still continues to whimper and presently he is sick on the floor. I mop it up as best I can with an L.C.C. swab and a newspaper. He looks rather green and we make him lie down for a bit. Presently he brightens up again, and goes out into the corridor. Yet again he lets out a howl – this time he has pinched his finger slightly in the sliding door of the compartment. I begin to feel that I do not envy the household on whom he is billeted.

Diarist 5445, F, Housewife, Otley, Yorkshire, 25/12/39

Christmas Day. James woke very early and rooted in his stocking. He was very pleased, particularly with a small anti-aircraft gun. This seems wrong in a fairly peaceful household – but what can one do?

Diarist 5231, M, Assistant Librarian, Bristol, 29/12/39

He spoke mysterious words giving the impression that he was able to wangle extra supplies of petrol. 'Father goes somewhere with a can, and comes back with a can . . .' was about his most explicit statement. Mr. Harwood, in self-defence, threw a mystifying smokescreen about the fact that he gets a couple of gallons a month from a neighbour. They looked secretively at one another, and seemed very happy in this semi-criminal atmosphere. There must be lots of people stealing down alleys to the back doors of garages, and getting a real kick out of it.

Diarist 5341, F, Shorthand Typist, Liverpool, 29/12/39

Rationing to be introduced Jan 8th. Butter, bacon, sugar.

Elderly man in shop: 'Don't believe it's necessary. It's only to find work for some of these people up in London. It's the same with evacuation – don't believe in it.'

2. MY DEAR, THIS LOOKS LIKE THE <u>END</u>

January to June 1940

merely be a matter of giving blood to a bank periodically,
which would be much less disagreeable than tramping out after a
raid, probably to no purpose. Mrs. B. says that at one West End
hospital she knows that they send ambulances to collect such
donors as are needed — now that would be more like! But of course
that would be a tremendous business and expense for the hospital.

     Took Mrs. B. to dine at the Ivy. She was very gloomy,
as usual. She doesn't jitter, but she does <u>gloom</u> so. She has
two favourite slogans, which she alternates: "My dear, this
looks like the <u>end</u>, doesn't it?" and "Let us eat, drink and be
merry, for tomorrow we die!" This last sentiment I find tolerable
only when I am actually eating drinking etc. - and very well too -
certainly <u>not</u> at 8.15 a.m., Mrs. B's. favourite time for telephoning.- But on the whole I find her gloom cheering rather than
otherwise. I suppose because my extremely argumentative nature
immediately assumes the opposition view-point. (I'm lucky in
this, as it means that my own phases of depression coincide with
improvement rather than deterioration in the situation.) I have

'She has two favourite slogans, which she alternates: "My
dear, this looks like the <u>end</u>, doesn't it?" and "Let us eat, drink
and be merry, for tomorrow we die!"'

35

The uneasy calm that hung over the closing months of 1939 begins to break into a storm of truly appalling proportions. The international situation degenerates rapidly – Denmark, Norway, Luxembourg, Holland, Belgium and France are invaded and occupied. By the closing days of June, Germany has possession of the Channel Islands and Italy has entered the war on their side. The only good news is the successful evacuation of many troops from Dunkirk – a comfort, but one dwarfed by the near certainty that Britain is next on the invasion list.

With Hitler looking unstoppable there is shock and helplessness, black humour and resolve. People suddenly find themselves entertaining new boundaries of potential suffering, with the inconveniences of the previous weeks and months reduced to trivialities in the face of this far greater threat. Many are still only passively involved in the war effort. They contribute through tolerating restrictions and doing what they're told – a state that seems conducive either to stoicism or fatalism, depending on their character. With the conflict happening elsewhere, and growing ever nearer, there is ample space for contemplation, depression and plan-making.

*   *   *

Diarist 5390, F, Shipping Firm Secretary, Glasgow, 03/01/40
Mother and I got talking about the reduced birth rate. I think that fear is the root of the trouble. In the face of worldwide uncertainty people are afraid to have incumbrances; also they don't want to be so 'inhumane' as to bring children into the world to go through the terrible future that they foresee. Mother thinks that women won't bring children into the world to be 'cannon fodder'; also the suppression of child labour was unjust

to poor parents who needed the money that their children used to bring in 'in the good old days'. Mother, however, is not very much interested in the problem. 'It is just talk, talk, talk.'

Diarist 5231, M, Assistant Librarian, Bristol, 03/01/40

I am, of course, affected by His Majesty's proclamation on National Service, but I've been rather carefully forgetting about it. So have mother and father. Only comment is mother's, who puts down the paper and says, 'It's beastly.' I used to occasionally mention my approaching army career, partly, I suppose, to shock, and enhance my importance in the family. I didn't realise how bad they all feel about it. Mother says that a while back Jean, my sister, was crying because I should probably have to go. Which is most unexpected and distressing. No one ever mentions the army, or the war, except casually, political discussion is at a minimum. The war was, for a few days, terrible and exciting. Then it was only fitfully so. Now, after being merely a bore for a while, it grows more fearsome. It becomes personal and menacing.

Diarist 5102, M, Student, Armagh, County Armagh, 05/01/40

I worked all day and called for Sammy G. at night to ask him to come down for supper (at Gladys' request). We went first to the Bughouse. He wanted to see the flick ('It's a Wonderful World') and though I saw it in Dublin last term I went with him, as it was his only chance of seeing it. In the middle of some gun-play in the picture, he alarmed me by producing a revolver. He also produced cigarettes, which surprised me, as I never knew him to smoke before. He says he's started smoking so that when he's out on duty, he can make some remark about wanting a cigarette, reach inside his coat and produce the revolver. It sounds feeble to me. I suggested that he should be called six-gun Sammy, but it would be inaccurate as there are only five chambers in the revolver.

Diarist 5054, M, Tea Merchant, Walton-on-the-Naze, Essex, 06/01/40

To London again this weekend. The discouraging outlook will not deter me from making the most of the present. In fact it is probably the cause of my doing so. I refrain from too much meditating on the ethics of the present situation, because to do so depresses me. I feel that I have a grievance against our Government. Before the war I had little sympathy with them, feeling that their policy, ever since the last war, contributed to this chaotic situation. (Although I admired Chamberlain's strenuous efforts to keep an impossible peace) I am a pacifist, but I am not sure that my position is not analogous with that of a member of a crew of a ship which is in troubled waters owing to bad seamanship on the part of the Captain.

Diarist 5402, F, Retired Teacher, Kingsbury, London, 06/01/40

Feel very depressed, and wonder whether I would not after all be happier if I left this empty shell of a home. Have no real desire to live alone. I still find that it is my personal grief for my mother – an old lady of 87 whom I would not for anything have back in this war-ridden world, – and not the thought of the millions whose sufferings are incomparably worse than my own, that really gets me down – though the war is a good second.

Diarist 5352, F, Art Student, London, 16/01/40

I went to a lecture at the Anglo-Palestine Club on 'Picasso'. The chairman introduced the speaker by saying how gratified he was to see a crowded hall on such a cold night, such a dark night, even for the blackout. The speaker started by saying the same thing, in different words, and added 'what a funny thing it is that war stimulates the public's interest in the arts' etc. I may add that it was a lousy lecture.

Diarist 5231, M, Assistant Librarian, Bristol, 17/01/40

There is an outbreak of military fashions in women's dress. Long, military-looking coats, and jackets with brass buttons and shoulder straps are not so bad, but today, in the post office, I notice quite a remarkable collection of war-inspired hats. There are two lightweight, blue, peaked caps, similar to those worn by chauffeurs, with soft tops (the caps I mean, not the chauffeurs), which are very popular with some of the younger girls around here. Then I am startled by a sort of shako, an improvement, a notable advance, on the ATS cap, and irregularly set about with buttons. And then, best of all is a middle-aged woman with a black hypertrophied forage cap, decorated with a little flat white-metal dog. Coo!

Diarist 5341, F, Shorthand Typist, Liverpool, 20/01/40

Went on walk to Hall Road. Couldn't see much on the river, but did see the destroyer in the distance. Sentry was on duty. Tried to take some photographs of the dog, but thought I'd better be careful in case anyone thought I was a spy or anything.

Diarist 5101, M, Chemist, London, 22/01/40

Feel that Germans are justified in their opinion of Churchill. He looks like helping England to lose the war. What with his friendly advice to the neutrals, which was badly put & justifiably misconstrued & his blustering ways, he has helped world opinion to go against us. We mustn't imagine the whole world sympathises with us, & has antipathy for the Germans. That is far from the truth.

Diarist 5199, M, Railway Draughtsman, Wilmslow, Cheshire, 24/01/40

General mentality these days: What a stupid war! How stupid that the nation allows the conduct of things to remain in the hands of the stupid bunglers who brought about the war! How helpless we are as individuals; and there seems no tendency to unite in fierce opposition – not even with simple scandals as SLAUGHTER ON THE ROADS. We are supposed to be fighting for democracy, but it seems as if democracy has lost its voice in England! For the newspapers and wireless are no indication of what people are thinking.

Diarist 5420, F, Housewife, Birmingham, 24/01/40

I read in 'The Mirror' that human hair is, or will soon be needed for the felt to line shells with.

Although I had always intended keeping my curls, nothing would give me greater pleasure than to think I had helped to line a bomb direct to Hitler. I must think it out.

Diarist 5231, M, Assistant Librarian, Bristol, 08/02/40

As I fumble for the pavement, tonight, in the blackout, a soldier comes up behind me, and, in imitation of Bing Crosby or someone, tremolos,

'Now that my romance is through,

May I bring romance to you?'

When a 'bus headlight illuminates me, he says, 'Aw, nuts!' cheerfully, and goes away.

Diarist 5102, M, Student, Armagh, County Armagh, 10/02/40

A letter from home this morning mentioned quite <u>definitely</u> that Sammy G. had joined up. For once, I won't feel pleased at the thought of going home. The war has taken all my best friends away – even my girl-friends have joined up.

Diarist 5396, F, Writer and Artist, Port Isaac, Cornwall, 13/02/40

The new Fougasse posters are very good I think and will do a great service to mankind if they can teach them to keep a curb on their tongues – for surely if the habit is induced it will not stop at military information, but must of a necessity through it being difficult to decide what information would be useful to the enemy and what not, be extended to all talk. What a thing to have achieved to have taught people not to gossip!

Diarist 5348, F, Music Teacher and Housewife, Rotherham, South Yorkshire, 14/02/40

I sat over breakfast and the morning paper. Nothing infuriates me more than the articles written by lady this or lady that explaining how she ekes out the meat ration. It is so ridiculously easy for people who have plenty of money to do so, since there are ample supplies of poultry, rabbits and fish. There is a chef on the wireless who also irritates me, because he is obviously talking to the well-to-do. What I should like to hear would be helpful talks to those who have an income of at most £200 a year and who cannot therefore afford poultry, rabbits at 2/10 each and any fish except herrings, which can pall whatever the boosters say.

Diarist 5332, F, Teacher, Cullercoats, Tyne and Wear, 19/02/40
I was tired and rather depressed all day. I said to a colleague at lunchtime 'I can stand the war and the weather separately, but together they're just a bit too much for me.' It was slushy underfoot, raw and cold.

Diarist 5212, M, Paper Salesman, Preston, Lancashire, 22/02/40
The wife of a captain in the regular army tells me she hasn't been to a cinema or had a night out for months – 'I have three children and I can't leave them on their own.' The eldest is 7. Her relations are all in Scotland and she is too proud to ask a neighbour to look after the children once in a while. It's a shame there isn't an association of 'fairy godmothers' to look after 'babies' at least once a month, and see that mothers, in the circumstances of my customer, enjoy an occasional spree.

Diarist 5240, F, Teacher, Watford, Hertfordshire, 24/02/40
While out shopping, I met a married woman of about my own age, with a seven-year-old boy. We talked about the amount of sickness about (German measles, laryngitis & colds) & the depleted staff in shops & factories; & so on to the war. She deplored its effect on

children's nerves, as, owing to the blackout & carrying of gas masks they are not allowed to forget it. Among other things she said, 'I shall be sorry when the light evenings come, for I feel so safe in the blackout, when everything is dark.' She expects bombing planes to come when it is light enough for pilots to see.

Diarist 5348, F, Music Teacher and Housewife, Rotherham, South Yorkshire, 26/02/40

She also made this comment on the blackout: 'I had tea this week with a Catholic who finds her guardian angel a great help in the blackout. When we came out, she strode on, led presumably by her guardian angel, and I fell flat over some sandbags. It may be a victory for catholicism, but I don't think her G.A. is a gentleman seeing that we were together.'

Diarist 5386, F, Doctor, London, 28/02/40

Our decorator (60) came this a.m. Was in last war. Was gassed but refused to get a gas mask this time. 'Put a wet towel over your face, & go off round the corner' was his advice.

Diarist 5356, F, Business Owner, London, 28/02/40

So many women lately are saying to me how deadly sick they are of life: what with the blackout (that seems to get them down worse than anything) the cold, frozen and burst pipes – nothing happening in the war – a terrible apathy is setting in. And the Govt. has entirely the wrong orientation in dealing with the Nation. If it turned round and said – look here, we'll work together – Instead of – look here, you damned well do as you're told and ask no questions – they'd be amazed at the response.

Diarist 5163, M, Park Keeper, Eltham, London, 02/03/40

A fine sunny day. All civil activities have settled to normal. Scarcely a gas mask is to be seen. I notice that when air raid shelters for the public are erected on open spaces the entrances are padlocked, so there is no anticipation of a sudden emergency. Fire and Police stations are doing away with sandbagging.

Diarist 5342, F, Housewife, London, 04/03/40

Decided to go to Mother but called in at Foster's on the way. She was out, but in the garden, not street. Not too pleased to see me as she was rather grubby & I, for once, dressed up. Everything there in apple-pie order. As much bedding as usual & hothouse full of fancy primulas & cyclamen. They kept it heated through all that bitter weather too. She said 'too bad they could not have any room for vegetables.' Seeing they have a double tennis lawn, I could not resist suggesting they put potatoes in part of it but was assured 'they simply could not do that, it would look so bad from the windows – of course, it's different for you.' Saw the elaborate shutters they have had made for their windows.

Diarist 5348, F, Music Teacher and Housewife, Rotherham, South Yorkshire, 09/03/40

John D. turned up for his lesson as usual, and late, so that I did not finish with him until 12-45. He told me that the experts said that the German measles had been sent over by the Germans. When I asked him what experts, he said just the experts, and I was not able to convince him otherwise.

Diarist 5240, F, Teacher, Watford, Hertfordshire, 09/03/40

For the following reasons, I shall be sorry when the war is over:

1. There is no unnecessary traffic on the roads which are much safer to cross.
2. The quiet in the streets at night and on Sundays is much appreciated. There is a garage near & this street was used for trials after repairs, as well as for weekly overhauls (Sunday mornings) before the joyriding in the afternoons & evenings.
3. There is far less dodging about on pavements in the evening, & much less trouble over dogs, on leads or free.
4. There is far less interference with the working of radio sets, neon-lighting on shops apparently being the cause before the war.
5. There is a chance to enjoy the moonlight & to see the glories of the night sky.

Diarist 5348, F, Music Teacher and Housewife, Rotherham, South Yorkshire, 10/03/40

We had an early tea and then John escorted Hilary as far as Sheffield while I prepared a bed for early carrots and turnips. All the spring cabbages that I planted in the autumn have been killed by the frost and snow. There is no sign of them. The broccoli are also deceased with one or two exceptions and only a few immature sprouts remain. So much for my dig for victory efforts. Incidentally I am not digging for victory so much as for a family supply of vegetables at as low a cost as possible.

Diarist 5285, F, Ambulance Driver, London, 11/03/40

Mr Wheeler arrived today to find us all in deck chairs in the yard. Nasty shock for him – he hates to see us not working – but the cars are all gleaming clean & no work to be found anywhere, for all his searching.

'Oh I wish something exciting would happen,' sighs Baker, 'Life is so dull.'

Mrs O'Reilly: 'When I got up this morning & saw the lovely sunshine I thought to myself, well I don't know, I've a good mind to send in my resignation & go out in the sunshine like I used to.'

Diarist 5435, F, Shopkeeper, Launceston, Cornwall, 12/03/40

We've got a notice in the shop asking people to bring their own baskets etc, because of what we've called the 'paper shortage' (meaning that we don't like paying 9/- a 1000 for bags to put their stuff in). Mrs P (London woman staying here with two kids) said, looking at it, 'Paper shortage, indeed, of all the ridiculous things – telling us there's a paper shortage & they're throwing away <u>tons</u> of it over Germany [in propaganda leaflet drops] – silly fools.'

Diarist 5352, F, Art Student, London, 24/03/40

I walked down to the Haymarket during the lunch hour. Crossing Piccadilly, I saw a very young R.A.F. officer, about 22, hobbling along with the aid of a stick and a girl's arm for support. He had lost a foot. Just behind him was a middle-aged officer in khaki, also limping. Then an R.A.F. of about 30 came along. His right arm was obviously paralysed. Just then I passed a placard saying 'Germans in Boulogne.' Two young girls, who were laughing behind me, suddenly stopped and one said 'I think this is Armageddon.'

Diarist 5228, M, Textile Warehouseman, Birmingham, 30/03/40

I told the boss I had joined up. He said, 'Take a tip from me. Adopt the fatalistic attitude.'

Examining myself I reckon that what I have done has not been inspired by more than 1 per cent patriotism. The reasons for me joining are:

1. To avoid being conscripted.
2. To get new experience.
3. There is a chance of going abroad. And it seems that I should never be able to afford to go abroad in ordinary life.
4. To feel more in line with my friends who have joined up.
5. To satisfy the women who say, 'Why aren't you in uniform?' Not that I bother about the opinions of females very much. But when they say that, however sweetly, they might as well say 'Coward' and hand you a white feather.

Out of these five reasons numbers 2 and 3 are the ones that have really urged me to join up.

Diarist 5014, M, RAF Trainee Pilot, Cranwell, Lincolnshire, 30/03/40
Am investing money in goods – shoes & clothing which are bound to be useful – & indeed a necessity & whose prices are bound to rise – I suppose this is in common with any people with surplus cash. The world is so unsettled that one must work for oneself as much as for others.

Diarist 5324, F, Garage Assistant, Snettisham, Norfolk, 09/04/40
Betty went to see [Mr. M's] wife, & she had hung out an old thick coat to air on the line. She said she had brought it out to flee with if necessary, as she says you want to look scruffy so that if a fund for refugees is raised you will be more pitied. We decided it would be better to wear your best clothes though.

Diarist 5240, F, Teacher, Watford, Hertfordshire, 10/04/40
The party was most amused, when after listening to the news of Denmark & Norway I said I would like to get Stalin & Hitler, and knock their heads together & then knock Mussolini's head on both of them. One woman accused me (in fun) of being very bloodthirsty, but another said that most women would like to do worse things than that to Hitler, if they could get hold of him.

Diarist 5123, M, Technical Process Controller, Birmingham, 10/04/40
The news has been assimilated now. There is very little mention of it today: very little more war talk than usual. This I think is partly because people are beginning to feel a little afraid. 'Germany is getting very near to us now.' Such mention of it as there has been accompanied by strong opinions on the lack of news of effective opposition, leading either to nervous apprehension or a condemnation of the Government for helping Norway 'as it helped Czechoslovakia, Poland and Finland.'

People are not as boisterous as usual but nearly back as normal, after yesterday's abnormal quiet. I was prepared for some reaction in the opposite direction because there is a feeling of impotence (as if one is hit but unable to lift an arm to hit back) which I thought might today find some audible or simple expression but it has not come yet.

Diarist 5205, M, Shop Assistant, Great Baddow, Essex, 22/04/40
In street. Saw a woman trying to get a small parcel into her gas mask case (one of the zip fastener type), which presumably did not contain her mask. 'It won't go in,' she said to her friend. 'It takes such a lot of things sometimes.'

<u>Diarist 5396, F, Writer and Artist, Tadworth, Surrey, 24/04/40</u>
As I take no part in [A.R.P duties] myself I have to rely on the stories told me by friends who are doing canteen work, to know what goes on during these duties. Knitting is the main occupation from what I can gather and I should think the wool manufacturers are reaping a fine harvest – if their supplies aren't being curtailed too severely and if Sir John doesn't cast his eyes on their profits.

<u>Diarist 5231, M, Assistant Librarian, Bristol, 06/05/40</u>
I am extremely bored by the war, and so, it appears, is everyone else.

<u>Diarist 5396, F, Writer and Artist, Tadworth, Surrey, 06/05/40</u>
The W's who live nearby, have, flaunting their daring gone over to France today for a holiday – an action typical of the selfishness of this age that even yet cannot understand how much their lives are to be disturbed and shaped by the war. Many, who thought that way, would call their action unpatriotic – unnecessary luxury in wartime – a view which would never occur to these typical and unthinking young people.

<u>Diarist 5401, F, Architectural Journalist, Slough, Berkshire, 10/05/40</u>
I shall always connect fine weather here with days of fearful tension. The forget-me-nots I planted during the week of crisis last summer are in full bloom and fading. Now I watch new rose trees and madonna lily and plan to plant more tulips for next spring. Next spring . . . I do not know what I shall be doing even next week. We are being warned to carry our gas masks again, to look to our

windows, to seek shelter at the first sound of air-raid sirens, to ascertain where the nearest First Aid Post is in our district.

Diarist 5390, F, Shipping Firm Secretary, Glasgow, 13/05/40

I had a very bad night, tortured with the sufferings of Belgium and Holland. I must have indulged in too much news yesterday, and as a 'defence reaction' I am steering clear of the papers today. The people with whom I work have got over the excitement of Friday by now, and back to 'normal'. Miss Bousie, however, clearly feels things very badly.

Diarist 5396, F, Writer and Artist, Tadworth, Surrey, 17/05/40

V. has been busy going round billeting refugees. I asked her if she had had much luck. 'Oh rather,' she replied enthusiastically, 'I think people have been marvellous. One man said they had no spare room but they would put up a bed in their lounge. I only came across one woman who was difficult. She was very sniffy and said she thought we had enough troubles of our own without worrying about other people's – silly creature couldn't see that other people's troubles in this case are our own.'

Diarist 5378, F, Writer, Farmer and Housewife, Campbeltown, Argyll, 20/05/40

I feel sick this evening; I have a kind of pressure at the back of my head, the same I used to get as a child after frightening nightmares. The rats are making a lot of noise under the drawing room floor: not that I mind them.

I telephoned to Oban, and then lay out on the grass reading Fleming's book about the Reformation, for this varicose vein in my leg had started, and I wanted to keep it level. The feelings that

Protestants and Catholics had for one another, feelings which, even ten years ago, one had supposed to have disappeared completely, are very familiar; only they didn't smash everything then, because they hadn't the mechanical means to do so. One gets a certain nostalgia for the post-reformation centuries, when tolerance was a virtue. It was a most beautiful day; I hated it being so beautiful. I have seldom been continuously in real country during May; one is assailed by sunlight and soft and brilliant colours, by a network of scents and birdsong; it is unbearable just now, it makes one feel guilty.

Diarist 5240, F, Teacher, Watford, Hertfordshire, 21/05/40

Met a young married woman (32) & we talked of the seriousness of recent events, the war of nerves, & the uncertainty of every-thing, & the impossibility of making any plans for the future. Her parting remark: 'It is good to wake up in the morning & feel that one more night has passed in safety.'

Diarist 5312, F, Nursing Sister and Hospital Tutor, Chester, Cheshire, 24/05/40

My day off. Had another bad night, and a most queer dream. I had been eating something, and there was a luggage label attached to the end of a piece of string hanging out of my mouth as I finished. I said to myself, 'Well, you can't eat that,' so I cut off the label, after trying vainly to pull out the string. It seemed as if my stomach would come too, so I swallowed the string again. Now what on earth could account for a dream like that! Went home for lunch, and then out for a walk round to Blacon. It was lovely and fresh out. Heard the King's speech. I thought the present tension would have made him stammer more, not less. He managed very well. It was a good speech. I wonder if he writes his own? So the

Germans are in Boulogne, but we seem to be closing up a bit behind them. I hope we can cut them off from the main body of the army. It seems a pretty tough proposition, though.

Diarist 5006, M, Office Manager, Tea Propaganda Board, London, 25/05/40

Visited by a journalist friend, early 30s, who is, to normal people, eccentric. He wears sandals, and is a strict vegetarian, his whole diet consisting of 3lb. of raw fruit and vegetables and 2oz. nuts per day. Must admit that he looks healthier than I have ever known him. He and I spent the day playing records talking etc. He is fond of philosophy and his present attitude is complete pacifism – non-resistance to aggression. He can make out a very sound case for his particular view, though I can't agree with all his arguments.

Diarist 5312, F, Nursing Sister and Hospital Tutor, Chester, Cheshire, 27/05/40

And here at the Chester Royal Infirmary we are apparently still carrying on as usual lectures and so forth, as dull as ditchwater, but necessary for the training of future nurses, I suppose. It is neither spectacular nor heroic, but the future must be secured if possible, or why fight?

Diarist 5348, F, Music Teacher and Housewife, Rotherham, South Yorkshire, 30/05/40

Spent the morning cleaning & dusting & marking papers, & after dinner went as usual to the Friends' group to help & mend & make clothes for the refugees. As usual I created diversion by spilling all the buttons, losing my needle & sitting on it & chatting nonsense. Mrs M. said that she hadn't laughed so much since last week. I refrained from saying that everything was so bloody awful that one could only laugh, even though the agony was rending.

Diarist 5348, F, Music Teacher and Housewife, Rotherham, South Yorkshire, 02/06/40

The cat decided to come with us & she followed us all the time, fleeing up a tree if any stranger appeared. Most of the bluebells were dead. We talked of the many happy hours we had spent in the wood in spring, summer and winter, & wondered if next spring we should sit there listening to the cuckoo and looking at bluebells under spring bushes. We felt sad, though we said little, for we seem to have reached the end of all things.

Diarist 5411, F, Convent School French Teacher, Blackburn, Lancashire, 04/06/40

Another air-raid practice. Used the Paris air raid as propaganda to get more money for [my fund to adopt a French refugee baby]. Was putting my money box away at 4 – when about 7 of staff set on me all at once – why a French baby? Plenty of British babies, or will be soon; probably all our own children will be refugees before long; (can't see political side – strengthening of Anglo-French union by practical works; or scholastical side – making the learning of French a real thing instead of a textbook thing).

Diarist 5006, M, Office Manager, Tea Propaganda Board, London, 05/06/40

My mother (65) and father (63) came over to see their grandson and were suitably thrilled. With them came my aunt (slightly older than my mother) who normally lives at Canterbury. My first words to her were 'Haven't they arrested you yet?' I knew she was keen on Fascism and had toured Germany last year and been much impressed. She still talks all the time in pro-German style, though I know she means no harm. She genuinely likes the Germans she met on holiday, and the present turn of events has really upset her.

Diarist 5396, F, Writer and Artist, Tadworth, Surrey, 06/06/40

These days _are_ exciting – every minute may bring a new development and it is all interesting – most absorbingly interesting. I thank my lucky stars that I am living in 1940 – and I pray to my gods that I _may_ live to see the end of it all – not so much because I wish to preserve my own life but because I want to see how it all turns out . . .

Diarist 5006, M, Office Manager, Tea Propaganda Board, London, 06/06/40

My particular annoyance is my 'second-in-command', a man of 63 who is supposed to be learning my job, in case I am called up. He is good-natured and all that, but a terrible bore. What is worse, he gets his ideas from newspaper headlines and the Daily Mirror! He is the perfect example of a man who thinks and talks in cliches. 'It's a small world after all . . .' 'We ought to sterilise every German.' 'By Gad, the Air Force is giving them hell.' 'Mark my words, my boy . . .' and so on, till one wants to scream.

Diarist 5388, F, Housewife, Harpenden, Hertfordshire, 11/06/40

Young woman in train started violently when the door was banged when someone got out of the train. Explained her state of nerves to me by saying her husband was in France and in great danger. That morning she had rounded on her 'betters' because the only thing that worried them was that their sweet peas were not doing as well as they would like. 'What about our men and me and my like,' she said.

Diarist 5240, F, Teacher, Watford, Hertfordshire, 11/06/40

In the window of a house was stuck the following notice, printed on a white paper about 6' by 3' & mounted on a darker paper of same shape & slightly larger : – (quoted from memory)

'There is no depression in this house, and there is no interest in the possibilities of defeat. They do not exist for us.'

Diarist 5348, F, Music Teacher and Housewife, Rotherham, South Yorkshire, 14/06/40

She said that Mr & Mrs G. had gone down to south Norfolk to their bungalow to arrange the new furniture. We wondered where they got the petrol from & hoped they would be caught. Mrs G. had called yesterday on Mrs F. to tell her they were going for a long weekend, complete with maid, & Mrs G. was sewing some pretty flimsy material which, she said, was for curtains. Mrs F. retorted tartly: 'I'm busy, too; knitting socks for the soldiers.'

Diarist 5285, F, Ambulance Driver, London, 15/06/40

Afternoon shift. Things are moving a bit too fast to keep track of them. Nor does there seem anything adequate to say. Very little commentary on the news bulletins. Though we all gather to hear them again these days, it's practically in silence. Were much more excited yesterday to see a balloon come down, having lost its tail, hauled in slowly, twisting & swirling like a goldfish in a bowl.

Diarist 5294, F, Schoolgirl, Edgware, Middlesex, 16/06/40

Mother has announced that she is going to put five pounds into National Savings. I myself belong to the National Savings group at school, and I give a quarter of my pocket money each week. I can't analyse my motives for doing so. I'm not easily taken in by propaganda about the nation's pennies winning the war, and reason tells me that 25% taken regularly off my pocket money means much more to me now than the two or three pounds I may manage to save will mean in ten years' time. I think that the 'Lend to Defend' slogan must either have captured the romantic streak in my imagination or that there is some attraction in having saved something, in having put it completely out of temptation's reach. Anyway the fact remains that I voluntarily give up money I could very well use.

Diarist 5348, F, Music Teacher and Housewife, Rotherham, South Yorkshire, 17/06/40

Then the news. So the French had capitulated. I couldn't eat my dinner. If we were to continue the fight alone, surely we should all be exterminated. If we too capitulated what humiliations would the Germans impose on us. We could not live under Nazi rule. I found myself planning to sell everything we possessed to pay our fares to Australia – anywhere where we could be free to live our own lives. But I kept busy all the afternoon, scrubbing the kitchen floor & ironing, to pass the time away until the next news was available.

Diarist 5427, F, Widowed Housewife, London, 25/06/40

Air-raid warning just after 1a.m. lasting nearly 3 hours. The first we experienced as I was away in Scotland at the beginning of the war.

I was unspeakably thankful to find that the noise of the siren was not terrifyingly loud: so many people had told me it was 'a horrible nerve-wracking din,' 'you can't get it out of your ears,' 'it makes you tremble all over just to hear it.' Loud and sustained noise always rattles me completely. I really am not responsible for my actions if I'm subjected for any length of time to a road-drill or a crying child at close quarters! So what I've really been frightened of all along was losing my head completely in the sudden panic-stricken awakening to an endless deafening howl. I never got so far as to worry about subsequent eventualities! But, I suppose owing to the fortunate position of this house in relation to that of the local siren, the noise was not at all distressing. Certainly it was infinitely less blood-curdling than even quite distant cats on the tiles.

I was so relieved to find myself perfectly calm and not at all shaky that I felt intensely happy; and I felt, too, a sort of exalta-tion because at last what we've all been waiting and waiting for had come.

Diarist 5427, F, Widowed Housewife, London, 26/06/40
I have decided to give up taking Picture Post: it has been nothing but pictures of corpses, and most detailed instructions for deal-ing with invasion by tank, parachute and so forth, for weeks. If it is necessary for us to learn to handle hand-grenades and other weapons, it is for the government to instruct us by issuing leaflets etc; not for a journal which sells as an unofficial illustrated news-weekly. I refuse to go on paying 3d a week for long accounts of how to defend a village street or take cover in a bare field – so interesting for a female Londoner.

Diarist 5006, M, Office Manager, Tea Propaganda Board, London, 26/06/40

In afternoon our telephonist (30-ish) came down to say that her boyfriend had rung her up. He said that there was a placard out in the City to say that we had landed on enemy territory and made contact with Germans. Great excitement over this rumour. Most of us of the opinion that perhaps troops had been landed in some Italian possession and the rest was newspaper placard stuff. 'They really are devils, these newspaper men. They chalk up stuff every night which makes me buy a paper I don't want, and there is never anything important in it,' said fem-sec (30-ish).

Diarist 5427, F, Widowed Housewife, London, 27/06/40

Took Mrs. B. to dine at the Ivy. She was very gloomy, as usual. She doesn't jitter, but she does <u>gloom</u> so. She has two favourite slogans, which she alternates: 'My dear, this looks like the <u>end</u>, doesn't it?' and 'Let us eat, drink and be merry, for tomorrow we die!' This last sentiment I find tolerable only when I am actually eating drinking etc. – and very well too – certainly <u>not</u> at 8.15 a.m., Mrs. B's. favourite time for telephoning.

Diarist 5427, F, Widowed Housewife, London, 28/06/40

To my horror I observe the dustmen tipping all the carefully sorted paper, bones, tins etc. into their cart together. Really this sort of thing is the limit. The maids – whom I've ticked off several times for not saving paper properly, etc. – were absolutely furious. I intend to write a raging letter to the Borough Council, but give up the idea; there are so many muddles, what difference does one more make, and surely it will be the wrong person who will get it in the neck – if anyone does. Besides, how can one take all this paper-saving seriously when, in spite of the government's agonised cries of acute shortage, books continue to appear in dust jackets and with at least three more or less blank pages at each end.

Diarist 5399, F, Retired Nurse, Steyning, West Sussex, 30/06/40

My sister from New York writes that she feels that the sun ought not to shine nor anyone smile or enjoy themselves, while this awful tragedy is going on. She feels that the bottom has fallen out of the world. Yes, it has, but we must not realise it too vividly or we shall not be able to carry on at all.

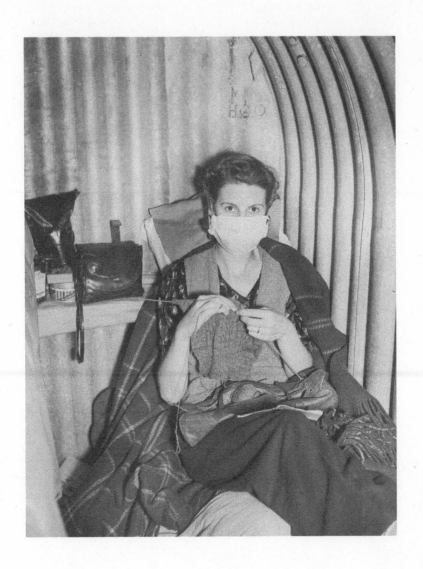

3. HE PRETENDS TO BE A WHISTLING BOMB!

July to December 1940

In the cupboard again part of the night. Decided to bring
a mattress down and a pillow and spent the night there.
Much better than keep on getting up. I asked mother for
a siren suit for my birthday present and we decided to
buy it the following day.
        My father is very facetious during the raids. The
longer they go on the higher his spirits appear to rise.
He rushes to the door in the hope of seeing a dog- fight,
rushes back and makes endless cups of tea, tells jokes
and even comes up behind you and pretends to be a whistling
bomb! It amuses me to see how different.ly my people
re-act. Mother keeps very quiet, and does not appear at
all frightened but gets annoyed with him when he dashes
about. We remark on this and she said she thinks they will
be forced to get " an air-raid divorce."

Monday 26th.
Start out with the intention of buying an air-raid suit for
me. First we went to Bournes but they had nothing I liked.
Then to Dickens and Jones who had the very thing at 4½
guineas but we could not afford more than 2.
Then to Swan and Edgars were they were horrible, trying
to be very feminine instead of tailored, bits of fur aand
coloured scalves hanging about. Then to Weiss in Shatesbury
Avenue. The sales girl said they had gone out of fashion
and most women prefer trousers and a sweater now. They
had nothing suitable either. Some terrible things like
striped pantaloons at 16/11. Eventually,ratherhot and cross,
I made up my mind to give up the idea and buy something
else with the money. We had some tea and then came home.
The raid warning came about 15 minutes after we got in.
Another night inthe cupboard but this time I caught a cold
and felt rather annoyed.

Tuesday

'My father is very facetious during the raids. The longer they
go on the higher his spirits appear to rise. He rushes to the
door in the hope of seeing a dogfight, rushes back and makes
endless cups of tea, tells jokes and even comes up behind you
and pretends to be a whistling bomb!'

Over these months the war becomes a closer reality. Death and bloodshed are no longer happening on distant battlefields; instead they're on the front doorstep (and in the back garden, and right there in the middle of the living room). The dramatic aerial combat of the Battle of Britain is accompanied by night raids, first on industrial cities and then on explicitly civilian targets. Its horrors will continue well into 1941 with many areas suffering weeks of round-the-clock bombardment. Elsewhere Hitler is making inroads in other parts of Europe, Japan enters the fray on his side, and a new theatre of war opens up in North Africa. However, while all these cause anxiety on the home front, the word on everyone's lips is 'Blitz!'

The impact of the raids extends far beyond the immediate horrors of losing loved ones, homes and possessions. The indiscriminate nature of the bombing feels to many more like murder than like war (a distinction, incidentally, that preoccupies the diarists in many ways throughout the duration) and many are shaken by the physical transformation of their neighbourhood landscapes. However, the helplessness often felt in the earlier months of the year is soon displaced by the practicalities of coping with loss of sleep and amenities, and just generally getting on with things. Strangely, the people in 'safe' areas seem to have a harder time emotionally, feeling guilty and – rather perversely – like they're missing out on an experience, or that they don't deserve quiet nights while others are suffering so acutely. Those being 'blitzed' typically seem to interrogate their feelings less closely because there simply isn't time.

* * *

Diarist 5427, F, Widowed Housewife, London, 04/07/40

It is appalling to see what mindless thoughtless sheep the public are. Someone reads an anti-Chamberlain tirade in a newspaper – perhaps one of the Daily Mirror's vile slanders – and promptly he forgets what he had thought never to forget, and joins the crowd in crying down the leader whom, less than two years ago, he had hailed as a saint and a saviour.

B. goes to the other extreme. She is so indignant over the general attitude to Chamberlain that she refuses to see any good in his supplanter. She's the only person I've come across who is anti-Churchill – she describes his speeches, which most of us think so magnificently inspiring, as 'catchpenny claptrap', and himself as a 'ranting demagogue'. I personally feel the utmost confidence in his leadership; my only doubt is whether he will be as successful as a maker of peace as he is a maker of war.

Diarist 5312, F, Nursing Sister and Hospital Tutor, Chester, Cheshire, 09/07/40

We're going to have a thin time for the rest of our lives, paying for all this. What a huge credit has been voted! £9,500,000 per day spent on destruction. And it hurts them to spend £1,000,000 more a year on education in peacetime! But even so we must destroy Hitlerism. It makes one's heart bleed.

Diarist 5402, F, Retired Teacher, Kingsbury, London, 09/07/40

A man who was doing some odd jobs for me said that he expected we should all be nervous wrecks before the war was over – but went on to remark that he had been much happier since the war started. His business had entirely collapsed, and instead of supervising men he was doing the work himself, & felt very much better in health. I told him about the Neighbours' Co-operation scheme. He said it would be a great relief to his wife, who often worried to think that they might be buried in their garden shelter and no one know.

Diarist 5348, F, Music Teacher and Housewife, Rotherham, South Yorkshire, 10/07/40

The conversation inevitably turned on the war. All were agreed that the rationing was the best plan & that we had suffered no hardships yet. The rationing of margarine would be felt, but we would put up with anything to secure victory. Mr B. said there would be no attempt to invade us. Hitler was trying to distract our attention while he got troops across to Africa. He said that we needed a dictator. All broadcasting should be stopped & the people should be told nothing about what was happening. He was of the opinion that such restrictions would help to maintain the morale of the people!

Diarist 5427, F, Widowed Housewife, London, 18/07/40

The local delicatessen, a small one-man business, informs me I can have a dozen eggs from there if I don't mind paying 4/-. I am so absent-minded that it never occurs to me that this is monstrously illegal; the government-controlled maximum price is 2/9. I merely think what very expensive eggs, but a whole dozen worth it at any price for the children – I feel most uncomfortable when I suddenly realise what I've done. But the eggs are already in isinglass, so I'm spared a mental conflict over the question of returning them – a conflict in which I'm afraid conscience would quite definitely be the loser anyhow. It isn't my first naughtiness in regard to the larder in this war, either, though I think it's the biggest.

<u>Diarist 5146, M, Agricultural Worker, Glasgow, 23/07/40</u>
There was a sound like an air-raid siren today but it was very, very short. Mother noticed it first, but I put her off by saying it was a bus stopping and that was the brakes howling. I'm afraid of air raids – they seem so creepy: like going through woods notorious for snakes. There's nothing to be done but 'wait on them getting you'. From this standpoint I'd almost rather be a combatant than a civilian.

<u>Diarist 5390, F, Shipping Firm Secretary, Glasgow, 02/08/40</u>
The prosecutions for despondency and dangerous talk, the Silent Column and the attack on Mr. Duff Cooper seem to have exasperated many people. Mr. Mitchell feels it badly – 'You can't speak now without being liable to get run in by a member of British Gestapo'. Mr. Mitchell does not know what has happened to his neighbour (who is out on £20 bail) but thinks the Police dropped the matter. This man had said, 'When we say we have lost 5 planes, we have lost 15, a major told me.'

<u>Diarist 5240, F, Teacher, Watford, Hertfordshire, 03/08/40</u>
Hotel Notice.
LIGHTING RESTRICTIONS.
The management having taken all Reasonable Precautions for the darkening of windows, any of the Guests showing a light do so at their own risk and are liable to Police prosecution.
  (I was struck by the aimless use of capital letters.)

Hotel Notice.
LIGHTING RESTRICTIONS.
The Management having taken all
Reasonable Precautions for the
darkening of windows, any of the
guests showing a light do so at
their own risk and are liable to
Police prosecution.
(...was struck by the aimless
use of capital letters.)

Diarist 5427, F, Widowed Housewife, London, 05/08/40

The defunct silent-column drive has been replaced by a salvage drive. All the papers have huge appeals every day, with pictures of housewives 'marching as to war' armed with lamp standards and dustbin lids, or hurling saucepans and bundles of paper at the heads of Hitler and co. If it is true that saving waste paper etc. is going to be made compulsory, surely these appeals are a waste of paper rather than a means of saving some? Anyhow, most people have been doing all that they're now asked to do for months past, ever since they were first asked to: and those who remain impervious to the example of their more virtuous neighbours are hardly likely to respond to a mere newspaper appeal.

Diarist 5231, M, Assistant Librarian, Bristol, 09/08/40

F—. a clerk (35–45) who always treats raids as a huge joke, said that he woke up for each warning and then went to sleep again. 'But I heard two bloody great <u>bumps</u>, shook our house terribly,' he said, amid laughter, 'And I nearly fell out of bed. And I could hear the thing cruising about. I'm over by A—. you know, he dropped some over our way. And then, oh, ten minutes or more, I should think after that, the siren went. So then I went to sleep.'

Diarist 5312, F, Nursing Sister and Hospital Tutor, Chester, Cheshire, 11/08/40

We had a girl about 20 years or so, admitted here tonight with a bullet wound of the abdomen – a young soldier showing off with a revolver, and how it worked. I don't think they should be allowed home with ammunition until they are experienced enough to realise its potentialities. The girl is very ill.

Diarist 5024, M, ARP Warden, Liverpool, 14/08/40

[I asked a woman about the] SUGAR RATION. Did you make any jam the last time?, Not me, what with fruit at 1/6d per pound, them that arranges these things are not working men or wives, listen to that man on the B.B.C he gives you recipes every morning for puddings etc and he calmly says an ounce of sugar, where does he think we can get it from? He's like Mrs Beeton, take six eggs.

Diarist 5368, F, Housewife, Manchester, 14/08/40

Some of the paratroops landed yesterday have been rounded up, but no one seems interested in them any longer. It's amazing what a capacity most people have for dismissing unpleasant facts from their minds. I personally find it rather alarming to think of Germans wandering around England, bent on sabotage or other evil.

Diarist 5427, F, Widowed Housewife, London, 15/08/40

It really is quite extraordinary how quickly one adapts oneself and ceases even to notice restrictions. The lavish habit of a lifetime can apparently be overcome in a matter of days, and economising becomes second nature. I wonder what it will seem like, some day, to have unlimited amounts of everything again? (touch wood). Will one go back to former lavishness, or will one's acquired parsimony have taken too firm a hold? I know a woman whose attitude to tea, butter, sugar – even bread – has never recovered from the last war; she can hardly restrain herself from wincing at the sight of a generous helping. I hope I shan't be taken that way: I prefer my natural wasteful extravagance to meanness!

Diarist 5349, F, Journalist, London, 16/08/40
My father was caught in a shelter under Holborn Viaduct Stn. – no light at first, no seats, cold cement floor, no smoking – for a whole hour. Shd. have thought the railway cd. have been a bit more public-minded. But the Southern Ry. is the least cooperative & helpful of railways. It doesn't give a damn – I've lived on it for 20 yrs now, so I know!

Diarist 5312, F, Nursing Sister and Hospital Tutor, Chester, Cheshire, 17/08/40
Went with Mother to see the plane – Got a piece for a souvenir. The police on guard gave it to me. They are not very big machines really, to cost so much money. The metal in the body seems terribly thin. Only the front part is burnt out, and the propellers are warped and twisted. At the tail, which is perforated like a pepperbox with bullet holes, is still a landing wheel with tyre on. There does not look much room for a crew of five. They were taking a collection for the local spitfire fund, most appropriate.

<u>Diarist 5340, F, Landed Gentry, Hatfield Peverel, Essex, 23/08/40</u>
One's relations & friends write to enquire if we are safe & to tell
of their air-raid experiences. One asked me to come & stay with
her 'If I would like a change of air raids.'

<u>Diarist 5250, F, Actress, London, 25/08/40</u>
My father is very facetious during the raids. The longer they go
on the higher his spirits appear to rise. He rushes to the door in
the hope of seeing a dogfight, rushes back and makes endless
cups of tea, tells jokes and even comes up behind you and
pretends to be a whistling bomb! It amuses me to see how differ-
ently my people react. Mother keeps very quiet, and does not
appear at all frightened but gets annoyed with him when he
dashes about. We remark on this and she says she thinks they
will be forced to get 'an air-raid divorce'!

<u>Diarist 5427, F, Widowed Housewife, London, 30/08/40</u>
Raid at about 11.30 for about an hour. I was in the street when
the warning went, shopping, about ¼-mile from the house; it's
the first time I've been caught away from home! I was interested to see the shop shutters going up and the people running,
so I didn't hurry back – everything was quiet except the
wardens. It struck me as extraordinary that some people ran as
though the devil were at their heels – I saw a woman very
nearly run over by a car in her blind rush, and another was
panting as though she would burst and kept gasping 'I can't
run any more, I mustn't run,' still running – while others saun-
tered along in the most leisurely way, finishing their shopping,
perhaps, before moving; a group of old women actually stood
talking in the middle of the street, perfectly unmoved by the

hustle and agitation round them, like rocks in the middle of a rushing torrent.

<u>Diarist 5153, M, Factory Manager, Leek, Staffordshire, 30/08/40</u>
I find it rather difficult to report on the past week. The intensified air raids have created an entirely new atmosphere. The loss of sleep sustained by people who have to 'keep at it' during the day is having a marked effect on their stamina. To be raised nightly by the wailing sirens is more than flesh & blood will stand up to for long. Added to this, is the apprehension of being killed by explosions. People who have charge of invalids & young children are suffering terrible strain.

Many are irritated by the complacency of the B.B.C & the stereotyped announcements of 'slight damage and a <u>few</u> casualties'. Rumours of heavy damage in various parts of the country are rife, and people vouch for the truth of 'what I heard from a man who was there when it actually happened.' What the BBC dismisses as 'slight damage' may mean the whole world to those who have lost their homes & relations. The '<u>few</u> casualties' mean intense grief & lifelong sorrow to those who have seen their parents or children murdered by Nazi airmen.

I find that the women especially are beginning to speak of 'how <u>daft</u> it is that this war is going on'. People want to live at peace with one another & the eternal question of 'what is it all about?' is asked poignantly by many.

That the world is gone mad, or at least the people are mad to allow themselves to be flung at each other's throats, is the increasingly strong conviction of thinking folks.

Diarist 5240, F, Teacher, Watford, Hertfordshire, 31/08/40
I appreciate the newest good night greeting of the B.B.C. 'Good night, everybody, and good luck!'

Diarist 5399, F, Retired Nurse, Steyning, West Sussex, 03/09/40
On arrival here, I found they had been watching the battles in the air, so it had been an exciting day all round. I felt so satisfied to think I had defied all the 'Amiable Adolf's' threats, and had gone for my usual holiday to Gloucester. To tell the truth I had not much wanted to leave home. I felt rather like the elderly lady of 80, told about in a broadcast, who said, if an incendiary bomb dropped on her house she wanted to be there to put it out. But I felt, if I did not go, it would be because I was scared, and I would not be ruled by fear, either to do what I did not choose to do, or to refrain from doing what I usually did. And I come back, more sure of myself (naturally) having made the effort, and prouder than ever of my country and people.

Diarist 5349, F, Journalist, London, 05/09/40
I view the idea of another long winter of war with acute depression. Every time I draw the blackout curtains, I think, 'How lovely, the day when we don't need to do this.'

Diarist 5927, F, Housewife, Portsmouth, Hampshire, 07/09/40
I couldn't help being struck by the amazing adaptability of we citizens – here we all were less than an hour after the raid completely undeterred by the thought of a repeat attack, all streaming out to see what had happened. When the war began, I, & I know heaps of others had the rooted idea that when air raids really started, we wouldn't dare venture outside our homes

except for a hasty dash to the nearest shop for absolute necessities & spend the rest of the time cowering indoors.

Diarist 5240, F, Teacher, Watford, Hertfordshire, 08/09/40
My sister showed me a little woolly coat that she had knitted entirely during raid warnings at night. Her husband called it her 'Spitfire Cardigan'.

Diarist 5250, F, Actress, London, 09/09/40
There was a terrific argument going on in the pub, a very drunk, middle-aged and rather dictatorial man was laying down the law. 'England can't lose. She'll muddle through, We are fighting for freedom, and in a few months it will be England for the English, none of the blacks and foreigners about.' Then a much younger man, either a milkman or a butcher aged about 27 joined in. He said things like. 'This is mass murder, we've never had anything like this before, it is shocking. I wonder we stand for it. They say we are doing the same to Berlin. I don't know, but it sounds bloody silly to me. We've got hours of flying before <u>we</u> get to Berlin, <u>they</u> are over in a few minutes. And what about our politicians, do they sit about in rooms waiting to be killed, do they? You bet they don't. Comfortable safe shelters for them and their women. All the comforts' etc: I must admit I felt this man was talking aloud what many of the workers must be thinking.

Diarist 5285, F, Ambulance Driver, London, 09/09/40
We have started using the phrase 'since the war started', meaning since Saturday afternoon when the great raid set the whole skyline ablaze; & all the hill-tops here (which give a fine view of the Thames & dockside & half of London) were covered with

sightseers between the first raid & the second. Bombs first dropped in this district on Friday, just a few – knocking over a church, & upsetting our phone at the station, which is still out of order after 3 days so that we have to work through the nearest Warden's Post.

Diarist 5205, M, Shop Assistant, Great Baddow, Essex, 10/09/40
The 'Daily Sketch' today: 'Six hundred enemy aircraft came and made heroes of our Londoners . . . on Saturday.' How the fact of being bombed makes anyone a hero I fail to understand. The nonsensical emotionalism which some papers are now printing is annoying and disturbing.

Diarist 5163, M, Park Keeper, Eltham, London, 10/09/40
The park now closes at 8 p.m. That 'blackout night' creeps on, eating its way into the evenings making them shorter and shorter. The old 'uns among the park frequenters sigh sadly as they remark the shortening of the days. Said one, speaking for the others: 'Have we got to have another winter of it? Long dark evenings penned up in the air-raid shelter is a dreary thing to look forward to. I dread the thought of it.'

Diarist 5157, M, Retired Policeman, Upton Wirral, Merseyside, 18/09/40
A day of air raids but no damage done locally: it causes a very great dislocation in the lives of the community and am beginning to think we will have to carry on until the bombs or shrapnel commences to fall. Post office closed and local shops three or four times a day. The people stand outside the shops while the staff inside discuss their own affairs.

Diarist 5402, F, Retired Teacher, Great Missenden, Buckinghamshire, 18/09/40

I wonder how long people will go on bearing all this misery, with never a glimmer of hope held out to them that anything will be done for them after the war. We're promised no 'land fit for heroes' this time – nothing but escape from a worse fate; – to be ruled in Hitler's interests instead of those of 'Jews & International Financiers'. It's surprising that people who have so little to lose seem to have no doubts about their choice – that is, if the B.B.C & the Papers are to be believed.

Diarist 5166, M, Student, Cambridge, Cambridgeshire, 20/09/40

Today I saw a Messerschmitt 109 in Hampstead Heath – but not brought down there – rather, brought up for the 'Spitfire' fund – that weird & wonderful system of paying for the war as if it were a charity (or is it?).

Diarist 5401, F, Architectural Journalist, Slough, Berkshire, 23/09/40

Artist friend Ruth was killed on Friday week ago. June wrote and told me. This has brought the war into sharper perspective. Ruth was visiting friends two doors from her own house in Adelaide Road. A direct hit. Her own house untouched. June has taken G. to a school in Cornwall and when she returns will, I hope, spend a few days with me here.

M. and I are convinced that we and our friends will survive this war. Is this wish fulfilment? She thinks that everyone caught by a bomb was fated to be so – One's number is on it or it is not.

Diarist 5202, M, Engineering Draughtsman, Aylesbury, Buckinghamshire, 26/09/40

Understand there will be practically no fire-watching exemptions, as factory comes direct under Air Ministry. Very interested in reactions. Keen men are jubilant, slackers are despondent.

Diarist 5199, M, Railway Draughtsman, Wilmslow, Cheshire, 01/10/40

The reports from London make me wonder how it is the war affects me so little. We have moved our bedroom to the ground floor, so as not to be trapped by the stairs being destroyed. We have a case + rucsac [sic] in the hall, ready to be snatched up as we rush from the house if it is falling because of a bomb. I have arranged the bed so that flying glass will not reach our faces. 'Then having all things done' – I feel we can sleep in peace, ignoring all the warnings.

Diarist 5427, F, Widowed Housewife, London, 03/10/40

Mrs. B. said: – 'Oh, my dear, <u>nothing</u> will ever matter again, once there's no more war! . . . Just to live at peace again will be enough to make life absolute heaven, no matter if we're all starving in the gutter and lining up in bread queues . . .'

I wonder to what extent she will feel the same way when – if ever – peace really comes?

Diarist 5349, F, Journalist, London, 04/10/40

The whole thing merges into one unending ordeal. I wonder if this is what winter means – one unending raid like an arctic night? The winter is a rather dreadful prospect, but doubtless we shall get used to it as we have got used to other things. For the most part I don't think or plan or get worried, because it wd. be intolerable if I did. As it is I have plenty both of energy & vitality; also cheerfulness.

Diarist 5341, F, Shorthand Typist, Liverpool, 11/10/40
Heard this morning that there was a demonstration in Liverpool last night by people from Soho Street, which is a fairly common quarter. They were carrying banners with 'We want protection, or peace at any price' written on them. These people have only been bombed once, and are the kind who wouldn't put out a hand to save themselves, and wouldn't be evacuated.

Diarist 5398, F, Housewife, Bideford, Devon, 14/10/40
The German air-losses are causing great glee! 'What was last night's score?' asks someone, every morning!

Diarist 5453, F, Housewife, Newcastle-upon-Tyne, 14/10/40
It's astonishing too how one takes the most astounding piece of news in one's stride now, as it were, as much that would in normal times have supplied us with a year's sensations, we swallow in a week, without great comment. I suppose our minds have reached saturation point. All we hear and read now has little further effect.

Diarist 5425, F, Architectural Assistant, London, 15/10/40
He adds. – 'I was nearly blown up yesterday when a lorry taking an unexploded bomb to Regent's Park changed rapidly into just an exploded bomb – (there was practically nothing left of the lorry) four soldiers killed & many passers-by badly hurt.

Such I believe are the 'fortunes' of war – Miraculous escapes – horrible disasters are the order of the day, but life goes on much as usual in spite of everything.

Diarist 5420, F, Housewife, Birmingham, 21/10/40

I put Jacq. in the bath after waiting at least an hour for the sirens to make their minds up. Just as she had got in the bally things went off, I gave her a quick rub down & out she came the quickest bath she's ever had. As she stood being dried she said 'Blast Hitler, I've left all that nice water & it isn't even dirty.'

That's the effect of playing with some East End kids who have taken the house up the road. Even likely people cannot 'stomach' them if they are anything like this family they are dreadful & quite sully the neighbourhood.

Diarist 5390, F, Shipping Firm Secretary, Glasgow, 01/11/40

On the bus I was sandwiched between two young ladies who talked in haughty tones over my head. I received the impression that they were former pupils of St. Bride's (Boarding School – very posh), Helensburgh. At any rate they are aristocratic enough to the extent of horse riding. One lives in Glasgow and the other, wherever her permanent home (though it seems somewhere about here) has been going about the South of England. The Glasgow Miss said, 'We have had the Police up three times about our blinds – a different blind each time – and next time they say they will prosecute us.' The non-Native 'In the house I was staying in the South they turned the current off for a week because a light was shown. We had to visit our friends every night. They dropped 4,000 (yes, four thousand) bombs on our Parish. It was continuous. Most people are getting worn out through lack of sleep. I slept through – the only one in the house who did – though the house used to shake all over and the ceilings fell. One day when the cook was in the pantry hundreds of tins fell on her, and she was black-and-blue.' (This was all retailed with peals of laughter as if air raids were the best joke in the world.) 'One of the maids was angry with me for sleeping through. She thought I <u>ought</u> to get up! When they knew I was coming to Helensburgh, they said, 'The Helensburgh people will love hearing the news,' but when I got to Helensburgh my friends there said, 'We always do have news here, if there is none, we invent some.' I got a lovely pair of fur lined gloves from a bombed shop, reduced from 25/- to 8/6'.

<u>Diarist 5212, M, Paper Salesman, Preston, Lancashire, 03/11/40</u>
It is hard to summon enough courage for sleep – I'm not afraid when the siren goes, but I am very nervous of the lone plane. We all are here but are careful to keep our fears from each other.

<u>Diarist 5244, F, Civil Servant, Harrow, Middlesex, 06/11/40</u>
Sam relates that at the meeting he attended last night bad reports were given of the evacuation to Harrogate. People have been buying up houses & getting 2 or 3 guineas for rooms – hence they have no liking for the Government's 1 guinea. So the billeting officer has had to take a policeman with him to get his billets.

<u>Diarist 5390, F, Shipping Firm Secretary, Glasgow, 07/11/40</u>
In regard to exaggeration, one gets to know whose stories to suspect. This morning Agnes was telling us on indisputable authority that a time[-delayed] bomb in London had destroyed 500 (five hundred) bungalows, and when she had gone out of

earshot, all over the room one heard 'I don't believe it.' We were more disposed to believe Miss Bousie, whose cousin had written to say a time bomb near her had destroyed 4 London houses.

Diarist 5035, M, Power Loom Turner, Huddersfield, West Yorkshire, 10/11/40

During the morning – the conversation turned on holidays – once when someone picked up an illustrated guide to Scarbro' and again when someone said – 'It will be grand when we can get back to normal again and have a real good holiday again' – then there was a chorus of – 'yes – won't it be grand'–

Diarist 5143, M, Student Draughtsman, Wigan, Lancashire, 10/11/40

So 'Peace in our time' Chamberlain's dead. I don't know whether to be pleased or not. I should have liked him to live long enough to see what a mess he's made, and how much misery he's caused.

Diarist 5314, F, Housewife and Farmworker, Tayvallich, Argyll, 15/11/40

Local people constantly ask me what my husband thinks of the war & how things are going etc. etc.. I never can tell them, because he never tells me, which is the safest thing! But he is the only man from the village who is an <u>Officer</u> on active service, & it is curious to notice how much faith everyone seems to have in the smallest comment made by anyone from their own part of the world who is more or less 'in the thick of things' – & they seem to pay more attention to him because(?) he is an officer than to the few lads (all young) serving as privates. Possibly the strong feudal feeling of the Highlands?

<u>Diarist 5324, F, Garage Assistant, Snettisham, Norfolk, 15/11/40</u>
Poor Coventry people. How bitter & hopeless they must feel today. How long can it go on? How many years must all live in fear of the unknown horrors that so many of us have not yet experienced? Churchill talking about 1943 & '4 last week. Can the people stick it?

<u>Diarist 5165, M, Soldier, Royal Army Medical Corps, Leeds, 18/11/40</u>
I said to a man: 'I've found several people who love this life.' He answered, 'Have you? I can't say that I have, not many like leaving their homes.' Myself I hate it, and have never met anyone who felt pleased about it. The war is cursed freely, but generally people expect it to last a few years, two, or three or five. There is no optimism. On parade a sergeant warned us we might be mobilised two or three years after the end of the war, so as not to crowd out the labour market. I heard a few sighs but no comment.

<u>Diarist 5419, F, Munitions Factory Worker, Birmingham, 29/11/40</u>
I dread the sirens now, and have to will myself not to lie listening for the flares and bombs, and find I do not get the rest out of my sleep like I used to. People's nerves are on edge and if someone makes a loud noise, everyone jumps, and laughs at themselves afterwards.

<u>Diarist 5425, F, Architectural Assistant, London, 05/12/40</u>
Friend from the Thames Patrol Service came to see us on his 24 hours leave; he seemed to have lost any great interest in the future

of the war, and has got into the way of rather concentrating on the immediate annoyances and mistakes of the organisation, which seem to be getting him down somewhat. He looks fit and tough and will never again be able to show a pair of smooth gentleman's hands!

Diarist 5128, M, Accounting Clerk, Bristol, 08/12/40
I have a note of the Great raid on this district on 2 Dec, when the neighbours stayed in their basements, & I had to extinguish 9 incendiaries unaided.

I kept no record whatever, after 2nd Dec 1940. My experiences having finally extinguished any pedantic wish of recording warnings.

Diarist 5240, F, Teacher, Watford, Hertfordshire, 14/12/40
We have been wondering whether evacuees in the town are the cause of so much shortage in goods such as cheese, condensed milk, & biscuits. Women with no job can go from shop to shop all day; & the limited amount of food stuffs can soon be sold.

Rationing should be extended.

Diarist 5285, F, Ambulance Driver, London, 17/12/40
Last night Mabel invited a bunch of the bomb squad in to play billiards – 8 of them, a nice crowd. Very much on their best behaviour: they shook hands solemnly & said thankyou to all three of us when they left viz Mabel, myself, & a boy from one of the ambulance stations who'd come in for a bath & a night in bed (he's bombed from his home & has been living at the station for weeks). Heaven knows who they took

him for – sitting by the fire in pyjamas & bedroom slippers (Mabel's, very pansy) & they were too polite to ask or make any comment.

Diarist 5342, F, Housewife, London, 19/12/40
Father has already renewed the 'Reader's Digest' for next year for H. Today received a further card from R.D. saying the Kessells have given us a year's sub. Really sweet of them to try to cheer our war hours. Question is, what do we do with 2nd copy? Not my place to dispose of H's, also do not want Parents to know we have another. I have ideas.

Diarist 5388, F, Harpenden, Hertfordshire, 20/12/40
I felt very sad when I gave up the keys of what was our very pleasant little home, but was consoled by the thought that many of our friends were sorry they owned house property. One friend wrote: 'I curse the day I bought my blasted (actually and metaphorically) house.'

Diarist 5399, F, Retired Nurse, Steyning, West Sussex, 23/12/40
A young wife of a neighbour who has joined the air-force has a refugee girl with her, and what a good thing it is. It gives her something with which to occupy her mind, so necessary now she is left alone. Her sister, who is driving an ambulance in London, was down for 24 hours. She told how one night they were called to a house with the ambulance. Went through the bombs, and found three well-dressed women half drunk in the basement, with bottles of whisky under their arms. They only wanted attention. When the ambulance got back to headquarters, they found a call had come in and five people had

died with no attention while they were away. No one to answer the call.

Diarist 5165, M, Soldier, Royal Army Medical Corps, Leeds, 23/12/40

About original excuses, he promised the first who came with a new one would get leave. 'He'll be worth it.' A man came to the Coy Office with a slip of paper bearing this:

'Sir,

I have promised my wife a baby for her birthday. Her birthday is in 9 months on Saturday. It was a very sacred promise made when we got married, and I want to fulfil it. May I have compassionate leave?'

The CSM got hold of the letter and shouted:

'Are you pulling my fucking leg?'

'No sir, it's true.'

'I never heard that one – by Christ . . .'

What happened to the man I don't know, but it made the whole Coy laugh as the story went round.

Diarist 5076, M, Accountant, Sheffield, 25/12/40

We switched the news on at 6.0 p.m. as my brother wished to know if the R.A.F. had been over Germany last night. He was relieved that they had not as we might then get Xmas evening in peace. Incidentally my brother says that the only news which interests him is 'what poor beggars got it last night'. When the air-raid news is over he switches off.

<u>Diarist 5153, M, Factory Manager, Leek, Staffordshire, 28/12/40</u>
People expected we should have to endure air raids <u>for a short time</u> as a prelude to victory, but they never thought we should be faced with months or years of bombing, and this prospect is very distasteful especially to those who are so ill provided for.

4. THERE IS A RHYTHM IN EVERYTHING INTO WHICH LIFE ENTERS

January to June 1941

11th February, 1941.

There is rhythm in everything into which life enters, and you see it in public morale too. There is a pulse and when the beat is strong you hear war talk everywhere, and when it is weak the war slips into the background – comparatively speaking. While I was not writing the diary, the atmosphere was "electric" with high emotions, but this week it is more like a damp squib. Miss Bousie, it is true, came back from lunch full of the boards she had read, this man had something fearful, and that man something else fearful, every board more fearful than the preceding one. I said, "These men are out to catch pennies, why heed them?", and then (such was my abstraction", You use the word 'fearful' different from me. Here in the dictionary it says 'timid', that is how I use it." Miss Bousie however constantly uses it as meaning "something that gives her fear". (I read over these shorthand notes on 22/2/41 and added "the pendulum has now swung round to intense again'. But the date on which I am typing is the 24/2/41 and we are back to the languid phase again).

We work under the most unpleasant conditions nowadays. Our Managing Director, Mr. Ferguson, is modelling himself on the slave driver in Uncle Tom's Cabin, and in several quarters the same idea is emerging spontaneously, "What would he be like in a blitz? Firemen, policemen, soldiers, etc., would never put up with it". Opinion varies between the belief that he would behave himself, and the belief that he would get manhandled. Of course I work for the nicest man in the world, Mr. Mitchell, and personally I am not affected.

Mother and I have gone over all our papers and locked them up in a deed box. (Actually everything is replaceable). I am determined to pack our suit cases, so that if we have to get away quickly there will be some system in what we carry away. I cannot but believe that the attempt at invasion will come, but Mother scoffs at the suggestion.

The Stornoway gentleman spent all Saturday morning, all Monday and all to-day with us. I like him now. There are only 2 coal merchants there, both contractors to the Admiralty, but the other man had manipulated things so that he was getting good supplies and our man nothing. We little thought that a quarrel between two competitors could ever be represented as a case for requisitioning a cargo or a ship, but we have managed to show the Admiralty, the Ministry of Shipping and the Mines Department that the bunkering of minesweepers was suffering, and our man is getting 650 tons loaded on Thursday.   Wed.

12th February, 1941.

'There is rhythm in everything into which life enters, and you see it in public morale too. There is a pulse and when the beat is strong you hear war talk everywhere, and when it is weak the war slips into the background – comparatively speaking.'

This is the eye of the storm, at least as far as people on the home front are concerned. Blitzes continue nationwide with no sign of abating in either frequency or ferocity. The bombardment from the sky is accompanied by a barrage of bad news. Internationally, things are looking bleak; the German occupation of Greece and their success on the battlefields of North Africa, plus the continuing neutrality of America, all dent morale. Adding insult to injury are the ever-increasing strictures on normal life, capped off by the shock introduction of clothes rationing in June. Whether this is taken harder than earlier casualties (like soap and sugar) varies wildly, but for many it is the cherry on top of an increasingly unpalatable cake.

People have largely adjusted to the new normal of life under sporadic attack. As the situation at home and abroad is processed, space seems to open up for gripes and grumbles. Some of these are directed at governmental restrictions (deemed either too stringent or too lax, depending on who you ask) but most are elicited by the perceived failures of other people's responses to, and contributions towards, the war effort. For every person angered by a friend or neighbour not pulling their weight (whether in avoiding voluntary work, not offering a 'billet' to evacuees or refugees, or simply not sorting their household waste for salvage and reuse) is another filling their time with creative dodges and exploits – shopping on the black market or exacerbating a medical condition to avoid conscription. Between them sits a positive, enthusiastic middleground of people thriving in the new environments, jobs and opportunities created by the war. Indeed, some are having the best time of their lives, exhilarated and energised by it all.

* * *

Diarist 5263, F, WAAF Clerk, Bideford, Devon, 01/01/41

I have been home on leave in N. Devon. I found it much changed, unrationed foods get more difficult to obtain. Cheese, biscuits, marmalade, chocolate especially. The town seems crowded with people. The streets are as they are in August in the height of the holiday season, but full of women, old women, who have come to Devon to save their useless skins. Old made-up hags, drinking coffee in the Cafés! Women with children I excuse, but there seemed plenty of young, married women about in trousers, with no children.

Diarist 5324, F, Garage Assistant, Snettisham, Norfolk, 02/01/41

This morning B & I had a terrible argument with Mr M. He is in a thoroughly awkward mood recently as his wife's evacuated relations are getting on his nerves & making him bad-tempered. Everything you say he contradicts. We had been talking to him for about 10 mins in which everything was wrong, then we got on to the war. He then began condemning all foreigners & because we began talking international co-operation after the war he became very bad-tempered about other nations, & ended by calling us pro-German & going off in a complete huff although we had said nothing pro-German but just not looked on the British as superior 'herrenvolk'. I notice that as the war goes on people get far more unbalanced & illogical in their arguments. Their hate prevents them from straight thinking.

Diarist 5341, F, Shorthand Typist, Liverpool, 05/01/41

Today, in spite of the cold – we are absolutely frozen up – felt springlike & thought of new clothes for spring. I suppose we shall have to make do with a lot this coming year. Personally, I'm going to enjoy myself to the utmost of my capacity. I'm sick to death of this cloister-lily existence – dull as ditchwater. No excitement, fun or games. I think the troops are having a better time than we are.

Diarist 5295, F, Cookery Demonstrator, Margate, Kent, 10/01/41

Got some chocolate biscuits in Woolworth's today. The girl serving them looks worn out. It must be a strain to have hordes of people swarming around for ½lbs of biscuits hour after hour.

Diarist 5401, F, Architectural Journalist, London, 12/01/41

A bomb fell somewhere near* and the building rocked. No one moved, there was scarcely even a murmur. When we came out Jules said, 'I am not given to singing the praises of the British nation but when I see the way we can behave when something like that happens I begin to think we are not such a bad race after all. Abroad there would have been pandemonium.' Perhaps Londoners are used to these shocks by now and anyway only the type who can endure them are in town now, the rabbits have long since fled as we in the country know. The excitable, panicky foreigner has left too. A visit to London is tonic.

*This bomb was I think the one that wrecked Green Park Tube Station

Diarist 5376, F, Teacher, Burwash Weald, East Sussex, 15/01/41

But this lazy farmer here is a 'sportsman & a gentleman' & he won't get reported although he has done no new ploughing; has not yet ploughed the old; has hauled no manure as every other farmer round has done; never dug ½ acre potatoes; never picked all his apples; cut none of his bracken for litter; has not thatched his ricks; because he would not see to a gap in the fence all his animals have strayed over a field of roots & greens & eaten them off in the Autumn so that now when they need them they are gone. Most days he helps his wife milk & goes up to the pub. But he's a gentleman. (To my mind he's the scum of the middle class & that's far scummier than the scum of the working class.)

Diarist 5278, F, Civil Servant, London, 28/01/41

Had seven incendiary bombs on house and garden (second lot) small damage. Dug an AA shell out of top lawn (or rather the bomb removers did) as tall as the kitchen table, as big across as a dinner plate, and over twelve feet down. Ruined the tennis lawn. But we never had a net . . . Helped clear up at midnight the wet mess resulting in our office from 3 fire bombs on the roof above, jabbed holes in the ceiling for the streams of unnecessary water the amateur firemen drowned them in. Watched the AA pompom on top of Admiralty Arch firing at enemies in my lunchtime! Mug. More than a hundred mugs did the same. And fire bombs were dropping at the time, by the Temple in the Strand, though we didn't know it as we stood in Trafalgar Square.

Diarist 5412, F, Teacher, Beckenham, Kent, 30/01/41

Got a bit of a shock today. Was told by a friend that the man next door has patented a gadget to prevent water pipes freezing. He has been offered £60 down and royalties after the war. Or £300 now for absolute rights. Asked if he should take the £300 or not. My friend advises the £300. He replied 'yes I think I will, the architect next door says to take the £300, most emphatically as we are going to lose the war.'

Diarist 5402, F, Retired Teacher, Great Missenden, Buckinghamshire, 01/02/41

The threat of invasion looms large again. It seems to me that people are utterly unprepared for the terrors & miseries that probably lie before us. All we have been told is that we must 'stay put' – & even that perfunctory direction has not been repeated since September, so far as I know. I haven't any idea what I ought to do – if anything – if I hear the church bells ringing. Above all I dread Gas, and the prospect of not being able to find out what is happening to one's relatives. Supposing the children in school were cut off, & we could never find out what had happened to them! Others have had to endure it, & I haven't the comfortable feeling that such things couldn't happen here. Quite a number of my friends have expressed the hope that a miracle will happen – I don't know why, when the innocent Dutch & Norwegians were left to their fate, it should be supposed that God must intervene to save Britain, though she is anything but guiltless of responsibility for the catastrophe of Hitler.

Diarist 5427, F, Widowed Housewife and Voluntary Worker, London, 02/02/41

I'm fed up with reading the papers, anyway. All this miserable atmosphere of suspense their reports and articles produce make me wish I were dead. One can't take pleasure in the recurring blessing of a quiet night for fear of what it may portend – as the Sunday Times points out today, 'the fact that Hitler has not yet raided supports the idea that he still plans to invade . . . raids would produce the maximum effect of surprise and distraction if synchronised with the big invasion, and . . . Hitler is saving them up for that purpose.' One can't even look forward to the spring, and the gradual return of warmth and light to a peering, shivering, cloud-bound world, since it seems that all one's peace and security depend solely on this long-drawn wintry misery of frost and fog: – 'Hitler is only waiting for favourable weather to unloose his full strength against us for the first time . . .'

Diarist 5420, F, Housewife, Birmingham, 07/02/41
I went to see my warden friend, she like me was out of sorts & ready to pack the job up, her husband too was fed up & depressed he was going to resign from the Wardens so's he could become a gunner on an aeroplane. The other wardens had been grumbling & had caused some ill feeling because 40 out of the 80 for this area had no helmets or outfits.

Diarist 5091, M, Evacuation Office Clerk, Barnstaple, Devon, 09/02/41
Another week started, another 168 aimless hours passed without the slightest sense of construction and appreciation. 'What is my life – I am tied down, my education has been stopped at the most criticle [sic] age of my life, what capacities have I to construct things and do things?' I asked myself as I walked along the sordid windswept street.

Diarist 5420, F, Housewife, Birmingham, 10/02/41
A certain percentage I must admit seem to be afflicted with wishful thinking, that the worst is over & that it cannot possibly be as bad as we have had, I think that is due to the rest we have had from bombing.

<u>Diarist 5390, F, Shipping Firm Secretary, Glasgow, 11/02/41</u>
There is rhythm in everything into which life enters, and you see it in public morale too. There is a pulse and when the beat is strong you hear war talk everywhere, and when it is weak the war slips into the background – comparatively speaking. While I was not writing the diary, the atmosphere was 'electric' with high emotions, but this week it is more like a damp squib.

<u>Diarist 5294, F, Schoolgirl, Edgware, Middlesex, 20/02/41</u>
During a History tutorial today I managed to draw History mistress, 29, socialist, onto the subject of the Altmark [naval incident, in which British destroyers attacked a German ship in neutral Norwegian waters, and freed 300 allied POWs held on board]. She says, 'I think Britain has overstepped herself with the Altmark. I don't want to be unpatriotic – I'm terribly glad those men have been rescued, they've been treated barbarically – but I do think we acted rather high-handedly. There's more than half truth in what Norway says. And the "Daily Telegraph" is very frigid this morning. It almost admits that Norway's in the right. I haven't read the Herald. Of course one should read two papers of opposing views to get a reasonably good idea of things, but I can't afford two newspapers since the war. But it's only the cheaper papers – I mean the picture papers – that make it sound so glorious.'

<u>Diarist 5285, F, Ambulance Driver, London, 22/02/41</u>
Signs of revolt yesterday among the younger married women, half-humorous half-serious, against housewifery as a life's occupation – 'I've been an unpaid servant long enough,' says Hodge, 'I'm not going back to that after the war.' Others agree

enthusiastically. They find the house gets run well enough in the intervals between ambulance-work, so why should it ever be allowed to take up all the time.

Diarist 5425, F, Architectural Assistant, London, 23/02/41

Went to the Officer's Sunday Tea Dance at the Grosvenor, the first time for a long while that I have seen the rich in all their grandeur, with all the accompaniments of snobbery and exclusiveness. The debs, sub-debs etc in battalions, straining themselves in their self-appointed War Job of entertaining the officers, and attired in the newest 'little frocks' from Marshalls and Peter Jones. We investigated the Shelter and I was amused and not surprised to see that it far exceeded the factor of safety required by the Ministry of Home Security.

Diarist 5240, F, Teacher, Watford, Hertfordshire, 04/03/41

A real wartime joke from a 7 year old. I was revising the story of Ulysses & Circe & asked what Circe warned Ulysses about when he was leaving her island. 'The raids,' said one. He thought that 'Sirens' meant air raids!

Diarist 5285, F, Ambulance Driver, London, 06/03/41

A gang of us went down to the squash club last night. Some played squash first then the others joined them in the bar. Played darts & ping-pong. Our party (all station people – same crowd that has been at previous parties) happened to hit the same evening as a bunch of R.A.F. celebrating someone's second stripe. So we took the carpets up & danced. A nice party. Everyone was drinking beer, for reasons of economy. The club had a very wartime appearance, what with that, & the uniforms, including stray A.R.P overalls, women in trousers & so on. Also much fuller than it would have been in peacetime. Going out at night-time has quite got back to normal now. The amount of blitz we expect to get these days isn't even worth lugging one's tin hat along for.

Diarist 5425, F, Architectural Assistant, London, 09/03/41

Cooking for the family. Was horrified yesterday at the price of vegetables now, I spent 1/4d on hardly enough rhubarb to make a small pie. Shopping is now a miserable business of frustrated hopes and altered menus not helped by the exhausted patience and superior 'Well I'm the boss now you see' attitude of many shopkeepers. Once so soapy and ingratiating to the customer with the big family they now don't give a damn.

Diarist 5390, F, Shipping Firm Secretary, Glasgow, 14/03/41

During the day our Granton (Edinburgh) Office when on the phone wished to know 'All about the German bomber that had been brought down in Argyle Street.' Later in the day the Lothian Association phoned, with the same request, and they had complete details too – viz. it was lying outside either Woolworth's or Marks & Spencer's. How we laughed, for of course, there's no bomber lying in Argyle Street at all. That is what rumour is like.

Diarist 5341, F, Shorthand Typist, Liverpool, 18/03/41

Letter from Herbert saying how proud he is to have people in the blitz area. He had apparently shown my letter (written during one raid) to many people.

Diarist 5205, M, Soldier, Peebles, Peeblesshire, 22/03/41

For a long time I have had a grave suspicion, rapidly becoming a conviction, that we are not fighting for freedom and democracy at all, but that we shall have to fight harder still against Fascism in this country when the war is over.

Diarist 5240, F, Teacher, Watford, Hertfordshire, 28/03/41

Teatime. Two of my sisters joking about food shopping. One had managed to get half a rabbit, & said she felt as though she had acquired a fortune!

Diarist 5076, M, Accountant, Sheffield, 30/03/41

Went over to my evacuee brother in the afternoon. He seems to be enjoying himself in the garden after being so many years in London with only a tiny patch. He has made a reckless investment in seeds, fertilisers, &c, but I am afraid has forgotten he is in the north and has planted and sown too early.

Diarist 5199, M, Railway Draughtsman, Wilmslow, Cheshire, 01/04/41

I and my wife had been feeling bitter that Vegetarians were not allowed additional cheese, which my wife regards as important. So we were gratified to hear announcement of special ration of ½lb each.

Diarist 5118, M, Surveyor's Pupil, Trowbridge, Wiltshire, 01/04/41

The person whose house was hit behind my Uncle's and totally destroyed, was out fire-watching that night. Being near his own house he saw it had been hit but went and put out my Uncle's coal shed fire before bothering about his own home. When he was questioned as to whose house it was had been hit, he said, 'You never mind whose house. Get on & help put these incendiaries out.' Leaving his own belongings to help people less able to look after themselves (my Uncle & Aunt are both over 60 & both have weak hearts) is typical, I think.

Diarist 5462, F, Civil Servant, Welfare Office, Belfast, 02/04/41

All the propaganda recently about gas & gas masks doesn't seem to have had much effect. I was down-town for an hour this morning, & during that time saw <u>one</u> woman carrying a mask; & she was obviously English. Schoolchildren carry them when going to school, (because compulsory) but not at other times.

Diarist 5419, F, Munitions Factory Worker, Birmingham, 09/04/41

At the pictures tonight I cried when the Ministry of Information picture was shown. I do not often cry; but the sight of the mother, and the little boy pinned under the wreckage touched a sore spot. It still seems unbelievable sometimes that my three friends are dead.

Diarist 5399, F, Retired Nurse, Steyning, West Sussex, 11/04/41

Only five days since war was declared on Serbia, and the last two days I have not dared to listen to the 'News', I cannot bear it. Yesterday I only glanced at my paper, and am thankful there is no paper today, so I can't know what is going on. I know it is terrible. On Tues. I said to the Bank teller that I felt very apprehensive about what would happen in Serbia, but he said I was foolish. That WE were there, and were prepared, far better than the last war. I tried to believe him, pretended I did, but I felt in my heart we were NOT prepared and Hitler was.

<u>Diarist 5108, M, Laboratory Worker and Lay Preacher, West</u>
<u>Hartlepool, County Durham, 12/04/41</u>
Entered Leazes Park where a middle-aged man showed us two bomb craters with almost paternal pride. Both had fallen after 'all-clear'. Gentleman volunteered that 'he' was probably trying for nearby barracks. Small crowd outside St. James' Park before gates opened. Eventually 20,000 inside, gas masks a novelty. Very little war talk, but one man from Coventry inclined to talk down local raid. Crowd slow to warm up, but enthusiasm high when Newcastle scored after 48 mins and very great as score mounted to 4–0. Tried to tea at Co-op but queue waiting outside café door. Went to second news theatre where two queues had formed. Some features duplicated but 'Yellow Caesar' very good. Quiet audience. Large crowds at Railway Station where express left 5 mins late, making up on journey. Very little activity in West Hartlepool streets. Ended with table tennis and draughts at Wesley Canteen. Good muster of soldiers.

<u>Diarist 5035, M, Power Loom Turner, Huddersfield, West</u>
<u>Yorkshire, 19/04/41</u>
Wife told me she had been to town, met a friend who had just bought some chocolate biscuits told her where she had bought them. Wife goes into shop & happens to know the assistant – she asks for half a pound of chocolate biscuits – assistant says glibly – 'We haven't any – we sold them out yesterday.'

Wife says – 'Well that is rather remarkable – I've just this minute left a young woman who has just bought some.' –

She looked her straight in the face and said – 'It's all right, but there's no need to lie about it.' The young woman, abashed, said, 'Well, she told you – but she'll get no more if she comes in again'!

Listened to Churchill's speech on the radio – the first time I had listened to the radio for a very long time. His statement that morale was best in the worst-bombed areas took some swallowing. 'You — liar', one of the other patients said.

May Day again! I was at work early in the morning, and didn't do anything unusual. The sun had come out, and it was a lovely warm day. At the office there was a lot of work to be done, all sorts of letters and papers to send off the dead men. It is a business when you die in the army!! They pay £4 for your coffin, and I believe it costs them nearly £5 to bury you. The lads didn't talk so much about death. There was a long argument about sport, Scottish footballers, and the relative merits of Middlesbrough and Glasgow Rangers. They were at it all morning, and most of the patients for discharge joined in. One can see that the enthusiasm for sport is far from being dead, even though there is no sport.

Two unconsidered aspects of the blitz: milkmen bereft of customers, & doctors whose patients have gone. What happens, when people's livelihood disappears overnight like this?

Diarist 5199, M, Railway Draughtsman, Wilmslow, Cheshire, 05/05/41

Also in conversation it was related that a bomb entered a house and went right through. The only occupant was a servant, who was not injured, but the bomb passed near her, and stripped off all her clothes, including her stockings! She was found naked & carried away & wrapped in a rug. Although she had been with the people a long time, she returned to her home in Derbyshire & refused to come back.

Diarist 5462, F, Civil Servant, Welfare Office, Belfast, 06/05/41

Less people were killed than in the previous blitz, as this one was mainly directed on city centre & shipyards; but we now have an unemployment problem of staggering proportions. Thousands & thousands are walking the streets, with only the faintest hope of being employed again till after the war. What is going to become of all these people, many of them home-less & bereaved (as they will be) as well as without work? [. . .] Press reports of the raid are nauseating. Of course they are hampered by not being allowed to mention any street or building by name, but even so, it shouldn't be necessary to turn out all the usual journalistic cliché & claptrap about 'stricken mothers' 'citizens courage & stoicism' 'traders carrying on with a smile' etc. etc. Truth is that people are dazed, worn out, many despairing, nerves & irritability every-where, evacuation & rest centres a mess of conflicting instruc-tions & overwhelmed by sheer numbers; thousands walk out of town every night to sleep in the fields & suburbs, local authorities were almost completely unprepared to cope with such a situation.

(As I was one of the ones who wishful-thinkingly held the theory we wouldn't be bombed I am in no position to criticise. The foregoing is merely a statement of fact.)

Diarist 5402, F, Retired Teacher, Great Missenden, Buckinghamshire, 06/05/41

My sister-in-law – not a critical person – went to the Pictures. She says she is surprised that Mr. Churchill should always appear with a cigar in his mouth, when we are told to avoid spending money.

Diarist 5413, F, Housewife, Berkhamsted, Hertfordshire, 11/05/41

Big Blitz on London last night. Husband was fire-watching on the roof of his office from 11 to 6. Up there with only A. to help. A. no good, so terrified that he could not even join the hoses properly. H. arrived home very late Sunday morning, grey and staggering with fatigue. He laid his head on my shoulder and cried like a child. When he could speak. 'That fire – it was awful, I thought it would never stop spreading.' This has taught me a lesson – This is where I am needed – this is my War job, to be ready and waiting for my men to look after them when they come home. I am glad to be needed. Now I know that although I longed to be doing a war job, joining the NAAFI, or away on munitions, this is my place and my task.

Diarist 5427, F, Widowed Housewife and Voluntary Worker, London, 12/05/41

Mrs. B. phoned up almost immediately after I got in, and told me that last night set the record for the number of calls to the ambulance station – they'd been called out twenty-three times. Casualties had been appalling all round the district, she said; all the local hospitals had been crammed, their front halls running with blood and lined with bodies, and they'd had to go outside their own zone altogether a number of times, which has never happened before. A fire engine and trailer had received a direct hit right outside the Edgware Road station, and all the men on it had been done for. She sounded very desolate and said it had all been too terrible for words, but at the same time she was at pains to assure me that it hadn't been a patch on the big Wednesday-night blitz of three weeks ago, which I'd missed . . .

Diarist 5250, F, Actress, London, 25/05/41

Caught the 12.15 train home. When I arrived an acute attack of depression descended on me, and has remained more or less ever since. As I write this it is May 25th. I think it is the thought of an invasion cutting me off from about three people that I am really fond of. Two in Devonshire and one in the Midlands. So long as I know I can reach them, if I want to, nothing can depress me, but the thought of anything happening to any one of them with-out my being able to rush there gives me a horrible feeling every time I contemplate it.

Diarist 5427, F, Widowed Housewife and Voluntary Worker, London, 01/06/41

The month opened with a startler in the form of clothes ration-ing, which, the morning papers announced, is to take effect immediately through the medium of the spare margarine coupons at the backs of our present ration-books. Well: Now there will be some trouble. Personally, I don't worry much, as clothes mean less to me than to almost any woman I know, and a good excuse for going about shabby will please me rather than otherwise; what I dislike is the prospect of yet more complications and red tape, which seem to invade one sphere of existence after another till life becomes an endless filling-in and clipping-out of forms. On the other hand, the thought of people like — and —, who have nothing in their vain and selfish heads but fashion and smartness, being 'stung' by the new regulations more than makes up for the prospective inconvenience which rationing will entail. How darn clever of the Government to have introduced the new scheme this suddenly, and completely unexpectedly, so as to avoid the devastating last-minute rush and scramble that would otherwise have taken place: and how wonderful that the secret was actually kept secret right up to the bitter end!

Diarist 5157, M, Retired Policeman, Wallasey, Merseyside, 04/06/41

No raid today. Had a good day gardening the only thing I am now doing to help the war. I have to look after an old mother of 87 at night which means I must be on the premises from about 8 pm at the latest otherwise I would go to some labour exchange and volunteer for any work they considered me suitable for. I feel very uncomfortable but being 67 they consider me on the shelf I suppose.

Diarist 5454, F, Women's Voluntary Services, Blandford St Mary, Dorset, 07/06/41

The night watchman has just been in to fetch the revolver from the office drawer. I enquired after his allotment and also a large stretch of barren ground up there which was offered to the W.V.S. free if we could work it. According to this man, the Town Council has spent a lot of money having the allotments dug and then has not let them but a farmer has taken 8 plots and ploughed them by tractor and will plant them presently, roots I suppose. He thinks more soldiers should have been allowed to have them rather than let them get knee high in weeds. Thieving is very bad and difficult to check. An A.F.S. man lost 30 broccoli when he had a run of fires and had to go to Bristol as well. A woman was caught red-handed with 3 but he had to let her go as she had 5 children.

Diarist 5462, F, Civil Servant, Welfare Office, Belfast, 10/06/41

Found a shop where they had for sale, unrestricted, tomato soup, tinned tomatoes, tinned salmon, tinned fruit, & other articles which one has come to regard as luxuries! Needless to say, I intend to keep its location a dead secret.

Diarist 5401, F, Architectural Journalist, Slough, Berkshire, 19/06/41

The cigarette problem is acute. Have failed to get any in Slough these last 3 weeks. The village tobacconist had yesterday a few Woodbines. In London last week I managed to get 100 and Verrey had collected some tens and twenties for me which I am trying to make last but with the greatest difficulty. I can NOT do without them. It shocks me to find that they have such a hold on me. Verrey tells me it indicates a craving for sex but frankly at the moment I would rather have the cigarettes . . .

<u>Diarist 5454, F, Women's Voluntary Services, Blandford</u>
<u>St Mary, Dorset, 23/06/41</u>

A farmer near the Military Police H.Q. has taken to putting his fiercest bull in with the cows to intimidate the soldiers and their girls from going through into the hay grass. It seems most effective and the hay will soon be cut if this weather lasts.

<u>Diarist 5240, F, Teacher, Watford, Hertfordshire, 24/06/41</u>

After afternoon school one of my boys asked 'Is that a new hat, teacher?' That's the first time I have ever known a small boy notice my clothes. I mentioned this to our senior assistant, who on the previous Monday had appeared in a very pale grey, cool-looking, suit. He overheard one of his boys remark, 'Hum, how many coupons, I wonder?'

<u>Diarist 5399, F, Retired Nurse, Steyning, West Sussex, 25/06/41</u>

Have been to Sidmouth to see my sister (69) who was evacuated from London. She seems to have taken a new lease of life, since her two months sleeping in a chair in cellar of the house at Chiswick. She made over sixty pairs of gloves and mittens last year for the seamen, and is apparently angry with me because I don't knit. I can't do it nowadays, but I do send money to the different ' "Comforts" funds' when I can spare it. I get all my own meals, and work in a big garden. She has no household or food cares at all. All is done for her.

5. THE WORST IS THE LACK OF A FUTURE
INTO WHICH ONE DARE LOOK

July to December 1941

Some friends came down from London — young women, but they had a taxi to & from the station, though they could quite well have walked or gone by bus. What a long way we are yet from Total war!
Sept.2.
A friend — who is sane on most points — thinks that this war had to be in order that the Jews should return to Palestine. She gets her information from the Old Testament. The last war, she says, ended as soon as Jerusalem fell!
Sept 3
The third year of war begins. Has it so far been as bad as I expected? For me personally, no. I have never been in a bad Blitz, & apart from other people's troubles all that I have suffered has been: an undesired change of residence; reduction of income & great uncertainty for the future of the remainder: perhaps some lowering of health owing to loss of sleep & great monotony of diet. Again leaving aside other people's sufferings, I think the worst is the lack of a future into which one dare look, or for which one can make a plan.

'All that I have suffered has been: an undesired change of residence; reduction of income & great uncertainty for the future
of the remainder: perhaps some lowering of health owing to
loss of sleep & great monotony of diet. Again leaving aside

other people's sufferings, I think the worst is the lack of a future into which one dare look or for which one can make a plan.'

The sudden entry of America into the war in December, provoked by the surprise Japanese attack on Pearl Harbor, concludes a six-month period full of change and intrigue. From Germany's declaration of war on their old allies Russia, to the assassination of the head of the French government, there is plenty of chaos and momentum. At home many of those who haven't yet volunteered are now conscripted and, as the year marches on, more and more people's lives lose their familiar shapes and change beyond recognition.

The home front atmosphere is held in tension between the practical and the philosophical. It's clear to most that there's a long time yet before the end will be in sight. For the pragmatic, thoughts of the possible duration seem to be deliberately banished in favour of knuckling down to the work at hand. Others are more questioning and are subject to a sense of growing discomfort, and inclined to dissent. Many feel hounded by an inescapable news cycle; with constant updates on billboards, newspaper front pages, cinema newsreels and ever-present wireless sets, the war is a relentless presence for all but the most determinedly isolated.

* * *

Diarist 5324, F, Apprentice Gardener, Empingham, Rutland, 08/07/41
Evening relaxing & writing. Had a 'bath' in the wash bowl in my bedroom. It is only 2' across & my behind can just sit in it, but I had to do something! Primitive arrangements are all very well in

this heat! I have got 'sea fever'. How I long for the waves. I have never been a summer away from the sea before. I am perfectly aware it would not be safe on the beach if I was at home, but . . . oh I dunno.

Diarist 5233, M, Unemployed, Newport, Wales, 13/07/41

At Oswestry was challenged for identity-card by an elderly & suspicious policeman. He wanted my age, where I was born, & why I was not in the army. He told me I did not sound like a Welshman; I told him it was a point of dispute whether Monmouthshire was in England or Wales.

Diarist 5364, F, Secretary, Kingussie, Inverness, 16/07/41

Most people I have spoken to seem pleased that there is to be another debate on war production. Apart from the bad impression produced in other countries, particularly the U.S, which seems to be particularly susceptible to any form of adverse news, it's alarming to hear of soldiers losing their lives for lack of equipment at this stage of the war.

Diarist 5004, M, ARP Worker and Food Packing Manager, Belmont, Surrey, 20/07/41

Many 'V's' are to be found here, on cars, gates, posts, walls and even on the street paving stones. This is to me very absurd. We are confident of victory here, and do not need the reminder. It has simply provided a glorious excuse for small boys. The surprising thing is that although 'V's' are to be found everywhere, I have not yet seen them being chalked up by anybody, and [this] does prove how easy it must be on the continent to do it unknown to the enemy.

Diarist 5250, F, Actress, London, 21/07/41

Had several conversations with people who expressed the opinion that 'life isn't worth living now'. Complaints about money, food queues, lack of cigarettes, and rationing of clothes seemed to abound. My hairdresser was optimistic enough to say that in his opinion the war will be over before Christmas.

Diarist 5001, M, Insurance Clerk, Newport, Wales, 22/07/41

Although we are experiencing the longest air-raid lull since the collapse of France, people are going all out to have their shelters ready for the autumn, being anxious, I suppose not to be killed right on the last lap.

Diarist 5341, F, Shorthand Typist, Liverpool, 23/07/41

Talking about it this morning, people can't understand:

a) Why, if there is a plane, more gunfire is not heard.
b) What our planes are doing.
c) Why sirens are sounded for one plane – not apparently a bomber.
d) Why the ridiculous censorship prevails. Surely the Germans know they are over L'pool, and yet they put one line in the L'pool Echo, saying A.A. guns have been in action in a N.W. town, when the whole population has been dragged out of bed! It seems that we are all children!

Diarist 5454, F, Women's Voluntary Services, Blandford St Mary, Dorset, 23/07/41

Mrs S, had been to a County meeting for the District Nursing Assn. There was tremendous argument about giving the Nurses a war Bonus, 3% is being found by the County and the local assns are to find another 3% of the nurses' salaries. It was approved by all but some of the districts are so poor and have to find money for cars that they could not face it.

Diarist 5364, F, Secretary, Kingussie, Inverness, 28/07/41
Oh for pounds & pounds of fresh, cream butter again. (I've no direct war comment today. All I can think of is delicious or varied meals!)

Diarist 5004, M, ARP Worker and Food Packing Manager, Belmont, Surrey, 28/07/41
During the raid an amusing incident occurred. A Home Guard came to me reporting that he could see a 'light travelling upwards'. After a prolonged looking at this 'light ascending', I had to inform him that it was a planet which had been moving for aeons of time! This incident does however show the keenness with which the whole countryside is watched during a raid, and the slightest thing noticed.

Diarist 5233, M, Unemployed, Newport, Wales, 31/07/41
From 11th to 17th July I went on a cycling tour to North Wales & back. Slept at Hereford on the first night. During the night there was a terrific thunder storm. I went downstairs & lay on the floor trembling with fright – yet I used not to be at all afraid of thunder. It is air raids that have made me so.

<u>Diarist 5048, M, Quantity Surveyor, Kilmacolm, Renfrewshire,</u>
<u>01/08/41</u>

Once more R. at war. This time over blackcurrants and oranges. She had found in Glasgow that blackcurrants were controlled at 1/3d per lb., while in Kilmacolm the nursery said 'controlled about 1/6d.' She asked if she would be getting them soon and the man did not think he would have enough off his bushes to go round. That means highest bidder gets the chance. A fat lot of use advising us to bottle the juice of ungettable currants. Also they sold her oranges and charged her 1/4d. Control price is 7 1/2d per lb., so she had the oranges weighed and discovered they weighed 1½ lbs. On the oranges being returned the man said, 'Oh, we must have given you the small ones,' and then solemnly warned his daughter to be more careful in future. Need we add that he didn't look too pleased! By the end of the war every housewife will be a good sleuth.

<u>Diarist 5004, M, ARP Worker and Food Packing Manager,</u>
<u>Belmont, Surrey, 02/08/41</u>

It is regrettable that despite the official appeals to the public not to travel this holiday, so many people ignored the injunction. It does seem that the Govt. do not take enough action in actually <u>preventing</u> the population from doing unnecessary travelling. Surely the Railway Companies should not be allowed to duplicate and even triplicate the main line express trains. This only assists the holidaymakers, and is not liable to discourage them. I am reminded of a very pertinent cartoon by David Low recently seen in the 'Evening Standard'. It depicted some people relaxing in deck chairs on a beach reading newspapers carrying headlines such as 'Russian success', 'Germans thrown back', 'Revolts on the Continent', etc. They looked extremely complacent about it all, but at the back of them loomed an enormous Nazi tank trundling towards them. A remarkable and timely cartoon indeed – and very necessary.

Diarist 5139, M, Temporary Farmworker, Stony Stratford, Buckinghamshire, 04/08/41

A young aircraft machinist complained to me that the forces don't always choose the right men for the jobs. 'Suppose they want a lorry driver: they'll call for volunteers: among those volunteers there may be five men who have been lorry drivers in peacetime: right: instead of picking on these men they choose five others (as if deliberately) who've never driven a lorry in their lives, give them two months training and then they think they're fit for the job when they might have had suitable chaps straight off.'

Diarist 5364, F, Secretary, Kingussie, Inverness, 07/08/41

A variety of sausage for supper which people only eat 'because there's a war on.' Nurse came in in a rage & said she'd never seen shops like those of Kingussie in her life. Even though customers were rationed they could not get the food. 'They have too many favourites among customers,' she said. 'They ought to have a food controller in each district. Look at my belt.' (She's becoming very thin.)

Diarist 5454, F, Women's Voluntary Services, Blandford St Mary, Dorset, 08/08/41

Met a woman who has been helping in a Nursery school in Devon. They were neither of them trained but both paid. It was held in the parish room and her work consisted of conducting the little ones through the church to get to lavatory. They loved this and whenever possible bolted into the pulpit. She told us their favourite game was air raids which they instantly resorted to if left to themselves but this the helpers discouraged which goes to prove how wise the authorities are to advise a trained personnel because all the child psychologists seem agreed in advising the encouragement of such play so that the air raid becomes a friendly thing and the fear is played out.

Diarist 5240, F, Teacher, Watford, Hertfordshire, 12/08/41
On coming in from shopping I found three large oranges. My sister had seen some, & had bought them for me. I enjoyed looking at them & waiting for supper time, almost as much as I did eating them. Each was big enough to be satisfying, & all the more appreciated because unexpected.

Diarist 5048, M, Quantity Surveyor, Kilmacolm, Renfrewshire, 14/08/41
Aunt K. still 'collecting' rations but R. did not rise to her repeated 'Oh! Can you get sultanas?' We have never made a practice of scrounging round our various friends and relations and see no reason why she should either. The beauty of all this is that these kind of people don't seem to realise that if we can get sultanas they can probably get something just as important which we can't. One doesn't mind helping people out of a difficulty but it gets a bit monotonous when they are perpetually on the hunt. We noticed that she had quite a good haul in her basket from E.'s grocer – including ½lb bacon! Our ration needless to say is finished and we are living on hope till Saturday.

Diarist 5425, F, Architectural Assistant, London, 24/08/41

A friend and I walking near Crowborough narrowly escaped a sticky end when an Army lorry skidded in a muddy lane and leapt the bank onto us, we fled from it but it knocked her down and she removed herself unhurt from between the front wheels; in the split second after I had picked myself up and seen that she had apparently disappeared under the lorry I found myself saying 'Well, it's happened' what 'It' was I don't know but I think it was just the awful nastiest situation that one's subconscious is always expecting these days.

Diarist 5004, M, ARP Worker and Food Packing Manager, Belmont, Surrey, 27/08/41

It is a very imaginative action on the part of the Dutch East Indies in arranging for our R.A.F. to drop gifts of tea to the Dutch people. It is doubtless true that some people in the occupied countries must despair of ever being released from their German masters, and this welcome reminder to the Dutch people will go a long way to restore their morale and hopes for eventual victory. I cannot imagine anything which would please English people more if they were in a similar position than the gift of tea 'from the sky'.

Diarist 5443, F, Office Worker and Volunteer Mobile Canteen Driver, London, 30/08/41

Our van is very temperamental today, but it is truly amazing how kind and helpful people are; whenever we broke down there was always somebody around who could give us assistance. Finish just before 6 and manage to get a lift to Charlton to see the first football match of the season with Chelsea. The crowd is quite large, nearly ten thousand, mainly servicemen and the football is excellent considering that many of the players are doing it on their half day off.

Diarist 5314, F, Housewife and Farmworker, Tayvallich, Argyll, 01/09/41

The other day we asked each other 'what would you do first thing if the war suddenly came to an end'? I.e. given money & opportunity, what would be your ideal of something to do?

All agreed the first thing would be to tear down the blackout & turn on all the lights in the house! The Londoner would go straight to London & dress up & go off to a party, & I must say I said I would like to get a very fast "cad's car" with the strongest searchlight headlights available, & drive very fast through a night somewhere, & dance the next night from dusk to dawn. I do miss dancing tremendously.

Diarist 5427, F, Widowed Housewife and Voluntary Worker, London, 01/09/41

Life at present offers for my taste a damn sight too little active pleasure to set against the unaccustomed displeasure of work – what with friends scattered & busy, & the lack of petrol, & the shortage & monotony of food & drink, & now the beastly long blackouts creeping in again. Everything seems reduced to a vast, drab boringness.

Diarist 5443, F, Office Worker and Volunteer Mobile Canteen Driver, London, 03/09/41

Casting my mind back over the past two years, I am still amazed that so many of us are still alive, especially when I think of our unpreparedness on this day 2 years ago.

Diarist 5401, F, Architectural Journalist, Slough, Berkshire, 03/09/41

Two years ago, we are reminded by Press and B.B.C, war was declared. For two years I have been lucky, living so happily here. But the time is coming when I shall have to make sacrifices, like everyone else ... There seems no hope of the war ending for years ... The future appears dreary and incalculable. I cannot expect anyone to understand what it will mean to me to give up my indolent cottage life. The problem of what to do with the cats, for instance, seems appalling. They have become individuals whom I love, who love and trust me. If the worst happens and I am pushed into uniform (I don't WANT to be pushed into uniform) ... no one will want to feed and care for 3 cats for me. Stella might be persuaded to have Dinah or the Kittyhawk, or perhaps M. or perhaps they would take one each. But that leaves Ginger. It seems inevitable that Ginger would have to go ... But here I go, worrying about things before they happen ...

Diarist 5402, F, Retired Teacher, Berkhamsted, Hertfordshire, 03/09/41

The third year of war begins. Has it so far been as bad as I expected? For me personally, no. I have never been in a bad blitz, & apart from other people's trouble all that I have suffered has been: an undesired change of residence; reduction of income & great uncertainty for the future of the remainder: perhaps some lowering of health owing to loss of sleep & great monotony of diet. Again leaving aside other people's sufferings, I think the worst is the lack of a future into which one dare look or for which one can make a plan.

Also in the evening I went to see some disgruntled fire-watchers in a nearby road. It appears the whole road is seething with discontent, and after a lot of discussion which was getting us nowhere, I decided to hold a meeting at my house of them all later on in the week. The chief grievance appears to be that all people should be fire-watching in the road, and some are not; another complaint is the longer hours which now have to be covered. There are many other complaints too – most of them too petty and trivial to bother about. You really would not think that the most terrible war in history is in progress, and that we here are almost in the firing line. Oh no, Mr. Jones still complains bitterly that he was by mistake called two hours before his spell of duty in error, and what is the so-and-so Post Warden going to do about it!

F. was keen to let the boys see St Paul's, across the ruins, thinking it was something which they would remember all their lives, so we went into the City after lunch. Strangely enough, having heard so much about the devastation and the grandeur of the newly revealed St Paul's, I was less impressed than I had expected to be. To people who knew the City well like my husband, who worked there for years, it must mean much more. Malcolm told me afterwards that he had expected to see far worse destruction and a much larger cleared area. In fact he said 'I should think Americans must think half the talk has been balderdash when they see how many buildings are still standing.' So much for my anxieties about the effect on the young mind . . .

Diarist 5399, F, Retired Nurse, Steyning, West Sussex, 17/09/41

It is strange how some quite good, honest people will do terribly dishonest acts, and not realise how wrong they are. A neighbour told me her husband had brought home two army blankets, for which he had paid ten shillings. He would not tell her how, or where, he got them but said she had better wash them. She is terribly shocked at him, and he is a fool, for that reason alone, if for no other. He has lost her respect by doing this. And they had enough blankets for all they need, so need is not the reason. On the other hand, when his mother heard of it, she told him to grab all he could get. This man would not steal, and would be shocked if anyone accused him of stealing, but he does not realise that receiving stolen goods is just as bad, and he must know these blankets are stolen. In the long run, he, a taxpayer, has to pay for them and all others stolen because such men as him encourage the trade in them.

Diarist 5390, F, Shipping Firm Secretary, Glasgow, 19/09/41

Last night I thought the A.R.P was out in rather large force, and this morning Miss Gibson told me that they were practising till midnight and were to start off again tonight on a 'gas incident'. Going along Hyndland Road I met Nessie Campbell and a friend on their way to this affair, and beaming at the prospect, and coming home I ran into Miss Gibson with a notebook looking for the bomb. These civil defence workers enjoy themselves. I wish, how I wish, I could be one with them, but that cannot be, and Mass-Observation is really a great blessing to me for though few people know about the diary, it helps to restore my self-respect and makes me feel I have a war job too.

Diarist 5290, F, Hotel Clerk, Windermere, Cumbria, 29/09/41

Today we had to answer a wedding invitation from a penniless knight, over 50, who must be marrying money because the invite was on a double sheet of handmade paper, one sheet quite unused. Printers ought not to allow it.

Diarist 5261, F, Factory Clerk, Manchester, 02/10/41

Notice from the papers that A.R.P volunteers will have to give coupons for their uniform. If I have to give coupons for my overall I shall refuse to accept it, & I think others will too. We volunteers seem to get the worst of it every time. We put in a full day's work & then rush out to our posts and do not get even our own bus fares, whereas paid staff do no more work than we do when we are on duty, they knit & carry on with their hobbies all day. Then after about 8 hours they are quite free, and I don't suppose they do any voluntary work either.

Diarist 5004, M, ARP Worker and Food Packing Manager, Belmont, Surrey, 03/10/41

It has been a practice of mine for some years to read the obituary notices in the press. Alas, these are now swollen by the addition of those killed in action. I notice frequently that the parents say 'Please, no letters'. What a tragedy is hidden behind these three simple words – Please, no letters. The poignancy of grief could not be expressed more feelingly. Only a mind split with anguish could have first written them. 'Please no letters' – a marvellous requiem for a man killed in defence of his country, but the grief is private.

Diarist 5254, F, Housewife, Stockport, Cheshire, 07/10/41

Got a letter from the Council this morning refusing an extension in hours for the Services Dance – the committee say to write again pointing out that we'll never be able to 'present the nation with a rubber dinghy' if we can only ask people to dance from 8.30–10.30. And who can be ready for a dance before 8.30 on a working day.

Diarist 5261, F, Factory Clerk, Manchester, 07/10/41

Went dancing again tonight. Walked home in brilliant moonlight – a real bombers' moon, but not even a searchlight appeared to remind us there was a war on.

Diarist 5307, F, Stenographer, Birmingham, 10/10/41

The people next door have a table shelter in their kitchen, and we went in to see it, to consider whether we should apply for one also. But we decided against it. The kitchen is the only room where one can have it, being the only room not over a cellar, and in there it takes up so much room that it would be a perpetual misery, even if it were for a few seconds once in a way a safe refuge. Transient danger compared to perpetual annoyance is a trifle. Most people who spent hours and hours of boredom and physical misery in their cellars or Andersons last winter now say they'd rather have the certainty or reasonable comfort with the relative risk of death (and it is only relative, because neither Andersons nor cellars are perfectly safe) than the certainty of discomfort with a small measure of protection.

Diarist 5004, M, ARP Worker and Food Packing Manager, Belmont, Surrey, 12/10/41

I spent this morning at a stirrup pump demonstration putting out incendiary bombs. Some of the people I took with me were quite elderly ladies, and it was good to see them rolling over and over in the fire hut first spraying and then jetting the burning bomb and surrounding fire. The human race is very adaptable, and a year or so ago they would have said it was quite impossible for them to lie in pools of water surrounded by dense smoke while trying to put out a fire. One of our answers to Hitler!

Diarist 5015, M, Student, Glasgow, 13/10/41

Several people in recent months have charged me with being unpatriotic in keeping a dog even although he eats only dog biscuits and domestic scraps. The first are made from flour unfit for human consumption while the latter would otherwise be thrown away since there is no collection for the utilisation of this material as pig swill in this district. In any case, how many spaniels can exist on the diet of the equally useless horse.

Diarist 5360, F, Health Visitor, Wallington, Surrey, 15/10/41

I can't think how anyone can afford to get married these days unless they both continue working, and live in furnished rooms, until after the war. I suppose it would be a good idea if they put their earnings into national savings to take out to buy all the things they want after the war.

I object to national savings, though, because so long as the Government have your money, they have the whip hand over you.

Diarist 5159, M, Unspecified, Chesham, Buckinghamshire, 19/10/41

For what must be the first time since the war the papers contain reports of several murders in London in the last few days. It is not a happy feeling that if Hitler does not kill you, there are either some murderers running about or some careless motorist who will.

Diarist 5199, M, Railway Draughtsman, Wilmslow, Cheshire, 29/10/41

Amusing banter in office about saving & spending. I ventured to ask 2 men how much they spent on smoking. A very assertive chainman with only about £3 a week spends 10/- or 11/-, but he defends this as he spends nothing on women (he is a bachelor) & very little on drink. The office chief whose salary is probably at least £400, spends about 2/-. Another chainman & myself were the only other men present (the others being out surveying, or not yet arrived) & we two are non-smokers; & the assertive chainman rounded on us for not paying taxes on smokes!

Diarist 5001, M, Insurance Clerk, Newport, Wales, 30/10/41

The most cheerful time of day is from the moment the 'all-clear' goes. The kids are packed off to bed again and we are fairly sure of a couple of hours' peace by the fireside and an undisturbed night's sleep. We cannot grumble these days. Yet those couple of hours of bedlam when we ought to be free from children are exasperating.

Diarist 5317, F, Office Worker, Leeds, 31/10/41

It is heartening news that the Limitation of Supplies (Toilet Preparations) Order comes into force tomorrow, thus ending the perfectly disgraceful black market in cosmetics. All sorts of people have been selling unbranded cosmetics at absurdly high prices, and I recently saw a short propaganda film illustrating the dangers of these unknown cosmetics. They can cause all kinds of skin eruptions and diseases. What I should like to know is why the fats and other materials allocated for cosmetic manufacture cannot be divided between the well-known established makers (Pond's, Yardley's, Elizabeth Arden etc.) and this home-made stuff cut out altogether? Such a regulation would be no more severe than restrictions imposed in other directions. I am surprised this problem hasn't been tackled before, when it affects the question of health.

Diarist 5017, M, Soldier, Ilford, Essex, 01/11/41

Four of our number are working on the Duke of Gloucester's Barnwell estate. This past weekend their weekend passes were cancelled and they were told to report back to the estate for a job of national importance. Rather disgruntled, they reported for this job of national importance, to find to their disgust that they were detailed to act as beaters at a shoot which the Duke had arranged for their mortification! Were they mad – but all to no avail. And not a penny not a crust of bread. Not even a thankyou was given to them.

It started with my mother saying what a waste she considered big dinner parties were with five or six courses and was very glad that the war had put a stop to them. My grandmother and aunt were most annoyed about this and said they always liked to give their guests a really good dinner, their maids liked it etc. I kept quiet, at first, to see what line my mother would take and almost felt that at any moment she would come out with the communist manifesto.

I simply can't understand these people who are petitioning for the abolition of night bombing [of Germany]. We have got to win this war, and the one arm which is stronger than the enemy's, these deluded people are trying to make useless.

Saturday. Loudspeakers bawl that Winston Churchill is due in town and ask us to give him a hand. As if anyone needs asking! Leave the people to just see the man and they'll yell loud enough, and so it proved. I was in town and had I run might have seen the big man as his car went up High Street, but somehow, I didn't bother. Don't underrate the chap, just can't see that a look at him wd alter my ideas one way or another. He's o.k. for the job he's doing.

Mentally I'm pushing the winter on as hard and hurriedly as I can go. Only about six weeks (just under, I discover on consulting diary) to the shortest day, thank God. I'm just a trifle claustrophobic about the blackout as it is, and it helps to bear it, to remember it has only got six weeks to get worse in before it starts getting better again.

Diarist 5240, F, Teacher, Watford, Hertfordshire, 14/11/41

A knock took me to the door about 7.30pm. It was pitch dark outside, & a deep voice said: 'Madam, you are showing a light!' I couldn't think where, & said so, asking where it was. 'It's here' said the voice, much less deep, & with a laugh in it. A friend had successfully disguised his voice, & had deceived me absolutely.

Diarist 5443, F, Office Worker and Volunteer Mobile Canteen Driver, London, 18/11/41

Mrs. S. told me today about a friend of mine named Ivy. A few months ago she was married to another friend of mine, one Ron who works in the Arsenal. Like everybody else she registered early in August and in due course was called up for an interview. The official at the Labour Exchange told her that she must work, whereupon Ron sallied off to the Exchange and told them that his wife was not going to work as he didn't want her to. The Exchange officials, apparently numbed by this outburst agreed that Ivy should stay at home. I do not wonder that women will not go forward for War work when they know of instances like this one. Ivy is a lazy girl and never liked work, she now wanders around doing odds and ends of shopping and has a good time generally. I know of a good many cases of this type and I am sure there are hundreds of girls who are doing as she is doing.

Diarist 5004, M, ARP Worker and Food Packing Manager, Belmont, Surrey, 24/11/41

This war, unlike other wars has shown us one thing, money is useless unless you possess the means of being able to spend it. Almost the whole of Europe is witnessing millions of coupons changing hands each week, but the paradox of it all is that there is plenty of everything for all if only nations were not so foolish as to go to war.

Diarist 5338, F, Civil Servant, Morecambe, Lancashire, 01/12/41

Only thing of note was that I had an egg for breakfast – the egg – my ration for about a month.

Diarist 5402, F, Retired Teacher, Great Missenden, Buckinghamshire, 02/12/41

Churchill announced conscription of women for the Services – and in the Telegraph there's an advertisement for a ladies' maid 'to maid one lady'. If the Labour Party will stand for this kind of thing, it's hopeless.

Diarist 5045, M, Nurseryman, Newick, East Sussex, 05/12/41

My annual Xmas shopping day in the town of B—. What memories this brings back of former years' Xmas shopping. Turkey, Plum Pudding, wine, innumerable presents, crackers, toys, jokes and surprises, materials for dresses in children's pantomimes, Xmas cards not knowing where to turn to get it all in in a day and now a rather aimless wandering to and fro for a few small presents and even these the Devil's own job to find.

Diarist 5321, F, Houseworker, East Ham, London, 05/12/41

Met Mrs T 'the nice lady', & we talked. She wants to chuck out the whole of Parliament, & have some fresh blood, including women. She would like to see an all-women parliament!

Diarist 5192, M, Civil Servant, Stockton-on-Tees, County Durham, 08/12/41

Sirens sounded as I was homing, and there was no doubt at all that the weekend's happenings had jolted people out of their lethargy, for there was far more jumpiness than there would have been a week ago; evidently nerves tend to become edged by these cataclysmic events.

Diarist 5390, F, Shipping Firm Secretary, Glasgow, 10/12/41

The belief that shocking things have happened, are happening and will happen in the Pacific is coupled with an inability to grasp the situation – one has to look at maps to find out where the places are – with the result that the war seems 'unreal'. It is what you feel in regard to 'Hamlet' inverted. There the tragedy seems 'real' and you have to remind yourself that it is an invention. Now you feel that the tragedy is an invention and you have to remind yourself that it is real.

Diarist 5226, M, Solicitor's Clerk, Maryport, Cumbria, 17/12/41

Loud-voiced miner's wife in bus asks us to give America a chance and wait till she gets going. America wouldn't hold back. We're too soft-hearted. And there's too many nobs in Parliament making money out of the war.

<u>Diarist 5216, M, Research Chemist, Broxbourne, Hertfordshire, 24/12/41</u>

Then K & I went out to a party at the 'Studio', I wearing my Hungarian embroidered tunic to show that I felt like a party. We took some scones and mince pies with us. There are about 14 people, mostly young & connected with the WEA, and they had an old copper water-bucket (from Venice, via my Mother) on the floor with beer in it, and just enough glasses & cups to go round. They had a Christmas tree and a small gift for each of us. We talked, and played games a bit, and I took K. home to feed Julia at about 10-45. When I went back some of them left and the last 8 of us sat and listened to gramophone records for a while. Home at about midnight, playing carols on my recorder.

<u>Diarist 5451, F, Housewife, Bedford, Bedfordshire, 30/12/41</u>

I met a woman today who declares that she takes no notice of any appeals – but burns all paper & destroys salvage. In her view the Government have no right to interfere with the even tenure of her life.

6. THEY DELIGHT IN GOING COUNTER
TO GOVERNMENTAL ADVICE

January to June 1942

'I know an elderly couple, very good kind-hearted people, whose lives have always run in the one smooth easy groove, who yet unknowingly are traitors to their country. They delight in going counter to governmental advice.'

Here, in the dead centre of the war, events are at their most global – the Allied nations (now twenty-six in number) start the year with a 'United Nations' declaration, a fitting gesture in a conflict that now spans every continent except Antarctica. For those at home, the Pacific becomes a frequent presence in the news but the war still remains close at hand. Air raids continue – including the 'Baedeker' blitzes, in which various cathedral cities and cultural sites are targeted – and American troops arrive to set up bases across the country, joining the many other nationalities (whether soldiers, diplomats or refugees) who have already arrived and set up home over the previous three years.

Action and industry are in the air, with a considerable proportion of the population now in uniform. For every male branch of the army there is a female equivalent: the Army has the ATS, the RAF have the WAAF, and the Navy have the WRNS (or the 'Wrens'). These auxiliary services support the combatant units in a myriad of ways. They are drivers and mechanics, clerks and analysts, and an essential part of the war effort (everybody wants to be a Wren, they're widely considered the most glamorous and to be in possession of the best uniforms). Morale tends to be higher among those who feel like a useful cog in the war machine, and lower for those who are grappling with old jobs bent into new shapes, or trying bloody-mindedly to push on with the life they had before the war.

* * *

Diarist 5427, F, Widowed Housewife and Voluntary Worker, London, 01/01/42
The first day of a new year is always inclined to be rather torpid – this one was no exception in spite of the war, & in fact last

night's celebrations only departed from pre-war standards in their expense & in the fearfully limited choice of drinks at vast cost – oh and of course in the microscopic size of the 'butter' portions. Crackers, balloons, paper hats, rattles & blowers were of absolutely identical quality with those of previous New Years & were just as lavishly distributed – presumably for the last time for years to come. And there were amazing numbers of drunks in all stages, from the flat out to the greatly plastered. I shouldn't have thought so many people could have afforded to do themselves so well at such terrific prices. One woman had semi-passed-out in one of the lavatories in the cloakroom, & had become hysterical; she kept sobbing that she felt so ill, she must go home to bed; but as soon as anyone attempted to move her she started screaming the place down. Three doctors, summoned to cope with her, were unable to do so & hovered nervously outside, not liking to settle inside the ladies cloakroom for what was obviously going to be a very long job!

Diarist 5045, M, Nurseryman, Newick, East Sussex, 02/01/42

As a relief from War and all its attendant worries I take my small son into B— and we go to a special children's Cinema show and lose ourselves in 'The Wizard of Oz' and 'Three little Pigs' and 'Ferdinand the Bull'. In a world of absolute insanity the quixotic happenings in these films seem sane by comparison. Thank God for Disney and his like. There is also a very ancient 'Chaplin' one of the old 'slapstick' kind which in those far-off days before Dictators strutted in the lime-light and stole Charlie's thunder we should have split our sides laughing over, but now it seemed quite unfunny.

<u>Diarist 5390, F, Shipping Firm Secretary, Glasgow, 04/01/42</u>
Elsie is very sore about the milk distribution for children in schools, and reports much the same as the Glasgow incidents viz. wastage and the undermining of Scottish independence. I think that the positive benefits of keeping the nation's children healthy outweigh the probable misuse of the scheme by some parents. But Elsie won't have any of that, 'If they can't afford to pay, they must do without. That is the only way to develop character.' My reply that 'If I were an expectant mother I should look to the nation to give me free milk' apparently proves that I am one of the people whose characters are undeveloped.

<u>Diarist 5451, F, Housewife, Bedford, Bedfordshire, 08/01/42</u>
The mysteries of coupon free curtains were explained to me today. I could never understand the discrepancies, but it appears that any material, curtain or otherwise, which should possibly be used for clothing must not be sold without coupons. I was shown a sacking roller towel which was labelled 'linen huckaback' & priced at 2/6. In spite of shortages, I consider that tradespeople often take a mean advantage of the present situation, by bringing out all their old & shop-soiled stock, which they had not the remotest hope of disposing of, & offering it for sale at handsome profit.

<u>Diarist 5205, M, Laboratory Technician, Potters Bar,</u>
<u>Hertfordshire, 10/01/42</u>
Noticed two more health posters, one on precautions to take against influenza, the other on precautions to take against scabies. The great drawback of both was that they had about five minutes' reading on them. I think pamphlets and radio talks

would be more suitable for health propaganda. Posters cannot deal with the subject fully enough.

Diarist 5261, F, Factory Clerk, Manchester, 13/01/42
Heard several comments today about the incivility of shop assistants. In most cases it is not the proprietor of the business who is to blame, but the assistants, who seem to have the same ideas as some factory workers and think they have their employers in a cleft stick. Mother's favourite expression in this situation is that 'there won't always be a war'.

Diarist 5233, M, Unemployed, Newport, Wales, 16/01/42
Had a frightful cold. Stayed in the house most of the time. Our landlady lit the fire before I got up & I sat by it reading. Could not stay in bed if had wanted to as our bed is a Morrison shelter.

Diarist 5401, F, Technical Journalist for Aircraft Factory, Slough, Berkshire, 27/01/42
Churchill has made another magnificent speech. Such imagination, sensitivity, vitality . . . he gives us masterpieces of modern oratory. Never a wasted word or a woolly sentence. Unstinted tribute to the Russians. We have sent all that Stalin asked for – to our own disadvantage . . . But the Russians in consequence have saved us Persia, India, Suez . . . He pleads with diabolical eloquence for a vote of confidence and I am sure he will get it.

Diarist 5149, M, Student and Civil Defence Worker, Exeter, Devon, 04/02/42

In discussion with university undergraduates on the topic of winning the war. The most generally expressed opinion was that we will lose the war unless everyone in the country is determined to win it. At the present moment very few people even think seriously about the matter. They are perturbed by bad news, and elated by good, but they never relate such news to their own lives, and their own work. The reason for this apathetic indifference is that (a) the full significance of losing the war is not realised, and (b) there is no ideal before people's minds of the conditions of living certain to be achieved if the war is won. In both these respects improvement can be sought through effective propaganda, – now sorely lacking.

Diarist 5199, M, Railway Draughtsman, Wilmslow, Cheshire, 09/02/42

Much talk in office about soap ration: some men seem to have learned details by heart. That shaving soap is excepted means that wealthy folk can use it for all purposes. At the office I am in charge of stationery & other stores, and for some months I have kept the lavatory supplied with a small piece of soap. (Each man has his own pieces of soap, but it is a convenience to have a 'communal' piece.) I had first supplied a larger piece, but this disappeared at once, & the smaller piece (not worth 'pinching') remained generally. Today, however, I have decided I must abandon this policy. At 9.30 I noticed no soap, so I put a piece, which had disappeared at 11.30, so I put another piece, which also soon disappeared!

Diarist 5331, F, Shop Assistant, Dewsbury, West Yorkshire, 15/02/42

Spent the day generally straightening myself up ready to start tomorrow on my task of self-discipline. The decision to make this mighty effort is the result of reasoning as follows:-

The world in general is in a fearful state, and we, in particular, are in a hell of a mess, whichever way you view our situation. This situation has not come upon us like the Flood. Our actions and inactions made it and they are caused by our muddled & selfish thinking and refusal to think at all. I mean 'our' actions and thinking, and not just our leaders', but those of each of us, including my own. Therefore, acknowledging I have a share in making the world what it is, if I am honest, I cannot dodge my duty, which is to atone by helping make the world what it should be. The first step seems obviously to be to clear from my mind muddle and self-centredness and to set it to work, and this I shall attempt.

Diarist 5412, F, Teacher, Beckenham, Kent, 16/02/42

The impregnable Singapore. This is a bad shock. Questioned people as to their reactions. Most people feel very upset. Most of the remarks were, 'Why did they keep on telling us Singapore was the Bulwark to the East, if it would be taken so easily?'

The Prime Minister's speech didn't go down very well either – resentment was felt at the half hour palaver before he got to grips with the business. Tuned in to Germany in the evening. Lord Haw-Haw in his best vein. Accused Churchill of being the worst sort of Dictator. A dictator masquerading under the guise of a democrat. The demanding of a vote of confidence stirred him to ridicule, every time Churchill blundered – he said – he held a pistol to the head of the British Public & demanded a vote of confidence. – Thought uneasily that there was something in this.

Diarist 5240, F, Teacher, Watford, Hertfordshire, 17/02/42
My sister told me that immediately after the rationing of bristles for brushes was announced by B.B.C., a woman went into the shop where my niece is assistant, & bought 30/- worth of brushes.

Diarist 5412, F, Teacher, Beckenham, Kent, 23/02/42
Had my hair shampooed & was given some 'Good Housekeeping' magazines to look at from America. The colourised reproduction of oceans of ham, pancakes, tomatoes & butter made my mouth water. It was really painful to contemplate. Showed it to the Hairdresser, she exclaimed 'disgusting', we sympathised with each other at the sinking feeling one got at the cinema when American meals were portrayed on the screen. Refined cruelty to send those scenes over here now.

Diarist 5256, F, Teacher, Thornaby-on-Tees, North Yorkshire, 24/02/42
10 year old child comes late morning & afternoon. Unusual. Ask reason and discover that Father has returned to the pit to work and does not live at home, mother is doing war work, & goes out at 6-30 a.m. Child is alone all day, a neighbour coming in to give meals.

Diarist 5443, F, Office Worker and Volunteer Mobile Canteen Driver, London, 27/02/42

My cold still being with me I paid another visit to my doctor who remembered today that I go to the canteen. She told me I must not go there again for at least a week, I must stay indoors every evening and avoid the cold night air. It seems too stupid in these days of terrible suffering to bother doctors at least 8 times for a cold.

Diarist 5239, F, Aerodynamicist and Housewife, Bolton-le-Sands, Lancashire, 02/03/42

Jack and I had an argument in the evening about the use of petrol. He has asked R. to go to the Lakes with us again next Sunday, and I said that I felt guilty about using the petrol, since we had already been there three times this year. He said that we had got the basic ration and didn't see why we shouldn't use it as we pleased. We don't use it for shopping or on short journeys. It's quite true, but I still feel guilty about travelling more than a few miles. It's partly that I am sure that other people will be wondering how we've got the petrol without realising that we have used hardly any of our basic ration all through the winter.

Diarist 5412, F, Teacher, Beckenham, Kent, 04/03/42

Visited Mrs H., W.V.S commandant. A local worthy telephones 'She had lost her dog, & is very grieved at his death. Could she have an evacuee?'

<u>Diarist 5378, F, Writer, Farmer and Housewife, Campbeltown,</u>
<u>Argyll, 05/03/42</u>

Margaret Crawford, one of our first teachers, came to the
canteen for a bit, but threw her weight about and didn't work;
Anna told her her conduct was lousy and they had a good old
row! During the holidays Anna drives taxis and lorries for the
family business – the remaining brother will probably be called
up – at Tighna Bruich, made 30/- in tips last holidays, partly
driving commercials to the farm houses, once an Education
Inspector! – cross with old friends who don't tip her!

<u>Diarist 5451, F, Housewife, Bedford, Bedfordshire, 06/03/42</u>

I know an elderly couple, very good kind-hearted people, whose
lives have always run in the one smooth easy groove, who yet
unknowingly are traitors to their country. They delight in going
counter to governmental advice. When told to save paper they
say 'go to h—' & spend every penny so that no one else shall
have the spending of it. When the wife told me how careless with
money her husband was, I mildly suggested that it is our duty to
save & help our country, but was told 'Oh! he wouldn't consider
that!' in a tone that implied that the public welfare was her last
consideration. Yet the man is a retired Civil Servant, holding a
government post.

<u>Diarist 5199, M, Railway Draughtsman, Wilmslow, Cheshire,</u>
<u>09/03/42</u>

Visitor from Potteries states that people earning good money are
spending lavishly on good furniture, carpets, etc., because they
cannot find enough of ordinary luxuries whereon to spend their
surplus wealth.

Diarist 5378, F, Writer, Farmer and Housewife, Campbeltown, Argyll, 09/03/42

Then the Seaman's Mission, where I had a cup of tea. Miss Llewelyn in fine fettle, explained how she liked going to tuck in the submarine men who sleep in the Mission, adding 'I've a mania for seeing sailors asleep.' I saw several of my old friends, who would wink at me all the time we were talking. Miss L explained how she believed in tradition and leadership, gave several stories of her childhood on some remote Dependency, said that she thought colours and noises were the same, she couldn't bear being in a room with daffodils because of the tinkling they made, etc. Some of the sailors like her, others say she's an old hen.

Diarist 5205, M, Laboratory Technician, Potters Bar, Hertfordshire, 14/03/42

The loss of thirteen Allied ships in the battle for Java is another great blow to our sea-power. But the mood of the 'Sunday Pictorial' seems to me the wrong mood altogether; its nauseating heroics leave me cold. There is no room for this sickening sob-stuff. What is needed now is a more purposeful mood, a cool and calculating, rational outlook. We cannot see clearly through this smokescreen of emotion. It won't matter much if we are to get fewer newspapers if this is the stuff they are going to befog us with.

Diarist 5412, F, Teacher, Beckenham, Kent, 22/03/42

Visit from a Westminster parent today, Mrs C, a nurse told a drama of the blackout.

She, as is usual in the case of Nurses, is scandalously overworked, was told to do a double night duty. Went home in early evening, (during daylight) put on the electric kettle & fire, made a cup of tea. Went to bed. Did not pull the blackout.

At eleven o'clock, she woke up in Hospital.

The glare of the electric fire caused the police to knock at the flat. No answer. Finally broke in & found Nurse C, in a pool of blood, on the floor. Bad uterine haemorrhage. The doctor at Westminster Hospital, after she had recovered (after a blood transfusion) said a few minutes more bleeding & she would have passed out. Today she thanks her lucky star[sic] she was too tired to pull her blinds when she went to lie down. Has no notion how she got on the floor.

Great excitement in the block of flats where she lived, of course the rumour was Mrs C had been MURDERED.

Diarist 5261, F, Factory Clerk, Manchester, 24/03/42

We have been besieged with visitors at the works today. They are chemists & engineers from Head Office who are helping with experiments. One of them is a German Jewish refugee. He has been down to the works many times & has always a great many insults to put up with both from staff & workmen. It galls the men to see a German walking about in better clothes than they can afford & with a nice comfortable job at Head Office. For myself, when I hear him insulted I cannot help feeling sorry for him. He has been in a concentration camp & his family is scattered in several countries. His parents are still in Switzerland & must be a continuous source of worry to him. He was at the works at the time of the fall of France. The tension that day was terrible & the boss suddenly discovered a plot to seize this German & put him in the river. He came back to the office at the double, grabbed the German & his belongings & rushed him off the premises. We did not see him again for many months.

Diarist 5399, F, Retired Nurse, Steyning, West Sussex, 25/03/42

I felt rocky this afternoon after trying to do a little extra work, and was going to bed, but sat out in the garden in the sun instead, and feel calmed and relaxed. There is nothing like sunshine and outdoor air for 'nerves'. The larks were nearly bursting their throats with song. The guns were going off around us (practising?). Last night I was up at 1 pm, and the searchlights were up over the moon-lit sky.

Diarist 5199, M, Railway Draughtsman, Wilmslow, Cheshire, 27/03/42

A man from next office came in to ask if anybody wanted razor blades at 2/6 per packet, I suggested that as he went around he should also suggest growing beards (I wear a beard: labour-saving). The comments made led me to remark that there are 3 things that most people would rather lose the war than give up: smoking, drinking & shaving!

Diarist 5202, M, Engineering Draughtsman, Aylesbury, Buckinghamshire, 31/03/42

Lunch at Brit. Restaurant. It seems to me that people here are becoming more sociable. Several now greet me daily, whereas hardly a soul used to speak to me. It takes a long time for Britishers to thaw.

Diarist 5004, M, ARP Worker and Food Packing Manager, Belmont, Surrey, 01/04/42

Under the stress of war the old customs are dying out. Nobody tried today to 'April Fool' me, and nobody I know was tried either. Previous years have been one long round of trouble until mid-day. I suppose it is now only schoolboys who honour the custom nowadays.

Diarist 5412, F, Teacher, Beckenham, Kent, 02/04/42

Got to the Hotel about 12.30. What a collection of people. It was weird, all the slice of the population between 20 and 60 had been cut off. There remained a few young families of army men, then a vast congregation of decrepit well-to-do people between 60 and 80 years of age. An old old chap looking like Oliver Lodge toddled about, another looking like the ancient tortoise at the Zoo blinked lizard-like eyes out of the folds & furrows encircling them. Aged sisters, some married & worrying about sons at the front sat shouting to each other owing to one or the other being deaf. Raddled old hags with gouty feet & pinned hair too lazy to make their own homes groused lethargically about the food. Waitresses, elderly & married walked uneasily on their flat feet & legs tortured with varicose veins. I was fascinated by the crowd, it was unreal, like an underground scene from Grieg's Hall of the Mountain King.

Diarist 5427, F, Widowed Housewife and Voluntary Worker, London, 03/04/42

I should think even this proverbially muddle-headed country has excelled itself over this 'business as usual' Easter. No two shops seem to be opening at the same time, & no one seems to know if

& when they'll be able to buy any particular sort of food for the weekend. Our butcher told R. that they had all along intended to close today, & that it wasn't till yesterday morning that they heard they were to keep open till 12!

Diarist 5192, M, Civil Servant, Stockton-on-Tees, County Durham, 05/04/42

On top of her other troubles, she had one solitary cigarette, & no prospect of getting any more till Tuesday: she would look at it, pick it up, heave a sigh, & put it down again. I told her I had a full packet in my pocket, but it didn't seem to help.

Diarist 5402, F, Retired Teacher, Great Missenden, Buckinghamshire, 10/04/42

Last week when I was alone all day I sat without a fire (it wasn't really cold) and felt all patriotic until I remembered that under present restrictions I couldn't benefit anyone outside the household by my economy – so today I had a fire.

Diarist 5176, M, Office Worker, Birmingham, 10/04/42

Going back to work after dinner A.W.L. of an Advertising Department picked me up in his car. He is using his last drop of petrol, he says. I asked him how he found enough to do at his job. He said they were doing only a little of 'good will' advertising, being 'like every other firm – and, for that matter, every individual – concerned for their position in the world after the war.' He thought the talk of patriotism was blatant hypocrisy, and that individuals, groups and organisations were only concerned in looking after themselves.

<u>Diarist 5443, F, Office Worker and Volunteer Mobile Canteen Driver, London, 17/04/42</u>

I decided today that I should be wise if I terminated my engagement, a difficult decision to make, but Henry wanted to get married and I was not willing, and he did not want to go on in this way. The peculiar thing about this matter is that in peacetime nothing like this could have happened to me, but time is so short these days and sometimes it is difficult to see things as sanely as we would have done in normal times. There have been moments this week when I would have stepped up the aisle quite easily, but my reason told me that this was foolish. Maybe I have been too cautious, anyway it is a bitter blow but at least Henry is going off abroad to do something worthwhile. I hope to be kept really busy so that I can get my mind off my own troubles.

<u>Diarist 5347, F, Civil Defence Telephonist, Hove, East Sussex, 23/04/42</u>

St. George's Day & my birthday. Reg called it my austerity birthday & gave me Savings Certificates. The girls at control gave me a book-token which pleased me very much. We are having a tea-party this afternoon with two of us celebrating birthdays – my 33rd and Joan's 22nd. We have got so used to having nothing to do that any excuse for a diversion is welcome.

<u>Diarist 5381, F, Warehouse Office Worker, Gateshead, Tyne and Wear, 26/04/42</u>

Went to allotment to help Father to dig and plant for Victory. We used to do this before the war, so maybe it is not only for this reason that we break our backs. Stayed there for two hours before lunch, and very much enjoyed getting the beds ready for sowing vegetables. An old man (to judge by his appearance he must be over 70) who knows father, came along to offer us his help. I was amazed to see a person so old, – he looked his age and was deaf – looking for work, not for any financial reason. Had he not been deaf I would have tried to find out his reason. But on the face of it, it appeared that he wanted something to do. Which led me to think that it is natural for people to work, and that we must see to it that no able-bodied man or woman is condemned to the horror of unemployment.

Diarist 5196, M, Army Clerk, Glasgow, 04/05/42
Spent Tuesday night dealing with Fire Guard queries and writing out warrant cards for some of my 400–500 Fire Guards. I should have an office staff but I shall perhaps earn the thanks of a grateful Government – and perhaps not. Incidentally, there are so many forms and regulations that I tell my people they must be careful not to put out a fire before filling in the appropriate pink form, but I shall have to cut that one out as I think some of them are beginning to believe me!

Diarist 5039.2, M, Factory Worker and Volunteer Fireman, Mansfield, Nottinghamshire, 06/05/42
Had medical today. Put in grade 4. Beforehand, told by many people, to exaggerate the nature of my complaint, so has[sic] to, 'get out of it'. Did not do so.

Diarist 5385, F, Writer and Secretary, Southborough, Kent, 11/05/42
Into our compartment come two ageing women. They have been travelling since early morning. Dressed drearily, but expensively,

with all the impedimenta of the well to do, they fill with bags & books & cases & themselves the parts of the compartment not occupied by Mother & me. At 3 o'clock, 15 mins before the train is due to start, they receive a tea basket, tea and cake. Astonishing cake it looks. Their comments show that its taste is as marvellous as its looks. 'What wonderful cake!' they say. 'Really pre-War. It is almost too sweet.'

Mother & I eye it quite greedily, with its light almost white colour & fine texture. Black currant-like dots also spatter the generous slices.

'Must have kept it hidden away somewhere,' one woman says.

She stares at me throughout the journey.

Diarist 5233, M, Factory Worker, Newport, Wales, 15/05/42
The unit is known as E.M.U. or Emu. I work mostly with a gang of women under the superintendence of a storeman. Two of the women are more foul-mouthed than anyone I have ever met before in my life. I have said before I find this sort of thing rather distressing. Yet both of them are very decent creatures at bottom – one is twenty-two with a husband in Egypt, the other a widow of 40 with one little girl. They speak with great affection of their husbands & of children generally, but that does not hinder them from indulging in this most revolting sexual chatter. (The phrase 'Target for Tonight' is current in a sense quite other from the film title). I am myself the object of a certain amount of banter because I have been married 5 years & have no children. It is not meant maliciously so I manage to stand it.

Diarist 5425, F, Architectural Assistant, London, 16/05/42

A week's leave. Down to Wiltshire. No wireless and no papers for several days; lying in bed late in the morning and going to bed by daylight, eating a lot and reading detective stories, a pastime I only enjoy when at the end of my tether. Also walked on the down and along the river in between showers, and attempted to sketch, dogged by rain and a very mobile bull that seemed always to be in the field where I was installed. Returned on Whit Monday – risking the crowds – in the emptiest train I ever remember.

Diarist 5454, F, Women's Voluntary Services, Blandford St Mary, Dorset, 21/05/42

Infant Welfare in the afternoon. I had to weigh the babies which is great fun. There are some nice babies coming now. Only 2 slummy ones the whole afternoon and they were not nearly as dirty as their mothers. A lot of them are first babies which accounts for their beautiful clothes perhaps but not for their grand bodies. Lots of them belong to soldiers' wives who have been to clinics wherever they have been. I wonder if they find it a way of making friends or if they feel they need the advice.

Diarist 5240, F, Teacher, Watford, Hertfordshire, 26/05/42

While I was at a friend's house an enquirer asked if my friend could promise to take in people for baths in the event of a gas attack. My friend gave a conditional promise: if the bath water happened to be warm, it could be used. If not, electric heat would take much longer than the required five minutes to warm the water.

Diarist 5402, F, Retired Teacher, Great Missenden, Buckinghamshire, 31/05/42

For some time I have been anxious to know the correct thing to do if one saw a parachutist landing. A member of the local Invasion Committee 'hasn't the faintest idea', and so far the only advice I can get is 'Arrest the man & take him to the Police Station' – 5 miles away. In this isolated spot, I should have thought it was important to know exactly whom to inform. I should go to the nearest telephone & dial 999 before doing anything else, but possibly the right thing would be to leave the lines free for the authorities. Why aren't we told?

Diarist 5381, F, Warehouse Office Worker, Gateshead, Tyne and Wear, 04/06/42

The Ministry of Information have a very active branch in the Newcastle area, and put on lectures and film shows very regularly. I attended practically all these shows last Winter and heard some very good speakers. The film shows, mostly M.O.I. ones, were also well worth seeing, and made me realise that the film as a medium of propaganda is an excellent thing. These shows usually last two hours, and consist of a lecture for an hour and a few short films. Recently I have not gone to them for a few reasons. Firstly, I am tired of the wrong sort of propaganda, and am not so interested now, in what is happening in the military sphere. I am more intent on planning for the peace, than fighting about how to win the war.

Diarist 5454, F, Women's Voluntary Services, Blandford St Mary, Dorset, 05/06/42

My bees swarmed but the Queen crawled up the leg of the spare hive and did not have to be taken in a skep. [. . .] Bees are nice to deal with. They seem so sane and well organised when the world seems hastening to its doom.

Diarist 5369, F, Writer and Voluntary Worker, Swansea, Glamorgan, 06/06/42

Somewhat revived return to work. Before the war I hated the little war clauses put into quotations & specifications stating 'in the event of outbreak of hostilities etc. etc.' One quotation today had the amazing clause, 'In the event of <u>cessation</u> of hostilities etc. etc.' Is this a precursor of the future? Notice, one section of the population who are coming to the front in this war are little boys. Already I hear they are demanding double time for Sunday for taking out papers. Now I find them enterprising on their own, with a cart & a wild pony borrowed from the common collecting rags & bones!

Diarist 5076, M, Accountant, Sheffield, 10/06/42

Later in the evening my niece remarked that 'As she had not started the war, she was not going to help.' However, she is thinking of joining the Air Cadet Corps 'because they have a nice uniform.'

Diarist 5369, F, Writer and Voluntary Worker, Swansea, Glamorgan, 10/06/42

I went horse riding in the evening. It was my first time. And they heaved me on to the horse with such vigour I nearly fell off the other side. Then when she stopped to eat grass, I nearly fell down her neck. Still it was fun. Life seems full of contrast & colour; The horror of war and the beauty of the hills. We had our usual beach party. About 8 girls and ten or a dozen of the Pioneer Corps, whom we seem to have undertaken to mother, & provide with tea every Sunday on the beach.

Diarist 5331, F, Shop Assistant, Dewsbury, West Yorkshire, 17/06/42

No biscuits for second week in succession. Customers so loud in their complaints that it might be bread they were deprived of. They have had at least half a pound per family per week since we came here and think the sky has fallen because they are not there as usual. Sometimes think we live in a bubble or glass case in this part of the world – the war makes so little <u>apparent</u> deep impression on us. The Japanese horrors, the starving people abroad, the fact that we are outclassed in Libya and are having ships sunk galore is nothing to us so that we get our 'extras' regularly, our cigs & matches & 'points' goods, our eggs & tomatoes. Perhaps if we were told the <u>whole</u> truth occasionally instead of one-sided truth or given the pill without the jam one might get the War deeper under our skins.

Diarist 5401, F, Technical Journalist for Aircraft Factory, Slough, Berkshire, 18/06/42

Small, irritating matters. The odd thing is that one accepts them, on the whole, cheerfully, and life continues to be, in the main, interesting and agreeable. We do things gradually in Britain. For instance, there was tremendous talk and gloomy speculation when the petrol cut was first instituted. 'What <u>shall</u> we do without a car?' An appalling privation . . . But in six months' time we shall be doing without our car, just as we are doing without bananas, grapefruit, butter, jam, stockings. When the idea of shortages is thrown at us we are shocked. Our imaginations paint a drab and pinched existence. But the shortage occurs, commodities are controlled or rationed or disappear altogether, gradually . . . and gradually we discover that we are doing with less or without. And life continues to be, in the main, agreeable and interesting.

Diarist 5425, F, Architectural Assistant, London, 22/06/42

The sudden and disastrous news of the fall of Tobruk. The evening papers full of widespread recriminations. The Standard's leader lamentably calling for explanations and for wisdom in finally learning the necessary lessons. We seem to have read the melancholy story so many times before. But lately disasters of this magnitude seem to make a less and less lasting impression on people, it's a blow at the moment but in spite of methodically losing every battle we do not seem to be losing the war so why worry! A curious feeling of remoteness from the battle sets in and as it is not immediately obvious to many people in their private lives what the loss of Singapore or even Egypt entails, and as we are monotonously fed on news of the vastness of American production and the consequent inevitability of final victory, these temporary setbacks, although a pity and require investigation, do not seriously disturb a public consciousness that has got used to the humiliation of continually being outwitted and outfought.

<u>Diarist 5196, M, Army Clerk, Glasgow, 29/06/42</u>

An outbreak of smallpox is reported in Glasgow and everybody is advised to get vaccinated. The clinics are thrown open and it is done free of charge, of course. By the weekend a quarter of a million people had been vaccinated. We had it done by our own Doctor at the weekend. Our chief fear was not of smallpox itself but of the possibility that if it gets worse we may not be allowed to travel and, of course, holidays are near.

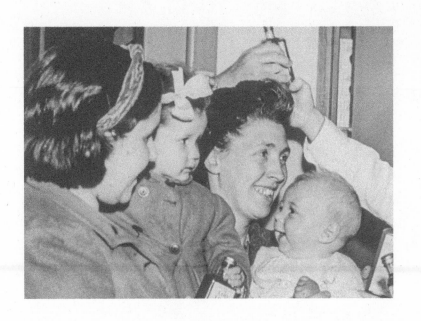

7. SHE IS QUITE CERTAIN WE ARE GOING TO LOSE THE WAR

July to December 1942

Saturday, August 15th.
A poisonous journey in a packed train to
Arbroath where I am going to see my mother
for the week-end. Found her struggling with
a large half-shut-up house and no servants.
Filled with dread at the prospect of trying
to keep off the subject of politics for a
whole 48 hours!

Sunday, August 16th.
If my mother goes on as she is doing she will
inevitably be had up for 'alarm and despondancy'.
She is quite certain we are going to lose
the war and her fanatical loathing of the
Government is such that I think she would
simply consider that they had been 'served
right' if we did lose. The ravings of a fanatic with Nazi ideology are not funny at any
time but when the proceed from one's mother
they lose any humour they might have had.

Monday, August 17th.
Back to Edinburgh by an equally crowded train
in a state of depression that only an evening

'If my mother goes on as she is doing she will inevitably be had up for "alarm and despondency". She is quite certain we are going to lose the war and her fanatical loathing of the Government is such that I think she would simply consider that they had been "served right" if we did lose.'

A difficult summer in the theatres of war sees Churchill subjected to a vote of no confidence in Parliament, but gives way in November to the first significant Allied victory of the war. It is termed, by Winston himself, as 'the end of the beginning'. Several weeks later the Beveridge Report, which has been in preparation for over a year, is published. It recommends the provision of social services and free health care for all in post-war Britain, radical reforms that – if written into law – will create a welfare state.

While there is plenty of scepticism about the government's desire to implement such sweeping change, many are optimistic that the report signals real progress. For the first time there is a concerted sense of looking forward, one distinct from the hope and optimism that was an intermittent feature of the preceding months and years. Instead of imagining The End they are now considering *beyond* it, and speculating about whether a better world might emerge from the ashes of this one. Many of the diarists begin to document smaller and more personal things, as if, able to refocus on their own lives a little while, they dare to plan and to dream.

* * *

Diarist 5369, F, Writer and Voluntary Worker, Swansea, Glamorgan, 01/07/42
The birthday of my two parents. Coming on the same day although 5 years' difference in age it has its compensations. One present usually does for both. This year, on the scanty war ration we felt the joy of humble celebrations. Two people under the same star and so different in temperament has entirely debunked any belief I had in the Zodiac system.

<u>Diarist 5365, F, Housewife, Watford, Hertfordshire, 05/07/42</u>
Unlike fowls and horses, cats and dogs have, mostly, only a sentimental value, especially in towns, and if they cannot live on what falls out of human safe consumption they should not be tolerated, much less have special food prepared and even killed for them. Farm dogs and cats justify their existence or get shot. House pets often get better fed than their owners. I know of one case where the people, vegetarians, drew and gave the dog both their meat rations plus what they could obtain in the way of dog-meat.

<u>Diarist 5013, M, Telegraphist, Doncaster, Yorkshire, 05/07/42</u>
A huge four-engined bomber passes over – quite low – I point and shout to Godfrey 'Look! A spitfire!' He gives me a look of unutterable disgust. My turn to laugh. I like teasing him a bit.

<u>Diarist 5399, F, Retired Nurse, Steyning, West Sussex, 08/07/42</u>
My niece with the new baby in Gloucestershire, told me that if she wanted the free cod-liver-oil etc, given out to mothers of babies, she would have six miles to go to the welfare station. Walk 1½ miles to a long-distance, infrequent bus, and take a chance of it being too full to stop for her, when she returned. The midwife told me that many of the village women did not go for their baby free rations because of the difficulty of getting there. I have written to Lord Woolton, and suggested that, in these places, the midwives, who have cars, and are always in the villages, and frequently calling on the new babies, should be empowered to take the free orange juice and cod-liver-oil to those who could not fetch it. His secretary acknowledged my letter.

<u>Diarist 5331, F, Shop Assistant, Dewsbury, West Yorkshire,</u>
<u>12/07/42</u>

B. went off to Blackpool yesterday. He says if the Government really meant us to stay at home they would stop the trains, but, he says, there are too many of them shareholders in the Railways to do that. Sooner he had gone than myself. Have no wish to travel twenty in a Railway Carriage and queue for permission to come home again. My way of holidaying is to lie in a deck chair in our little garden and read 'Moby Dick' and forget the war.

<u>Diarist 5369, F, Writer and Voluntary Worker, Swansea,</u>
<u>Glamorgan, 12/07/42</u>

Our beach parties are now famous, and our hostess is an Austrian refugee of 18½ who looks 25 and acts 30. You sure never would recognise the little refugee, who landed forlornly upon us, dressed in a white Hungarian pinafore, looking like an English girl about to be confirmed, except for those eyes, no English girl about to be confirmed ever had eyes like that, – black, flashing Viennese eyes. But even then I had thought she had a nerve to come to a foreign country alone, & not knowing a word of the language. But now she knows more slang and American idioms than any of us. She gets her own way from sheer force of personality. When she says hands off so-&-so & so-&-so it is hands off. We talked about our jobs – pre-war mostly. Danny was an apprentice in the printing trade, & Howard in the cotton trade, & Schoefield of Sasskatchewan – however you spell it, was a film artist painting the background scenery.

<u>Diarist 5390, F, Secretary, Ministry of Fuel and Power, Glasgow,</u>
<u>13/07/42</u>

In the course of conversation I asked Mrs. Lamb how David's children had stood up to the blitz at York. They are 3 and 5 and took it as a lark. The 5 year old boy has a splendid joke that he often repeats; he tells the three year old sister 'If you are naughty I will drop an oil bomb on you and you will be burnt up.' This never fails to produce amusement. (Personally I should try and stop that joke by failing to be amused by it).

<u>Diarist 5039.2, M, Factory Worker and Volunteer Fireman,</u>
<u>Mansfield, Nottinghamshire, 27/07/42</u>

Heard that a whole street in Derby had been bombed to the ground in a raid last Thursday. I know for a definite fact that no bombs were dropped on Derby that night. That as[sic] been a feature of this war that I have particularly noticed. People do like to exaggerate, they like people to think that they have important exclusive news, and there is usually a lot added to the story.

<u>Diarist 5381, F, Warehouse Office Worker, Gateshead, Tyne and</u>
<u>Wear, 29/07/42</u>

I will try and make a survey of British Restaurants in the near future. I pass one on my way to work, but as they only open for lunch and tea it is always closed. This is the first one opened in Gateshead and is called the Mayor's Restaurant. I have heard that it is very well patronised. It is situated in a slum area, and it probably is very useful for poor working class people. I have not patronised these B.R.'s as I do not eat in restaurants at all, in view of the fact that I am a practising orthodox Jewess (sounds frightful, but I really am quite normal) and I am not permitted to eat meat if it is not prepared according to Jewish ritual.

Diarist 5233, M, Unemployed, Newport, Wales, 01/08/42

I write this month's instalment under most depressing & discouraging conditions. The job I had as a sorter at the Post Office that was to tide me over at least until October, when I intend to try to get a job with the Ministry of Supply at Cardigan, was lost after only four weeks. They said I could not sort quick enough; I was not making the requisite progress. And my shop in London which I have held onto so long, though without any profit, will at last have to close down. It is making a loss, & the landlord refuses to reduce the rent. So the only thing is to sell the fixtures & fittings & cut losses. I owe £300 to the bank. My father will lose that, less what the fittings realise. He does not complain or reproach me in any way, but I don't like it. I've always been more or less dependent on him, & though we are now on very good terms, we have had enormous disputes in the past.

Diarist 5381, F, Warehouse Office Worker, Gateshead, Tyne and Wear, 09/08/42

I travelled with a boy of 11, who had been spending a holiday with relations in Glasgow. He was an intelligent child and told me he had just passed for York Grammar School. His one ambition was to become a pilot and bomb the Germans, even if it meant waiting for the next war. War has a terribly long reaching effect on young minds, which welcome the chance of destroying and killing one's fellows.

Diarist 5401, F, Technical Journalist for Aircraft Factory, Slough, Berkshire, 10/08/42

The Nazi plane which paid us a visit on Saturday was seen by nearly every other person 'just above my house'. One of our typists was at the fete which he machine gunned. No one was hurt but a row of deck chairs was shattered. Reports of bombs that fell vary in number from 9 to 2. Damage to some lorries parked by railway line, an old factory building and a waste space. Two policemen killed.

Diarist 5415, F, Restaurant Owner, Edinburgh, 12/08/42

Bought my first sweet ration. Seldom ate sweets in peacetime but fancy I shall now buy them monthly: probably partly because I've 'got a right to them'!

Diarist 5376, F, Teacher, Burwash Weald, East Sussex, 12/08/42

2 evacuees are leaving us. The aunt took a cottage here after the mother was killed in a London raid – now they are returning. We think it mad. London will get raids again. The 8 year old's nerves are hardly right yet. Y'day she went as white as a sheet when told it was her turn to go to the dentist. At first she wept whenever spoken to, almost looked at.

Diarist 5415, F, Restaurant Owner, Edinburgh, 16/08/42

If my mother goes on as she is doing she will inevitably be had up for 'alarm and despondency'. She is quite certain we are going to lose the war and her fanatical loathing of the Government is such that I think she would simply consider that they had been 'served right' if we did lose. The ravings of a fanatic with Nazi ideology are not funny at any time but when they proceed from one's mother they lose any humour they might have had.

Diarist 5118, M, Engineering Assistant, Trowbridge, Wiltshire, 23/08/42

Considerable concern felt at the outbreak of foot & mouth disease in the Trowbridge Area: now in 35 localities: all the cattle affected are slaughtered. As well as losing the meat (the carcasses are buried) the milk goes west. Several villages around have had their milk supply 'go dry' & it has had to be brought from other districts. Some people accuse the Jerries of dropping infected starlings from their planes when they come over, but I expect the birds came over of their own free will!

Diarist 5076, M, Accountant, Sheffield, 25/08/42

One of our wealthiest clients asked us for our opinion about the purchase of a factory on war work. His idea is to provide a post (as Director) in essential work for a 'flame' of his, and so save her from compulsory enlistment in the Forces. We warned him that it was likely to be an expensive investment as the after-war prospects are not good.

Diarist 5402, F, Retired Teacher, Great Missenden, Buckinghamshire, 26/08/42

Had an unexpected visit from a 20 year-old relative: very clever, & a newly-fledged BSc. 'Did I hear someone say that Mr. Churchill had visited Moscow?' she asked. I can remember being terribly interested in the Boer War as a schoolgirl – we all were. I can't understand the apparent indifference of the young people I have met to this war when their own lives are at stake.

Diarist 5196, M, Army Clerk, Glasgow, 28/08/42

Had to get the Doctor for Anne on Thursday – she had a chill. Doctor says she is run down – after a month's holiday! She also warned us of her nervous disposition – but this week's funny story is the best yet. She has to have fresh fruit and vegetables. The former we can't get and the latter she won't eat.

Diarist 5256, F, Teacher, Thornaby-on-Tees, North Yorkshire, 02/09/42

'OPEN SECOND FRONT NOW' whitewashed on hospital wall boldly & clearly. Miss H. is excited & interested & remarks on returning from lunch that an effort has been made to rub it out which has only succeeded in making it more noticeable. Miss D. reads it with curiosity but makes no comment. Neither refer to policy or origin.

Diarist 5233, M, Unemployed, Newport, Wales, 03/09/42

Our landlady told us that listening inadvertently to the broadcast 'Gestapo in England' & hearing 'Mr. Churchill has gone to Berlin to ask for an armistice' she thought for a moment that it was true, & felt a chill at the heart. Were there any others?

Diarist 5390, F, Secretary, Ministry of Fuel and Power, Glasgow, 03/09/42

We have been mystified by the reappearance of [the budgie] Dick's sparrow friends on the kitchen window sill – when we stopped feeding them, they retaliated by striking Dick off their visiting list. Now we see that they are after the parsley seeds on the plant Mother brought back from Berwick. Sparrows are dear to me, and it is a real regret that we can no longer feed them. The emphasis is all on pigs nowadays. All the scraps must go to the pig bins.

<u>Diarist 5089, M, Postal Sorter, Bristol, 04/09/42</u>
Mum related the story of how a British soldier lost his temper in Marks and Spencer's Cafe waiting for the girl to serve him with a cup of tea. He had travelled all night from Scotland – and was now going on to S. Coast for embarkation. He had not been able to get a cup of tea at the station. The girl behind the counter at Marks would not take any notice of him – and he said 'If I was a bloody Yank she would be slinging her arms around my neck.' A lady in the queue sympathised with him – but advised him not to make a fool of himself – saying 'we think the world of our British Tommies.' She paid for a cup of tea and a sandwich for him. He declined this at first – but afterwards accepted it.

<u>Diarist 5016, M, Analytical Chemist, Iver, Buckinghamshire, 08/09/42</u>
A friend of mine had a suitcase packed by his wife, ready at hand in the house, so that he could grab it quickly in the event of bombing. Last week he looked it through and found it contained the following things – 1 very dark grey suit, 2 shirts (rather old) – 1 pr pyjamas (fit for the making of dusters), 2 prs of pants – a pair of white buck-skin shoes – and – an opera-hat!!! To quote him 'All I needed to make me ready for the city was a banjo.'

<u>Diarist 5434, F, Psychiatric Nurse, Gosforth, Newcastle-upon-Tyne, 14/09/42</u>
I am making myself a very warm housecoat out of an airtex blanket & if that is wrong I can't help it as I started this coupon

rationing with very low stocks – & my shoes are such items – & we are trying to keep within the fuel target. I am also making mother a jacket out of half a rug. It's so successful I hope to get another one for myself & I am making myself a cape from a mackintosh ground sheet.

Diarist 5311, F, Housewife, Sutton Coldfield, Warwickshire, 14/09/42

Hear 1 o'c news and at the end an appeal by 'Our Stuart' for any fishing tackle and equipment that anglers have to spare for the benefit of soldiers who find themselves near rivers and streams, but unable to fish in their spare time because they have no tackle. I wonder if the Russian soldier has time to fish at this moment. Dear me, if the English take their pleasures sadly, they take their wars light-heartedly. Second Front or no, and with all due sympathy for a huge army idling away its time in this country through no fault of its own, this latest appeal does seem a bit thick.

Diarist 5192, M, Civil Servant, Stockton-on-Tees, County Durham, 15/09/42

Cycling home with Leslie, who berated me soundly because my wife has suborned his to join the gang who do duty at the canteen, thereby condemning him to get his own tea on a Wednesday and every 5th Sunday. I agreed that it was hard on him, & suggested that he & I take alternate Weds. for preparing tea for two, first at one house & then t'other.

Diarist 5100, M, Personnel Manager, Birmingham, 19/09/42

I've neglected this diary for a fortnight. Feeling off colour mentally & physically for reasons difficult to explain. Life seemed most infernally flat & dull. Work less exacting, labour turnover much less than previous months. After working hours restless & bored & unsettled. Found myself almost wishing for a raid & looking back on the blitz period as a time when life had a real kick in it.

Diarist 5199, M, Railway Draughtsman, Wilmslow, Cheshire, 21/09/42

Life proceeds placidly: could easily forget a war is on. Office colleague (lady tracer) whose brother has been called up, is very bitter because he gets army pay although working in a factory, while civilians get much larger pay. They are free after working hours, but he has army duties, polishing buttons, etc.

Diarist 5347, F, Civil Defence Telephonist, Hove, East Sussex, 26/09/42

I haven't written my diary in some weeks. I think I am so mixed up in my mind about everything that I don't know what to think or where to start. Nearly every argument I have been involved in lately, I have been on the opposite side to the majority so I cannot trust myself to express an opinion lately for fear of being thought odd. I must confess to myself that I am going through a stage of re-adjustment, I suppose many people are feeling bewildered with life just now but I feel that it is not only the war that has caused my confusion except in so far that it has made me meet many people who I suppose have influenced my views to some extent. Then, I live in the two environments, & although I hate self-deception of any sort, I seem to be two different people. For one 24 hours I am a woman with a job & personality of her own & the next I am my husband's wife & however much you try to keep your own outlook & opinions it is difficult not to confuse them with your partner's especially when he is a person whom you think you would esteem even if he were not your husband.

Diarist 5402, F, Retired Teacher, Great Missenden, Buckinghamshire, 01/10/42

A local lady says 'Why should we go cold & miserable when the West End shops still run lifts to take customers upstairs when they could quite well walk up?' Another said 'I think there's something in the idea of refusing to economise & forcing the introduction of rationing.' 'But,' said I, 'can we afford to? I shouldn't like to lose the war.' 'You may not like it if we win, either,' was the reply. Very true: Europe under Hitler would be better than a Europe in which all government had broken down. I often wish now that Germany had won the last war.

Diarist 5052, M, Teacher, Selsdon, Surrey, 03/10/42

We are asked not to start fires till Nov. 1. So far I have succeeded, clothed in an overcoat, wrapped in a rug, and footed in a foot muff I found which had been given to Mother by my brother years ago and which she never used! How little did one foresee then the circumstances in which I should use it!

Diarist 5039.2, M, Factory Worker and Volunteer Fireman, Mansfield, Nottinghamshire, 04/10/42

Land Army girl I know, brings home a dozen eggs every week-end. Hardly fair, in view of the few that we get. Anyway, I would have them, given the chance!

<u>Diarist 5309, F, Office Worker, London, 06/10/42</u>

I've just come in from an M.O.I. Committee meeting which had some interesting aspects. There is a queer tug-of-war goes on at these affairs between the timid, conservative, don't-let's-carp-and-criticise, leave-it-to-the-experts tendencies, & the sharply critical, won't-be-put-off-with-blarney, something-ought-to-be-done attitude: it is queer because the two attitudes are not always expressed by the same groups of people.

<u>Diarist 5307, F, Stenographer, Birmingham, 07/10/42</u>

One of my young colleagues, a girl just 21, is in a state of being semi-engaged to a lad invalided out of the R.A.F. She herself will be called up, probably to one of the services, in a month or two's time. But the lass is so determined that when she does get married (although they are not even thinking of planning the date yet) it shall be a Proper wedding, that she has already bought her wedding veil, for fear they should go off the market, and is now moving heaven & earth to get a 22 carat wedding ring! Ever since the war I have been wondering about this attitude. My common sense says it is so stupid & wrong to waste money on such empty conventions as a white wedding and all its paraphernalia, but my common sentiment says, Well, there's something rather good about saying Hitler be damned, I'm going to have a Proper Wedding in spite of everything! By and large I should say it does very little harm to the war effort, and a whole heap of good to morale, to go bald-headed for the frills & finery.

<u>Diarist 5076, M, Accountant, Sheffield, 09/10/42</u>

My wife is helping at a friend's office. The Managing Director there disagrees with women fire-watching, and says he would not let his wife go. 'I do not suppose Ellen Wilkinson is doing any in spite of her fuss,' he remarked. He blames all government muddles onto the Labour Party, or as he calls them, 'Bevin & Co' and concluded 'I used to be a sympathiser of the Labour Party, but I am not now.'

Diarist 5261, F, Factory Clerk, Manchester, 12/10/42
Mrs. M.C., the woman who cried because she has to fire-watch, should be on duty tonight, but has made the excuse that her husband is ill. This sudden illness is very convenient.

Diarist 5423, F, Housewife, Bradford, West Yorkshire, 14/10/42
Bradford has been notified that buses & trams are to stop running at 9pm after next week except for war-workers. Everybody I have met today is furious. Wonder how the bus conductors will find out who are bona fide war-workers? There will have to be some system of issuing tickets at the works – after the style of the discs which the blind people have. Of course, there'll be a lot of 'evasion' – I don't envy the conductresses in the 'blackout' this winter.

Diarist 5376, F, Teacher, Burwash Weald, East Sussex, 23/10/42
Lunch conversation turns to atrocities in Europe. The head says no doubt it's unpleasant to have the Germans in occupation & there are restrictions but she thinks the atrocity stuff is rumour & propaganda. It's no use labelling all Germans as bad & the English & especially the Canadians commit atrocities too. She takes a slightly lofty, amused attitude to those who believe in these reports.

Diarist 5335, F, Teacher, Bedford, Bedfordshire, 23/10/42

More discussions over fires: usual argument 'Other people have fires.' 'It's absurd to say no heating this month: how do they know what the weather will be?' 'I bet that Churchill & Wootton aren't freezing themselves.'

Diarist 5004, M, ARP Worker and Food Packing Manager, Belmont, Surrey, 02/11/42

I bought my sixth torch today. Again a different size to the five I already possess. The explanation why I have bought so many can be summed up in the word 'batteries'. Whatever size torch I seem to possess the shops fail to have the appropriate battery. It is very sickening to have to buy one torch after another in order to get a battery, but what is a chap like me to do who cannot see in the blackout? On A.R.P duty I of course use the official torches, but a recent edict has come around which restricts their use, and I have to be careful, if only as an example to others.

Diarist 5331, F, Shop Assistant, Dewsbury, West Yorkshire, 02/11/42

Then we got on to the subject of illegitimate war babies. One said she'd heard there were hospitals full of them and the Government was going to bring them up.

I wonder what sort of a race we shall have in future when everyone is sorted out back to their own country. A somewhat mixed one I should think. All these Poles & Americans & Dutch & Norwegians are bound to leave some traces. But this is the horrible part of war, worse than the slaughter – the loosening of restraining & decency, the stealing & the graft.

<u>Diarist 5199, M, Railway Draughtsman, Wilmslow, Cheshire,</u>
<u>04/11/42</u>

I rarely emerge from home in the blackout, but returned wife's library books at County Library. Wilmslow is a silly place, without a proper library open at convenient times: only 7.30 to 8.30 Wed. evening. To me it is unnerving: I bashed my temple but did not break specs. People all about roads, boys running about amidst cycles & traffic. Neighbour (wholesale greengrocer: woman) told my wife motoring in blackout is very unnerving because pedestrians are all over the road. Especially I noticed airmen & soldiers emerging from public house & going about roadway.

<u>Diarist 5427, F, Widowed Housewife and Voluntary Worker,</u>
<u>London, 07/11/42</u>

B. came up with John for the day & night. She said what did I think about the Libyan news, 'everybody' seemed tremendously excited over it & to feel that we were really getting somewhere at last: She went on to say that while it was certainly a welcome change to have news of success instead of chronic failure, she herself couldn't help feeling rather dubious as to the importance & permanence of the victory in progress, because it was all so much the same as what had happened before, first to our side & then to theirs. Personally I must confess to feeling absolutely & entirely apathetic. I shan't feel any more interest in this war till its end actually really comes, & even then nothing will go back to what it was – or even improve for some years. It's too late to repair the damage now & one can only hope there won't be too much more of it.

Diarist 5287, F, Housewife, Salisbury, Wiltshire, 12/11/42

Nothing at all worthy of note. Met a lot of grumblers grumbling at insufficient meat ration. Suppose this cold, wet, miserable weather makes us all feel we'd like something good to eat to cheer us up a bit. But we're all a long way from starving & for the 4th year of the war, I reckon we're going very well.

Diarist 5240, F, Teacher, Watford, Hertfordshire, 12/11/42

On the return journey I was in a train at blackout time. The ticket-collector came along & said: 'Blackout time; every one please pull the blinds.' Within ten minutes, two people, a girl & a soldier had pushed the blind nearest them aside to look out.

Diarist 5271, F, Local Government Clerk, Bury St Edmunds, Suffolk, 19/11/42

Find out why Assistance Board won't pay compensation to woman who sent her artificial leg to be repaired & it got bombed – she says the firm were bankrupt & the Govt. took it over & that's why Assistance Board won't pay. If they won't pay, find out if we will.

Diarist 5157, M, Retired Policeman, Wallasey, Merseyside, 21/11/42

Reading press in the papers about the forthcoming Beveridge report on social change after the war I can already see the warning light exhibited by vested interests. What reason have we to think that human nature has changed during the last 3 years, we all know that at times it is capable of great sacrifices but those times are rare and exceptional. Am I only a cynic or a foolish old man if I form the opinion that we will sink back to our old condition after the war plus a few improvements and advances which normally take place.

Diarist 5443, F, Office Worker and Volunteer Mobile Canteen Driver, London, 24/11/42

Felt really dead today and spent it in bed with a hot water bottle clasped to my middle. Odd, how when one feels bad, the news seems unimportant; nothing short of the Armistice could have moved me today.

Diarist 5045, M, Nurseryman, Newick, East Sussex, 02/12/42

A nurse I know of told me one of her patients who had been totally crippled for life by war action. To while away the time he took to making little rag toys. My nurse friend gave him a small handful of cotton wool with which to stuff them. A nursing sister who saw her do so snatched it away not only upbraiding my nurse friend for giving it but turning to the cripple said 'and you too ought to have known better than to take hospital stores. Don't you know there's a War on?' Further comment is unnecessary. My nurse friend said she felt like spitting in the other woman's eye but of course under our rigid code of discipline she just had to stand aside and say nothing.

Diarist 5004, M, ARP Warden and Food Packing Manager, Belmont, Surrey, 05/12/42

I have noticed since biscuits were 'zoned' that in this part of the country only the very plain varieties are reaching us. Chocolate covered biscuits are completely unobtainable, and I suppose this is because the firm supplying biscuits are not allowed to make other than very plain varieties. Previously we had the choice of at least six manufacturers, all with varying products. I realise that this sort of thing is quite unimportant in war, but I am afraid it foretells the state of things which may arise when we are at peace. With all this talk of nationalisation, I rather fear that individual tastes will not be catered for. I agree that it is not sense to buy Oatcakes from Scotland when they might just as well be made here, but supposing they are not made in the South, do I have to go without oatcakes, even though I am passionately fond of them? On the other hand I have seen lorries carrying Peek Frean's biscuits on the Great West Road travelling towards Reading, and coming in the reverse direction lorries from Huntley & Palmers bringing biscuits to London.

Diarist 5401, F, Technical Journalist for Aircraft Factory, Slough, Berkshire, 07/12/42

Red Cross 'Bring and Buy Sale' for Prisoners of War on Saturday afternoon. No one seemed to know who was organising it or what to do, but by time I arrived stalls had been arranged and sale was in progress. I helped J.W with side shows – we were patronised largely by children. Our trade slackened by 4.30 when I abandoned my post to get some tea and look round other stalls but all the best bargains had gone. Various foods were being raffled – sugar, home-made jam, eggs etc. Had a few words with my Commandant – her mother is very ill. There is no hope, and very little that can be done for her now – 'Before the war,' said J. sadly, 'one could take them abroad, buy special delicacies, get companionship but now there is nothing. One can not even get domestic help.'

<u>Diarist 5338, F, Civil Servant, Morecambe, Lancashire, 09/12/42</u>
We were warned by our Fuel-Warden this morning to be careful to put lights out as soon as it is possible to work without in the morning, as some of the residents had complained of their being left on too long. I think it's time some of these Morecambites set about sweeping their own doorstep, instead of prowling round to spy on the Civil Servants. Everything about us is wrong. There were complaints about our having milk in the mornings when Morecambe people 'couldn't get it for children'. Then there were letters to the paper about girls leaving the offices at 4.30 – that by a holidaymaker who had been 'working hard all the year' (as if we hadn't) – Now we are using too much light. I suppose it is really just the general objection to having us in the town at all.

<u>Diarist 5261, F, Factory Clerk, Manchester, 12/12/42</u>
Went to town with Norbert this afternoon & saw the film 'Mrs. Miniver' & enjoyed it very much. For an American-made film of English wartime life it was exceedingly good. The only thing that didn't seem right was the part depicting the outbreak of war. It was depicted as coming as a shock to us, whereas in reality we knew it was coming & knew when it would be announced.

<u>Diarist 5205, M, Laboratory Technician, Potters Bar, Hertfordshire, 18/12/42</u>
Still trying to get out of doing fire-watching on Christmas night, so that I can go home for Christmas. Even if the journey isn't really necessary, I think a visit home is a legitimate excuse for travelling about once a month.

Diarist 5443, F, Office Worker and Volunteer Mobile Canteen Driver, London, 19/12/42

We are all very interested in what will happen to Corporal D. who comes into the canteen every day. He was sentenced yesterday to 2 months imprisonment. Apparently he sold silk stockings to girls at the camp without coupons, this all happened about a year ago, but retribution has overtaken him now. Actually I think he has been unfortunate, at that time thousands of people were involved in this illicit trade, and the police have got hold of a few unlucky persons, to be held up as examples. If he is finally sent to serve his sentence, he will be discharged from the R.A.F., then automatically called up for the Army when he comes out of prison, and thus a promising career will be ruined.

Diarist 5035, M, Power Loom Turner, Huddersfield, West Yorkshire, 20/12/42

I have been making use of the British Restaurant for quite a while now, and having a regular cooked meal every day, and I didn't always get this before, actually I have put on more weight, and weigh more than any time in my life.

Diarist 5240, F, Teacher, Watford, Hertfordshire, 20/12/42

At the railway station, I was interested to see a tall zinc box near the barrier, with a notice asking people to drop in their finished-with newspapers & magazines for distribution to hospitals & among troops on the same day. A splendid idea on the part of the Evening Standard, I thought.

<u>Diarist 5447, F, Clerk and Housewife, Sheffield, 23/12/42</u>
War seems satisfactory in a slow fashion. I get horrid presentiments that 1943 is going to be hideous, but I feel that we can't avoid it, so let us get it over, and oh God, let us do things properly afterwards so that we don't have more wars.

<u>Diarist 5311, F, Housewife, Sutton Coldfield, Warwickshire, 25/12/42</u>
We have tea on our own by lounge fireside, and I have only small jam tarts and chocolate biscuits by way of sweet things. I used a packet of Madeira cake mixture to try to make a sponge sandwich, and put dried egg into it, but the darn thing went pudden-y in the oven, and it looks as though it will have to be given to the dog. Poor long suffering animal! Still, I'm not going to have it said that my cake wasn't even fit to give a dog! I lament though about the waste of fat. Bang went four ounces of marge.

<u>Diarist 5045, M, Nurseryman, Newick, East Sussex, 30/12/42</u>
December the last month of the curious year of 1942 has produced quite a few matters of interest for us here. To begin with I have gone up one in rank in the Home Guard and now find myself where I left off in the last war i.e. full Lieutenant and here I'm likely to remain for there are now far too many old dugouts up above for me to hope for any more promotion unless the Jerries come over and bump some of them off.

8. THIS IS JUST RIDICULOUS OFFICIAL PERVERSITY

January to June 1943

'In spite of the recent further increase in the milk ration, we
are still not allowed any milk for morning or afternoon tea,
nor a cup of tea at lunchtime. This is just ridiculous official
perversity.'

Over the first half of the year the Allies build on the major progress they made at the end of 1942, and it's clear that the tide has turned. Victories in Russia and North Africa are followed by the capture of Sicily in June – a triumphant moment. The British public, who have been used to hearing about strings of losses and retreats for three long years, are treated to a slew of good news. Success on the battlefields is not, however, echoed on the home front, where far-off victories offer little compensation for ever-worsening shortages, ever-tightening rationing and ever-increasing taxes.

With the novelty of victories wearing thin, many turn their focus and attention to how things are being run – and they often don't like what they see. Complaints about bureaucracy, red tape and lack of sense are rife, and some are preoccupied by the societal inequality that has survived and thrived despite the (literally) levelling experience of the Blitzes. People are sceptical of how the government is handling things and are generally more inclined to link their dwindling quality of life with internal political decisions, rather than external enemies.

* * *

Diarist 5412, F, Teacher, Beckenham, Kent, 05/01/43

Nearly had a rumpus at breakfast this morning. My eldest sister, pious, who runs a Mission House in Wiltshire, is here to help to nurse my mother. The 8 o'clock bulletin was coming through as we sat at breakfast. The announcer said the Russians have captured another 20,000 men killed, wounded, & prisoners. Some 40,000 trucks, & 5,000 guns, & millions of rounds of ammunition. The Night Nurse, who is not over-bright said, your sister F, says she can't believe what the Russians say, it's quite impossible for them to capture so many men.

Why, said I, why is it impossible. What about the 40,000 we lost at Loos in 1915, and the quarter of a million of Frenchmen lost before Verdun? My other sister, twin to F, said smoothly 'The figures are quite fantastic.' I exploded.

Diarist 5100, M, Personnel Manager, Birmingham, 05/01/43
When the sergeant bought [Smith] in I asked him what the trouble was. He broke out into a very incoherent sort of protest & was obviously very upset & then to my horror he burst into tears & cried noisily.

It was a distressing experience. I hate to see a man cry. I put him in my interview room to get over it & sent for his foreman. When the latter came we found Smith with his head slumped forward on his chest & his eyes. I had to shake him to bring him round. Then I sat down & got him to talk. He's one of a family of 17 & apparently has an excessively high blood pressure which results in outbreaks of violent temper. He used to have these when younger & his older brother's remedy appeared to be to punch him across the room. He talked on, stumbling & partly incoherent, exhausted by the outbreak of a few minutes before, holding his head which was aching. We washed out the suspension, called for a car to take him home & told him to see a doctor. We also told him when he felt these attacks coming on to go & tell his foreman so that on receiving some instruction or order he would not fly off the handle as he does on such occasions. But I'm desperately conscious that I can't help the poor chap. One feels guilty of merely passing on the job to someone else. We need not only a resident doctor but a psychological clinic as well these days, when we get such people sent to us by the Labour Exchanges. I wish there was some omnipotent body one could send these people to to be looked after. I wish one could devise some system of making their lives more bearable, of rehabilitating them & caring for them without giving such help the 'institutional' flavour they regard with such (often justifiable) horror.

Diarist 5004, M, ARP Worker and Food Packing Manager, Belmont, Surrey, 13/01/43

Mr. Bevin's recent speech telling a meeting of workpeople that they must not expect immediately after the war to have their liberties quickly restored, is a sharp reminder to those who expect, (and there are many) that with the coming of peace, conditions and circumstances will immediately improve. If these remarks had come from a Conservative man, no doubt an outcry would have been raised, but as Mr. Bevin is known to be such a champion of liberty, people realise that as he said it, the necessity must be great.

Diarist 5039.2, M, Factory Worker and Volunteer Fireman, Mansfield, Nottinghamshire, 14/01/43

Don't think L.W. will ration bread until absolutely forced to. It's good filling food. Anyway, there is a lot wasted. We waste it. I know a chap who doesn't like the wartime bread. Says it's soggy in the middle. A loaf lasts him a week. A good many people I know are not keen on it. I like it.

Diarist 5412, F, Teacher, Beckenham, Kent, 17/01/43

Wondered how on earth we went through this night after night in 1941. The barrage was simply colossal, the flooring shook, & the walls seemed to shiver from time to time. Wish I could settle down & knit or something. I simply want to smoke, & you can't smoke much in a small reinforced room. Wandered about wondering where the ginger cat had gone to, he is terrified by raids. After 3 hours the ginger cat's boy friend came streaking in, during a lull, then in came a ghost of a ginger cat. I've never seen such a terrified beast in my life.

Diarist 5399, F, Retired Nurse, Steyning, West Sussex, 17/01/43
A girl here (21) was called up for service, and told she must join up in one of the Forces. She is doing cooking six hours a day, in a restaurant, which will have to close if she goes. Also taking care of her father (63) who is working hard doing agricultural work, and also growing a large amount of vegetables on his garden and allotment, and taking care of two other gardens. A very useful worker. He comes home wet and cold, and needs some food and a fire. This girl has been his housekeeper since she was 14. At the local Board, at Worthing, he was told he must find a housekeeper. But if a woman is free to come and keep house for him, she can do other things, and he couldn't pay much for anyone to come, if she was any good at all.

Diarist 5199, M, Railway Draughtsman, Wilmslow, Cheshire, 22/01/43
A letter of mine appeared in the 'Wilmslow Advertiser', criticising the Ministry of Labour for able-bodied men being not used efficiently, while elderly folk are discouraged & insulted, when applying to be utilised, by being required to fill up forms with many irrelevant details, including particulars of education from age 12. Various people have commented favourably on this letter.

Diarist 5240, F, Teacher, Watford, Hertfordshire, 31/01/43
For the first time the Blood Transfusion Service was open on Saturdays & Sundays, & apparently this was very popular. There

were about 12 people waiting when I went in about 4.10. In conversation, others, too, mentioned that they did not expect to see so many there.

During the 'operation' I told the nurse about my recent illness, & she suggested taking less. But I told her I had asked my doctor's advice before coming. The nurse said she wished everyone did that. Far too many, women mostly, faint, collapse, or feel ill, & then mention a very recent illness excusing themselves by saying that they really wanted to give their 'pint'. The nurse said that the staff would rather not be worried by such people.

Diarist 5239, F, Aerodynamicist and Housewife, Bolton-le-Sands, Lancashire, 01/02/43
After listening to the one o'clock news D. said, 'The war will be over in two months.' We all disagreed violently. J. and P. thought that they would not be out of uniform for five years. D. said 1945 at the latest.

Diarist 5348, F, Housewife, Cheadle Hulme, Cheshire, 04/02/43
Carry out baby's bath water. Mrs M tells me not to put in pail. I say 'it's a shame to waste it – Gov't says we are to be careful with water'
Mrs M – 'oh well, if we did everything the government says —'
Me: – 'we might win the war'
Mrs M. (widow of Sergt-Pilot) – 'We've done our share towards winning the war, haven't we Anne?' (child aged 3)

Placard reported from Manchester Fish Shop

WE HAVE PLENTY

OF PAPER

PLEASE BRING

YOUR

OWN

FISH.

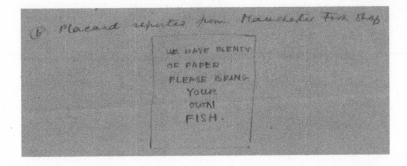

Diarist 5399, F, Retired Nurse, Steyning, West Sussex, 10/02/43

Measuring my brain power against the members of the Brains'
Trust I find in many ways it is far more active than theirs. For
instance, a question was asked last evening, about whether we
should consider posterity – something to that effect. Nothing
definite was said, but my mind flew instantly to the way we waste
coal – 70% of the heat is wasted up the chimney in open fires,
and we almost force other nations to buy from us, so as to enrich
certain members of this generation. Yet we are using up our
supply very fast, and can get no more through all eternity. In
comparatively few years, coal, that took aeons of time to lay
down, will be used and gone, and nothing but ashes to show for
it. The Brainy people never mentioned this.

Diarist 5402, F, Retired Teacher, Great Missenden, Buckinghamshire, 13/02/43

There's a little café in Wycombe where there is one teaspoon, chained to the counter – so many spoons have been stolen they will risk no more. The pens in the Post Office are also chained. I feel so ashamed, & hope the Americans won't notice.

Diarist 5256, F, Teacher, Thornaby-on-Tees, North Yorkshire, 14/02/43

Meet friend who has been evacuated in country for a good while. Talk about 'after the war'. She says there will be a fight for the Beveridge Plan because there are too many rich people who do not want to lose what they have. I tell her that I am keen to go to London at Easter to listen in at the N.U.T. Conference. She seems envious but says, 'Trueman (her husband) will not hear of my going while there's a war.'

Diarist 5088, M, Chemist, Manchester, 15/02/43

After dinner collected fire-watching money, and had a chat with Haughton (a neighbour); he has made his garden into a lawn again, for his child to play on, the results he got as a vegetable garden were too poor to warrant him continuing.

Diarist 5210, M, RAF Corporal, Warrington, Cheshire, 15/02/43

To me, the great question of the moment is, – 'When & where will the Allies strike?' It is obvious that it must be soon, before the Germans can regain their breath, & I feel that stretchy feeling of waiting coming into me that I always get before running or going in to bat. How will the invasion, when it comes, affect me

& Dora? Have the Allies really got the strength & the brains & the organisation to put this thing across at the first attempt, without wasting time or men's lives? The next few months will undoubtedly be the testing time. The consciousness of this makes me extra impatient of all the unreal & ridiculous bull-shit we have to inflict upon the men here. Our favourite refrain, when ordered to do something particularly stupid is: – 'And there's thousands dying in Russia!'

Diarist 5157, M, Retired Policeman, Wallasey, Merseyside, 17/02/43

I have read a good acct about the Beveridge report and I consider it is hard for us middle class who have never suffered from unemployment to realise what a nightmare the absence of security is to many decent working men. I sincerely hope they will secure it in the post-war world. It will be necessary however to deal very drastically with the work-shy people who are quite a considerable percentage of all sections of the community.

Diarist 5076, M, Accountant and Volunteer Police Constable, Sheffield, 23/02/43

My brother came on one of his rare visits in the evening, and even then rushed off to be back home by 9.0 p.m. He is still leading a gentleman's life, working for three days every other week and receiving full pay, doing a bit of Home Guard to liven things up at the weekend, and drafting letters of excuse to the Ministry of Labour and National Service to account for his failure to turn up at the requested interviews.

<u>Diarist 5443, F, Office Worker and Volunteer Mobile Canteen Driver, London, 26/02/43</u>

This morning Mother received a letter from a complete stranger enclosing a cheque for two guineas, in which she said that she had heard of our plight from my father's sister (Aunt Win) and as she was in a very similar position herself two years ago, she hoped my Mother would not be offended with the gift, but would get herself something which she needed. This really touched us, and made me feel that there certainly is a lot of good in this world.

<u>Diarist 5271, F, Local Government Clerk, Bury St Edmunds, Suffolk, 02/03/43</u>

Another letter from Ministry of Health about the wall [blocking the hospital light] says that the reason for building it was that Major Beatty wanted it for the protection of his racehorses. Well, of course, though in an L.C.C. hospital a man's life was not valued at as much as £50, racehorses fetch almost incomparably higher figures. What is man! Lower than a racehorse, even lower than a great many pedigree dogs, & this after preaching to him for centuries that he is in the image of God.

<u>Diarist 5239, F, Aerodynamicist and Housewife, Bolton-le-Sands, Lancashire, 03/03/43</u>

Mother read the paper at breakfast while I made toast, and told me that all the news was good. She said, 'I never expected that we would recover so quickly from the setback in Tunisia,' and 'I expect that London will have a raid tonight, after Berlin,' and 'I have not sympathy with Gandhi. He recovers from his fasts too quickly.'

<u>Diarist 5415, F, Restaurant Owner, Edinburgh, 11/03/43</u>

The Head Cook gave me notice again this evening and I spent three quarters of an hour soothing her into changing her mind. The immediate cause was a row from the Manageress for using all her month's fish ration in a week. But in fact the trouble goes deeper than this. All our suppliers spend their time offering her more than she has a right to in the way of food, and the strain of refusing when she has nothing to serve to the customers is obviously severe, and more than she should have to put up with. The said suppliers should, of course, be reported by us for their behaviour but as they are the only first class ones in the town we cannot afford to antagonise them: and so the vicious circle is made up.

<u>Diarist 5355, F, Teacher, Neath, Glamorgan, 21/03/43</u>

Rather surprised when landlady came hurrying back to put on Mr. Churchill's speech – she usually isn't very interested. Neither am I, but this speech was rather different. Haven't heard any other opinions, but it struck me as being a very unsatisfactory speech – disliked the recurring note of self-satisfaction and the 'I-know-you-don't-like-it-Johnny-but-it's-awfully-good-for-you' tone, the declaration that the Cabinet can promise nothing except the probable continuance of the war and the later detailed suggestions which will surely, as he must have realised, be taken as promises. The Government is obviously well aware that the country is not satisfied, and appears to think the safest method of quelling the dissatisfaction is to insist that the war is not over yet. Some of our politicians are going to find life considerably more uncomfortable when it is over than they do now.

Diarist 5052, M, Teacher, Selsdon, Surrey, 22/03/43

I have been told that our flour – and bread – is being doctored by calcium – and possibly other drugs – to 'keep up' the health of the nation. If so I think it is ridiculous, as many people don't need calcium and it doesn't agree with them. If true it would account for a good deal of the internal trouble which I have had since early January, and for the suppressed colds which are always so much more difficult to deal with and to dispose of, than the good old 'streamer'.

Diarist 5399, F, Retired Nurse, Steyning, West Sussex, 26/03/43

We went out to a cafe for lunch. She said she went out to dinner several times a week, otherwise she could not manage at all. She could not live on her rations. I said, I did, and was well and did not lose weight, and millions of others the same. She is living in a flat very luxurious 120 pound a year, and has been trying to get something cheaper, but she said, 'I am not going to let myself down in the world and live in a poor place. I have kept up my position with my husband for the last twenty years and I am not going to come down.'

All this, and your soldiers, sailors, airmen, and merchant seamen dying in agony to keep HER world safe around her. And the Tory members of Parliament fighting to stop Mr Bevin's bill to give decent conditions in hotels and restaurants. The sooner this sort of world crashes, the better, and I hope I live to see it. Why should other men die that these may live on in comfort?

Diarist 5399, F, Retired Nurse, Steyning, West Sussex, 28/03/43

After reading Gollancz 'Let my People go', to do with the persecution of the Jews, and how little is being done by our Gov. to help, even the few who get away, I wrote to our MP Lord Winterton, and said I wanted it to be put on record that neither I, nor anyone I knew, would object if all the Jews who could get away were admitted here. We would be glad and relieved if something was done to help them. He wrote that although it was tragic, the Jews were not treated worse than any others on the Continent, that numerically no more Jews had been killed than Poles and Czechs. That he was Chairman and Br. representative on the International Comm. set up before the war to deal with refugees. I wrote back that I despaired of my country, and that we did not deserve to win. That he, the Br. representative and Chairman on such a comm. evidently knew less than I did about the sufferings of the Jews. And that if he felt they were not worse treated than others in Hitler's power why did he not protest against the House of Commons standing to show their horror of what was being done, which Mr Eden had reported to them. Now he writes that my statement [in my letter, that] 'We don't deserve to win the war' is [a] most serious statement, and he considered it disgraceful. 'A number of people have been prosecuted under the Emergency Powers Act for making statements very similar to this.'

I'm not scared at his covert threat, because I know he wouldn't like his letter to become public, as it would if he started prosecuting me.

Diarist 5261, F, Factory Clerk, Manchester, 01/04/43
Mrs. F., one of the part-time clerks, doesn't seem a bit friendly. She has proved very snobbish with some of the workers. One old packer declares he would like to give her a good tanning across his knee. I knew there would be this kind of trouble if any

middle-class people ever came here to work. I should say there is only one person, including the management, who has any real claim to be educated, & that one is a useless product of a Public School. Everyone else seems to have started work at the mill at the age of 14 (or earlier) & to have naturally succeeded to various jobs as they became vacant by death or illness, irrespective of whether they were fitted or not. Anyway maybe the experience of being among rougher people will be good for Mrs. F.

Diarist 5385, F, Writer and Secretary, Southborough, Kent, 03/04/43

From my bed I see Civil Defence Workers & VADs trekking off down the roads to join the procession. Southborough War Weapons' week begins today. Already also we have bought a buttercup for the Crippled Children's Fund. Mother grumbled. Yesterday the Missions to Seamen people came imploring. Twopence here, 2d. there.

Diarist 5110, M, Vicar, Boston, Lincolnshire, 05/04/43

The troubles caused to families by [evacuated] children not writing are great. I often have to write to the Authorities to find out about youngsters. For some months I have kept a list of such letters, & the interesting fact is, that, with one exception, the youngster who hasn't bothered to write home is an only child.

Diarist 5239, F, Aerodynamicist and Housewife, Bolton-le-Sands, Lancashire, 06/04/43

They have been taking blood from a lot of people in the office, but I would not volunteer to give any again, for I can ill afford to spare it, and I want all my energy for this job.

Diarist 5443, F, Office Worker and Volunteer Mobile Canteen Driver, London, 10/04/43

Had a busy time today on the Van, I love driving around on a nice day, a lovely feeling. I wonder if private people will be able to get cheap cars after the War, I would love to get hold of a little car for myself, even a baby Austin would suit me. Nevertheless I expect it will be years before ordinary people will be able to afford luxuries of this kind, probably this will be wise, because we ought not to have cars in England (even little Baby Austins) if people in other countries haven't enough to eat.

Diarist 5186, M, Shorthand Typist (hospitalised), Woking, Surrey, 12/04/43

Much comment and discussion on the Increases of Taxes on Cigarettes, Beer and Cinema Seats. In consequence very little notice taken of the capture of Sousse, etc. Two men 'threaten' to give up smoking as if they were doing someone an injury, whereas the 'powers that be' acknowledge that they are trying to cut down the consumption of tobacco. I am afraid I derive a good deal of private amusement from all this as a non-smoker.

Diarist 5447, F, Clerk and Housewife, Sheffield, 12/04/43

I notice that the old men in the Park who sit on the benches and arrange the entire war abroad and at home, now speak of 'these 'ere Russians' where they used to refer to 'them there Russians'. May one draw the conclusion that they feel a little nearer to the Russians today?

Diarist 5331, F, Shop Assistant, Dewsbury, West Yorkshire,
12/04/43

To the W.V.S. after words with B.H. who flatly refused to go,
saying it was only a gossip shop and what good did they do. As
she has never raised a finger or done a stitch of knitting I thought
this was rich.

Diarist 5401, F, Technical Journalist for Aircraft Factory,
Slough, Berkshire, 21/04/43

Not only left light on in bedroom in February but again about
4 weeks later and the whole performance of policeman climbing in
after dark when I was out, to turn out light was repeated. Excused
myself from attending Court for first Summons and was fined
30/-. On the second occasion was charged with breaking Black
Out regulations and Wasting Fuel. When these Summonses arrived
all the men at the office set on me saying that second fine was
likely to be very heavy and that I ought to obtain legal advice.

Diarist 5240, F, Teacher, Watford, Hertfordshire, 24/04/43

The centre of Exeter was a mess, with more bomb damage than
I saw in the centre of Manchester. My friend at Pinhoe had made
a new garden, banked up with large red stones from the bombed
St. Lawrence's Church.

Diarist 5205, M, Laboratory Technician, Potters Bar,
Hertfordshire, 05/05/43

In spite of the recent further increase in the milk ration, we are
still not allowed any milk for morning or afternoon tea, nor a
cup of tea at lunchtime. This is just ridiculous official perversity.
Yet when the Public Health Committee came down yesterday

they had the best of everything. That is the sort of thing which makes one feel like joining the Communist Party.

Diarist 5429, F, Secretary, London, 07/05/43

A letter in the Chronicle this morning which says just what I have been saying recently about food queues. It is becoming a fetish, and you can tell by the complacent look on people's faces that they think they are doing the right thing by lining up – they remain rooted to the spot. Whereas I cannot stand more than two minutes without twitching and peering to see when I am going to move up. This woman says she has four children, and never queues for anything, and I fully agree with her that half the queues are due to people's acquisitiveness – something is going, and they are afraid of missing something which others are getting. If their time were really precious, they would be only too glad to be able to dispense with all non-essential items. I think as a matter of fact many of them take the opportunity to have a good gossip.

Diarist 5186, M, Shorthand Typist (hospitalised), Woking, Surrey, 13/05/43

Latest occupation, making up the ideal nurse from a combination of several. What about a basis of Nurse Lambert's wonderful nursing capacities, organising and disciplining qualifications, and eyes that talk as they flash, with the addition of Nurse Hierons' housekeeping propensities and Nurse Bolt's loving kindness and sympathy when one is ill and her kittenishness on other occasions. What a combination! During a blanket bath when completely nude a flashing eye appeared between the screens. – Nurse Lambert to see how we are getting on.

Diarist 5293, F, Factory Worker and Housewife, St Albans,
Hertfordshire, 15/05/43

Visited the headmaster's wife at the church school, during the morning break, the children went gathering stinging nettles which are hung to dry and collected later by W.I. organiser of the dried herb collection, despite stings they seem undaunted. This is work which the village has done for many years, as there is a large and old established Herbalist Firm in Dunstable, whom – before petrol restrictions – came to the recreation ground and paid the children for their collections and gave instructions, as each herb came in season. The largest collection being of elder-flowers which grow profusely in these parts.

Diarist 5402, F, Retired Teacher, Great Missenden,
Buckinghamshire, 17/05/43

I heard two young WAAFs discussing the war & people's reaction to it – I was quite surprised; of late I hardly ever hear a casual conversation about the war, though earlier it was quite usual.

Diarist 5233, M, Radio Operator, Newport, Wales, 20/05/43

This job would suit Tom Harrisson [founder of MO], & certainly suits me. When I think of my brother in a prisoner-of-war camp, of two of my friends in Africa & another on a tank landing craft, I sometimes think fate has been too kind. But then I think of all the bad luck with jobs I have had during the past 2½ years & I think it is about time the luck changed. It makes less difference to my life than most jobs would have done as on two of the three turns I am free during the day time. I am therefore able to combine the advantages of being out of work with those of being

in work. I continue as before to do the shopping for my wife, &
much of the cooking, washing-up, & other domestic chores.

Diarist 5307, F, Stenographer, Birmingham, 21/05/43

At one of the said [book]shops we were mystified and annoyed. It
was a large and very untidy place that we knew had been blitzed a
couple of years ago, but the small door was open and we pushed
inside and started to wander round, but the proprietor immediately upped and said No, he couldn't allow that. If we would tell
him what we wanted he would look for it, but he couldn't have
anyone burrowing around, because he'd been blitzed and everything was in a state of chaos. Well, that from the proprietor of a
second-hand bookshop, whom one would expect to make the
major part of his living by allowing people to burrow around until
they were tempted to buy, seemed absurd. Besides, all the other
people we visited had been blitzed, too, but they had done something about it – moved to new premises, or patched things up. How
on the mortal earth that man has managed to make a living during
the past two years with that sort of policy, I cannot imagine.

Diarist 5268, F, Housewife, Arborfield, Berkshire, 22/05/43

Conversation overheard while waiting in the fish queue. (NB. I
don't usually wait in queues, but this was a short one, and there
was sole!) Man looked like retired Colonel of a type I didn't
know existed any longer. Woman – well, she had the 'right'
accent, and shabby clothes, so I should think she was 'new poor'
and hated it.

Woman: Look, there's a black soldier – no, he's an officer!

Man Can't be.

W. Yes, it is, American probably, no, I know he's French –

Senegalese I expect. Well (with contempt) they can keep him!

<u>M.</u> By Jove yes! Mind you, these fellows fight well, and they're good fellows in their way, <u>provided they know their place.</u>

<u>W.</u> I was talking to some American boys the other day, and I said: How do you manage when these fellows get back home? Is there any difficulty? And they said: Well, they know their place, they know they're (she turned her thumb down) and we're (thumb turned up.)

<u>M.</u> (with enthusiasm) That's it! The utter rot you hear talked nowadays, as if they were our equals. As if they <u>could</u> be!

(I left the queue to avoid saying something frightfully rude – or hitting the speakers!)

<u>Diarist 5369, F, Writer and Voluntary Worker, Swansea, Glamorgan, 27/05/43</u>

Received call-up papers. Feel my life is being diced up in a wine glass, by someone standing on the edge of a precipice. Boss – to whom I have suddenly become absolutely indispensable – charges silently & sullenly around like a resurrected bison, finally writing a long letter to the M. of L. demanding my exemption.

<u>Diarist 5214, M, Retired Railway Official, Leeds, 01/06/43</u>

Why should the king and queen waste petrol going by car to Ascot races? That question was put to me and I had no answer – I could not justify the waste. Has M-O any views? You might mention it in your next bulletin. <u>If you don't, you daren't</u>!

<u>Diarist 5004, M, ARP Worker and Food Packing Manager,</u>
<u>Belmont, Surrey, 03/06/43</u>

Another spot of bother today in connection with a parade of Wardens in connection with 'Wings for Victory'. Once more, volunteers are called for, and once more all wardens refuse to go. If there is anything more calculated to cause bad feeling, it is this question of parades. They see no point in it, whilst unfortunately the local Borough seek every possible excuse to stage parades.

<u>Diarist 5331, F, Shop Assistant, Dewsbury, West Yorkshire,</u>
<u>05/06/43</u>

Olive & Auntie to supper. We discussed sleeping & dreaming. B. said he never waked to consider whether he slept soundly or not. Auntie has slept on her sofa partly dressed ever since the first air raids. Olive described a frequent dream she has where she is apparently flying high in the air & cannot get down, but is wandering all night over church steeples & mill chimneys.

<u>Diarist 5118, M, Civil Engineer, Trowbridge, Wiltshire, 06/06/43</u>

Disgusted my parents this morning by getting busy with laying more paving – actually 'crazy-paving' – and on a Sunday morning! It was unheard of before, but when I explained that I should <u>never</u> get it done if I didn't use every available moment, no more protests were forthcoming. Not that it would have made any difference if there had been!

<u>Diarist 5256, F, Teacher, Thornaby-on-Tees, North Yorkshire,</u>
<u>13/06/43</u>

D., married last November, is expecting a baby much to the disgust of her mother who says they should have waited until after the war. She lives at home & her husband is in the army. She has a good job & her mother is considering the financial loss. She vows she will not look after the child.

Diarist 5261, F, Factory Clerk, Manchester, 15/06/43
To see Vera Lynn in a film based on the story of her own success. She is not nice looking, but has a very lovable personality. Think her voice is on the 'common' side.

Diarist 5401, F, Technical Journalist for Aircraft Factory, Slough, Berkshire, 19/06/43
The frame of my glasses snapped on Thursday and as I was in town this morning I took them along to my opticians. The woman in the shop told me that repairs will take quite a fortnight. I had dallied with the idea of having completely new frames of a different colour for a change but I was not encouraged. Evidently supplies are very limited. Cases are now made of cardboard – she told me to hang on to my leather one like grim death as it could not be replaced and she made me take it back with me as they did not want the responsibility of keeping it.

Diarist 5415, F, Restaurant Owner, Edinburgh, 25/06/43
Husband arrived through this evening and we gave dinner to a nice couple who have been in Edinburgh for some months and who are now moving on as usual. It may add variety to life, but it is annoying all the same that one can never keep contact with any one person for more than three months these days.

9. I REFUSE TO LET MY MIND CONSIDER WHAT IS SAID

July to December 1943

'I listen parrot-fashion time after time to accounts of torpedoed ships, crashing planes, burning people, and refuse to let
my mind consider what is said.'

Significant progress is now being made on and off the battle-fields, with the retaking of strategic islands in both the Mediterranean and the Pacific, the publication of the Keynes plan (advocating an international monetary fund to provide temporary aid for nations' economies) and the foundation of the UN all jostling for headlines. A shiver of excitement accompanies the unconditional surrender of Italy in September. Here, it seems, is truly tangible progress – proof that the Allies will surely win the war.

These moments of hope and relief offer windows of levity in an atmosphere that is otherwise largely one of great fatigue. Attitudes vary enormously, in what is perhaps the widest breadth of feeling at any point in the war. While some are jubilant about the progress that's being made and are full of optimism for an end that seems convincingly nigh, others are pessimistic and can't see how a world worth living in will emerge from the carnage. Attempts to build that new world include widespread strikes over issues like gender equality and the minimum wage, which will grow in size and frequency in 1944.

* * *

Diarist 5420, F, Housewife, Birmingham, 02/07/43
Shall I say the one prevailing spirit is just Plodding. Great news comes through on the radio, people go on serenely, just as many turn out to work, in fact quite a lot have been working overtime recently.

Diarist 5307, F, Stenographer, Birmingham, 03/07/43
I have done more gardening of late than ever in my life before, & am really beginning to fall in love with it, as I never thought I

should. We have only a small garden at the back & it has been trenched & bombed & generally knocked about in quite a frightful way. But when S. came back to live with us we made it over to him, for he is a passionate gardener & had left a lovely place behind, & he has converted our sorry little dump into a green & pleasant plot that looks for all the world like a Dig for Victory Demonstration Allotment, so bursting is it with produce.

Diarist 5353, F, Housewife, Barrow-in-Furness, Lancashire, 04/07/43

I thought when I saw the inner city people 'why cannot we all go back to the "little communities" where people know each other, where life can centre & focus & not frittle & spread till it evaporates in the fierce heat of noise & clang – or stifles & stagnates in city streets where no one cares enough to say 'good morning – it's a lovely day – have you heard from Tom & what did the doctor say about Mary's throat!' I wish I could have waved a wand over the harassed thousands of people at the stations – giving them the assurance that 'staggered holidays' with accommodation to suit their tastes, pockets, families etc would be their 'right' after the war.

Diarist 5240, F, Teacher, Watford, Hertfordshire, 08/07/43

One of my boys brought a banana, wrapped in his handkerchief. A sailor had come home with a bunch, & had given one to all the children in the street. I took it round to all the staff, & said 'Prepare for a shock!', & was rewarded with gasps of amazement, & almost unbelief. The Head held it up, & showed the whole school, like a curio.

Diarist 5415, F, Restaurant Owner, Edinburgh, 11/07/43

Dined tonight with an Aunt and Uncle who (though not particularly old) live in a past age. The food is still excellent and there is a very old butler to serve it: and my uncle complained that he had only ten dozen of his really good sherry left! I came home early feeling slightly hysterical and invited one of my neighbours in for a drink to take 'the taste of the evening out of my mouth'.

Diarist 5429, F, Secretary, London, 19/07/43

Strange how quietly people are taking the very good news on all fronts. After a day or two, it seems as though we had never had anything else but good news, and people immediately begin to speculate as to whether – the burning problem, Shall we or shall we not have to have the blackout for another winter?

Diarist 5352, F, Art Student, Northampton, 26/07/43

Just then I heard a plane coming over. We all rushed into our lavatory, but nothing happened, and when it went away we came out. Mummy and Daddy went up to bed at 3.30. Bella and I waited. She got bored and played her mandolin, we drew the curtains back and saw the dawn. Then I said, get prepared for a row now, all the birds will start to screech. With the first shrill call of the dawn came the wonderful note of the 'all clear'. To me it is a perfect note, both musically and spiritually. When it was over we had one more piece of chocolate each and went to bed.

Diarist 5423, F, Housewife, Bradford, West Yorkshire, 02/08/43

The only way to influence people to stay at home & keep railways clear is to turn people's minds to their own sons, husbands or other relatives – tell Mrs. Smith that she is endangering her

son's life & lengthening his absence from home if she goes galli-
vanting on holidays. 'Vital war necessities' conveys nothing to
the general public.

Diarist 5157, M, Retired Policeman, Wallasey, Merseyside,
05/08/43
Have been doing some of our own shopping as our general maid
has left us. Having a large garden we have not a regular greengrocer and now with this shortage or rather disappearance of our
soft fruit it is getting difficult to get any. I go into a shop and ask
for apples and tomatoes today. 'Sorry but we have only enough
for our regular customers,' so that's that. We are largely to blame
ourselves – I mean everyone because there are a number of rapa-
cious people who go from shop to shop and will strip a shop or
district like a swarm of locusts.

Diarist 5399, F, Retired Nurse, Steyning, West Sussex, 12/08/43
I have had air-mail letters taking six weeks to come from America.
I suppose the planes are too crowded to allow the mail to be sent,
and it is wrong to fill them up with these unwanted women
'entertainers'. Surely we have enough screeching women in this
country to 'entertain the troops'. Another such woman was in a
plane that crashed at Lisbon, as has been stated every time she
sang her silly songs in radio programs. Possibly, if she had not
been on it, the plane would not have crashed. It is just the extra
'one more' that causes the accidents.

Diarist 5429, F, Secretary, London, 12/08/43
Why is it that people will insist on going away, despite all warnings as to the discomforts of travelling, food difficulties, etc.

They won't be done, so long as trains run they will fight to get inside them. It struck me that there was something of the conditioned reflex about their behaviour – August is the time when one takes the kids to country or seaside, so, all other circumstances notwithstanding, to the country or seaside they go. Or perhaps it is more like the behaviour of animals or insects who get the urge instinctively to migrate or 'swarm', without knowing what it is all about. However, no doubt people who live in nasty slummy districts without gardens really do need to get away, and I absolve all such. But a large proportion of the crowd seemed to be well-dressed young business women, prancing along with suitcases just as though there were no war on, lumbering up the trains and adding to the general turmoil.

Diarist 5233, M, Radio Operator, Newport, Wales, 14/08/43

While however I do not believe that hate propaganda of this sort can do anything but harm, I by no means underestimate the atrocities & their significance. They do not prove the Germans are different from anyone else; they do prove the extraordinary depravity of the human mind when subjected to certain evil conditions & influences. I hope after the war that tribunals will be set up to examine such cases as impartially as possible, & that the perpetrators, where their guilt has been proved beyond doubt, will be shot on the scene of their crime. The majority should be allowed to get off rather than that any innocent should suffer. There should be a sufficient number proved guilty to satisfy anyone not suffering from indiscriminate bloodlust.

Diarist 5271, F, Local Government Clerk, Bury St Edmunds, Suffolk, 14/08/43

I do not like this world, & wish I had not been born into its welter of blood and greed. If Christ achieved nothing then certainly I am not likely to, so it was merely bad luck to be created. I will own I listen parrot-fashion time after time to accounts of torpedoed ships, crashing planes, burning people, and refuse to let my mind consider what is said.

Diarist 5331, F, Shop Assistant, Dewsbury, West Yorkshire, 15/08/43

Depressed over many things, chief among them winter shortly to be upon us, and the blackout to hand this very night.

A good many people seem to think the restrictions will be relaxed somewhat and better street lighting be given, although nearly everyone thinks that we shall be for it sometime during the winter, either with gas or without. But certainly, opinion seems to be that Hitler will have a 'good crack' at us before going under.

Diarist 5076, M, Accountant and Volunteer Police Constable, Sheffield, 19/08/43

An old couple, in the middle 70s, called in the evening. They had slept through the recent alert, but were knocked up by the warden after the alert. The man answered the door, but went straight back to bed, a sensible thing to do in my opinion. The man, an ex-blacksmith, thought that the Germans should be wiped out. He had come to this conclusion because of the awful atrocities that had been committed. Incidentally he expressed sympathy with the Jews – he seems to be the first non-anti-Jewish person I have met for some time.

<u>Diarist 5233, M, Radio Operator, Newport, Wales, 28/08/43</u>

As for the spate of treacly slush which is continually poured out, I like it no better than swing & I am equally sedulous in avoiding it. There is one song however which some might consider as coming in this category, that I have taken a liking to; it seems to exhibit sincerity & honest feelings. It is called 'Saving Myself for Bill' & expresses the deep love of the average woman for her absent man, an ordinary but individual & unique Bill. Another popular song, of a different kind, which I like is the cheery one with the chorus:-

'Who's sailing the ships, who's flying the planes,

Who's manning the tanks & the guns?

The Smiths & the Jones, the Kells & Cohns;

They're all democracy's sons.'

I am glad the Cohns are specially mentioned.

My wife has just told me in emphatic language that she does not agree with me about 'Saving Myself for Bill'. I feel hurt.

<u>Diarist 5256, F, Teacher, Thornaby-on-Tees, North Yorkshire, 02/09/43</u>

Book Salvage Scheme – Badges for all children & in addition special awards of Generals', Colonels', Captains' & Sergeants' Badges to children bringing 100, 75, 50, & 20 books. Thousands of books roll in to school & it is fascinating to see what reading matter people possess.

<u>Diarist 5324, F, Hostel Worker, Gloucester, Gloucestershire, 03/09/43</u>

Can it really be 4 years today? I must have been quite a child when it began! I was certainly far less experienced of the world

& its peculiarities in those days. Now I am home again, I am convinced that those carefree pre-war days can never come again. Home will never be the same to me. I hope to remember it always as my happy youth when tennis, swimming & dancing were regular happenings & the rest of the world was uncared about. I don't think I could ever settle again in this village. I used to think I would never get on so well with people who had not known me & my family for years. Now I know that friends are soon made & that in life people come & go & in a fresh place a start can soon be made.

Diarist 5214, M, Retired Railway Official, Leeds, 06/09/43

Another chap and I were instructing two R.A.F. sergeants in the mysteries of cribbage and a discussion arose out of the fact that they were fed up with their retention as instructors when they wanted to go on 'Ops.'. Amongst other things one of them told me that if a sergeant is injured in flying he loses his stripes and corresponding pay, etc. They were very bitter about this and I entirely agreed with them. It is on a par with the Government's reliance on the R.A.F. Benevolent Fund. A 'Benevolent Fund', forsooth! The very name stinks! Such a Fund ought to be illegal and the few to whom so many owe so much should be assured of generous, really generous, treatment for themselves and their loved ones.

Diarist 5447, F, Clerk and Housewife, Sheffield, 08/09/43

Yesterday as I was preparing tea there was a knock at the door and there I found a 26-year-old wife living in one of these flats with whom we are on cordial terms, her husband a bomber in the RAF. Her face was wooden and she jerked out, 'Mrs U.,

Henry is missing,' thrust the telegram into my hand. Of course I just opened my arms and took her in and let her have a good weep the while I cursed audibly this blasted war. 'He isn't dead. I'm sure he isn't dead. He was home only last Wednesday. He's alive somewhere and worrying because he knows I'll get this telegram to upset me.'

Diarist 5240, F, Teacher, Watford, Hertfordshire, 08/09/43
Most unusually, I listened to B.B.C news at 6 p.m. & so heard the announcement of Italy's capitulation. After a few minutes there was an excited knock on the door, & my neighbour wanted to talk about it. She found it hard to believe, & wanted me to verify what she had heard.

Later, two sisters & a brother-in-law all agreed it was splendid news.

Diarist 5205, M, Laboratory Technician, Potters Bar, Hertfordshire, 10/09/43
Went down to Clacton to stay with relations for weekend. It seemed much more altered than Southend had done – barbed wire all over the place and streets barricaded, most of the hotels occupied by soldiers, gardens allowed to go to waste, many shops shut, the pier closed, only a tiny bit of the beach open, and comparatively few people about. But I am told that it is better now than it was when the evacuation 'scare' was on.

Diarist 5402, F, Retired Teacher, Great Missenden, Buckinghamshire, 14/09/43
Had a letter from my German friend, saying that she has a little daughter, & speaking most highly of the treatment she is

receiving in hospital. It made me quite proud of my country to think that an enemy alien & her illegitimate baby should be so well treated. I can't bear the bulldog breed, & am not drawn to lions, but I do appreciate tolerance & kindness.

Diarist 5076, M, Accountant and Volunteer Police Constable, Sheffield, 15/09/43

Two blackout offences and a cyclist riding without lights formed the sum total of the incidents on my police beat this evening. I had to get a man out of his bath to attend to one of the black-outs. There seems to be a general carelessness with blackouts and I really should have complained at several more places.

Diarist 5186, M, Unemployed Shorthand Typist, Woking, Surrey, 16/09/43

The Manager of the Electrical Engineering Offices met me on the doorstep and told me straight away that what he wanted [to employ] was a young girl of 18. What, I suppose, can be called an 'office-girl'. The offices of the solicitor were upstairs, so that was no use to me. I began to wonder where the reported labour shortage was, but of course I have to remember that my lame-ness is a severe disability. The beauty of the job I had last year was that the 'Office', in a tent, was, so to speak, built up round my stool.

Diarist 5293, F, Factory Worker and Housewife, St Albans, Hertfordshire, 18/09/43

My experiences is limited I know, but I do hear from all sections of the people, and among the men folk complete cynicism reigns on the subject of Post War Planning and promises, only the women hold tentative hopes for the future, and I wonder if ever it will be recorded what a silent but heavily burdened part the women at home have borne in being constantly surrounded with the moans and bitter criticism of their sons and husbands, in or out of the services, and yet have kept themselves morally uplifted and carried on.

Diarist 5005, M, Army Officer, South Ascot, Berkshire, 27/09/43

The Brains [on the panel] consisted of an Army officer, a secondary school mistress, a local clergyman, a technical college school master, a local doctor and a Scottish sergeant in the A.E.C. The thing that particularly struck me was that all the questions that the audience, which consisted of four or five officers, four or five A.T.S, half a dozen Wrens and the remainder Army M.C.Os, asked, were on some Post War planning subject and yet more striking were the replies all of which whether they were from the clergyman, doctor, schoolmaster or army officer, plumped straight for out and out socialist planning. Even the doctor who was not a young man and who held a responsible position in Colchester was in favour of a state medical system.

Diarist 5205, M, Laboratory Technician, Potters Bar, Hertfordshire, 03/10/43

The military situation continues to be satisfactorily handled, but the handling of the home front leaves very much indeed to be desired. The recent outbreak of strikes are an instance of this. Much of the blame, as far as one can judge from newspaper reports, seems to lie with the miners, who are acting in an irresponsible way, but there must be something radically wrong for such widespread unrest (and the strikes have not been entirely confined to the mining industry). Some papers say that the real reason is the Government's failure to take any action towards social and economic improvement at home.

Diarist 5443, F, Office Worker and Volunteer Mobile Canteen Driver, London, 11/10/43

At lunchtime today I passed Mr. Bevin [the Minister of Labour] in the Strand – he did look an unattractive man – amazing to think that such an insignificant looking individual has the fate of so many millions of people in this country, in his hands – I wonder how long he will last in power?

Diarist 5423, F, Housewife, Bradford, West Yorkshire, 12/10/43

I have never heard such a hopeless voice on the wireless as that of the man who said that he wanted a regular job after the war and added 'It isn't much to ask'! And in all conscience it isn't! I often say to myself when I see a poor, little, undersized soldier in battledress 'What has that poor fellow to fight for?' I feel ashamed that such as he should have to undergo the horrors and torments of war, after a hell of a life in peace, & very little to look forward to when the war ends.

Diarist 5039.2, M, Factory Worker and Volunteer Fireman, Mansfield, Nottinghamshire, 16/10/43

Blast walls were put up in our district, some 1½–2 yrs ago. Whether they had them or not was left entirely at the discretion of the householder. Most people consented. 12 months ago, people began to get tired of them, they were in the way, they made the houses dark, etc etc. Now the council are pulling them all down again.

The foreman on the job, says he has never seen such waste in his life, both of time and money. Still, there is money to be thrown away in wartime.

Diarist 5271, F, Local Government Clerk, Bury St Edmunds, Suffolk, 20/10/43

We went into National Gallery to talk & the wartime pictures there screamed from the walls. If that 'art' lives, future generations will definitely believe we lived in Hell & not on earth.

Diarist 5110, M, Vicar, Boston, Lincolnshire, 22/10/43

Had some more Income Tax grumbles. I have noted that when there is not much doing on the battlefields (I mean nothing spectacular) these grumbles come up in a quite regular manner, it is either 'Income Tax' or 'High Wages of Munition Workers'. Then something spectacular happens & for a time all is forgotten again.

Diarist 5460, F, Railway Clerk, Newport, Wales, 23/10/43

On Friday nights I fire-watch. Last Friday I went to the dressmakers early in the evening. Whilst I was covered in pins and pieces the alert sounded. I leapt out of the dress and started back up the road. I had about half a mile to go but I could see the searchlights up over [illegible] and was terrified that the new guns would start up before I got back. It was very dark and running madly I fell. Even my aches did not stop me running on and I fell into the house before anything happened. My knees were both swollen and are now yellow with bruises. There was no gunfire after all. Noel says I should have stayed indoors but I was supposed to be on duty and I should hate not to be found there.

Diarist 5338, F, Civil Servant, Morecambe, Lancashire, 01/11/43
We discussed possibilities of settling down after the War and she thinks it won't last much longer. We both think it is foolish of government spokesmen to keep trying to depress people by insisting that we must expect a long struggle.

Diarist 5186, M, Shorthand Typist, Woking, Surrey, 04/11/43
The office [based temporarily in the boss's house] wanted a candle for use in sealing registered parcels, so the butler was asked if he could supply one. He quickly produced one from a drawer-full. Apparently, once a candle has been started it cannot be used again. Is there a war on?

Diarist 5103, M, RAF Flight Officer, Bourn, Cambridgeshire, 04/11/43
A discussion on the 1939–43 Star and on medals in general. One man urged all medals ought to be abolished as so many deserve one and after all the inward satisfaction of a job well done is the real reward. Another urged the need of maintaining the service tradition and the desire to have special deeds commemorated. A third was against medals like the 1939–43 Star as it was quite impossible to draw a line between Commandos, RASC, Fire-watchers and all grades of civilians. My own view is that the 1939–43 Star will cause more dissatisfaction than satisfaction. London, Hull and Plymouth fire

guards have done more than many in the forces and many part-time fire-watchers have done their bit well. Campaign medals in this war are quite meaningless.

Diarist 5415, F, Restaurant Owner, Edinburgh, 06/11/43

Last night on arriving home I found a card on the hall table telling me to attend this evening at a given address for the first of a series of lectures (3) on firefighting. I considered 24 hours' notice a bit cool but was prepared to try and make do: but I rang up this morning to find out from the man who runs the fire-watching for our block what name I should fill in on the card in the space of Street Leader. When I was told in a voice of suppressed fury that I was to disregard the card as it has been sent me by another group in the street who have nothing to do with our block and (apparently) spend their time interfering. As it suits me much better to get my training at the restaurant I shall wait to do so, but if this is how the new scheme is being run it seems a pity.

Diarist 5337, F, Housewife, Fritwell, Oxfordshire, 09/11/43

Had to go to Oxford in the morning to see my herbalist, Mrs L, luckily Walter had to go so went comfortably in the car. Cold still rather troublesome. Mrs L very nice as usual, and wants me to go on just the same for another 4 months. Talked to the nice pair, Mr and Mrs Ingram who run the shop, neither have been even outside Oxford since the War started, and they have not had a holiday for 6 years. Seems too awful, they look awful, but declare they are quite well.

Diarist 5004, M, ARP Worker and Food Packing Manager, Belmont, Surrey, 09/11/43

I heard today of an interesting experiment at a local church. Since the war the church has not held a service in the evening during winter because it has not been blacked out. Last Sunday they held a service in the dark with only pale blue lights to guide the worshippers to the pews. Only well known favourite hymns were sung, and the minister preached in almost total darkness. The experiment was an enormous success and the church was filled to capacity.

Diarist 5256, F, Teacher, Thornaby-on-Tees, North Yorkshire, 20/11/43

Football match – almost a local Derby. Many Hartlepool supporters. Jibes 'Can't you take it?' Borough fans 'You won't have a man left at the end of the war.'

Diarist 5401, F, Technical Journalist for Aircraft Factory, Slough, Berkshire, 20/11/43

The long evenings have begun. The kitchen blackout I leave up all the week (and the cottage beams on a Saturday morning when I take it down before going to work because it knows that the kitchen will have two whole days of whatever sunshine there is and that there will be a fire in the range!).

Diarist 5380, F, Voluntary Worker and Clerk, St Albans, Hertfordshire, 25/11/43

When I reached home about 4.15 I found that my landlady's teacher friend had brought us an extra pint of milk between us. She gets milk for the schoolchildren & occasionally orders an extra pint which she sells to us! This is definitely Black Market (except that she makes no profit out of it) and I suppose if I were strong-minded, I should refuse it, but I am specially fond of milk & when my meat & bacon ration for the week is finished I live almost entirely on a quick-cooking concoction of vegetables, milk & cheese. As I'm not usually home till 7 or half past in the evening, I fool myself into believing that I haven't time to plan out and cook anything nourishing for my evening meal without milk, so I just accept it, partly to avoid offending my friend. Such are the feeble excuses which induce comparatively honest individuals to do what they would condemn in others.

Diarist 5402, F, Retired Teacher, Great Missenden, Buckinghamshire, 09/12/43

Our coalman called after a five-weeks absence – he generally comes once a fortnight, but he had been ill, then the lorry had broken down. How dependent we are on individuals these days!

Diarist 5447, F, Clerk and Housewife, Sheffield, 12/12/43

Thus does war muck about the lives of men and women [and cause them to have affairs] and I for one sit in judgement of none of them. God alone knows what I would have done in similar circumstances. Men and women were not made to be separated at all let alone by anything so violent and uncertain as war is. Moreover, sexual intercourse is heady, and those who have experienced it young naturally seek more, and Nature knows and cares nowt for our codes of behaviour. Few young folk are brought up with any idea of self-discipline, and most of those who keep straight do so from religious fear, or fear of parents, or just fear of consequences . . . Or they are never tempted. Blessed he who is never tempted! To such come no problems. But how dull!

Diarist 5307, F, Stenographer, Birmingham, 13/12/43

I've come to the conclusion that my own morale has been affected to a surprising degree by the greater availability of onions this winter than last! I've always liked that humble vegetable, but am amazed to find what a vast difference its presence makes to the many stews & 'made-up' dishes which wartime catering calls for.

Diarist 5324, F, Hostel Worker, Gloucester, Gloucestershire, 20/12/43

The hostel staff is busy getting ready for Xmas. The Farm Club geese have been guarded night & day in case they get stolen. The caterer said every time she wakes in the night she dashes to the window to see if the geese are O.K.

Diarist 5331, F, Shop Assistant, Dewsbury, West Yorkshire, 23/12/43

Very irritable this evening through (1) being over tired with shop work, (2) wondering if the baker <u>will</u> deliver all the bread he promised tomorrow & how I shall placate customers if he does not, (3) reading the whole of 'The Brothers Karamazov' this week when I am too tired to take it in, (4) eating too many mince pies, (5) having to listen to R. Frankau's show which is the B.B.C's prizest flop up to now.

I went to bed at 9.30pm so I didn't see the old year out. I am hoping that 1944 will see the end of the war but you never know and I remember some years ago on a chapel notice board a text or whatever you like to call it which said 'You can go a long way when you're tired' and it is possible that the Germans will be able to do that if pressed hard enough.

10. GUTS ARE NOT PRETTY!

January to June 1944

8 – APR 1944

30.3.44. In the Present Parliamentary crisis, the position is, that though the Govt. is sure to get its vote of confidence over the clause in the Education Bill relating to equal pay for men and women, it has lost the confidence of the public over it. I, like other women, take it that on the broad view Mr. C. is opposed to equality and will fight it. Logically this doesnt follow, of course, because on narrow points of procedure Mr. Butler was trying to steer the Bill through the shoals of the Burnham Scale, and the Govt. claims that the issue is now purely one of "confidence", and that the general principle of equality is not at issue. On the other hand, this equality is a burning question and has been waiting near the surface of things just for such an occasion. And I think it will now be fought out -- if not in the life of this Govt. at least with increasing bitterness and virulence, unless the powers that way are prepared to compromise once they have saved face.

One office colleague, who "typed for the suffragettes," in the old days, said energetically this morning: "Churchill has done for himself.... Stubborn old devil." Another said, "He's a fool. The whole thing is completely silly." She added that, while she believed women were just as good as men, men ought to get more - men teachers ought to get more pay than women teachers - in consideration of the families they had or would have to support. And of course there's the crux. If only the principle of equal pay could be established, and then some system of allowances - in the army way - could be evolved without penalising the man with a kids looking for a job - you would get something! Women wd. suffer bitterly and worst over any measure that reduced the power of men to get married and have families.

The whole thing is a pity, I suppose, and hardly the time to stage a sex war. But the time wasn't chosen deliberately; it just growed of itself, out of the depths. And now, for the Govt. deliberately to flout the Commons and ignore its voice, will kill completely any faith the public has in its democratic will. We do not want a benevolent autocracy to arrange our future for us. We are not grateful that everything is to be done for us above our heads, to be hung up like a stocking on Xmas morning. If Churchill isn't very careful he will lose all the love and admiration he has enjoyed ---many of us will remember that we distrusted him once in the issues of peace --- and public figures fall from grace very quickly. In that line we are a ruthless and fickle people!

The sex war is in being, anyhow. But a woman colleague said: "I'm just livid over all this. I think it's frightful. Fancy Churchill behaving like that...I thought his speech on Monday was awful -- just pure party politics. It just confirms what I've always said, he's not the man for the peace. He's absolutely pig-headed. I think it was a fine of the men who did stick up. It was grand." The fact is, that most fair-minded men are for equality on principle, and many women, for various reasons are against it in practice!

As regards strikes; a colleague of mine - the ex-suffragette-inclined one, thinks that the Govt. at beginning of war shd have taken a strong line and promised to shoot every striker... just as a soldier refusing to fight shd. be shot. See that today there is tremendous seethe and ness of strikes and strike temper everywhere. I wonder how long it is before we have a strike of women workers - striking as a body of women, I mean? The trouble is, that this is not a war merely of armies and fronts, but a gigantic convulsion, going down to the bowels of things. And guts are not pretty!

'The trouble is, that this is not a war merely of armies and fronts, but a gigantic convulsion, going down to the bowels of things. And guts are not pretty!'

Around the globe the Allies are making steady progress, inching forward in each and every theatre of war. Their pace, however, is achingly slow. On the home front, the public are waiting on tenterhooks for the big invasion (and hopefully liberation) of Europe – a plan that Churchill and the government have been hinting at for many months. It is not until 6 June that D-Day, when the Allies land on the beaches of Normandy, releases the months' worth of tension. A week later, the first of Germany's V1 flying bombs (swiftly nicknamed 'buzz-bombs' and 'doodle-bugs') begin to land on British soil. Their effects will be felt acutely over the rest of the year.

These months are marked by an eagerness to 'get the invasion over and done', a sentiment complicated by an awareness that tens of thousands of lives will be lost. Many seem desensitised, numbed by five years of exposure to the impossibly high casualty statistics from civilian massacres, blanket bombings and whole crews going down with their ships. For others, loss of life is an invisible backdrop to daily life, ignored and unnoticed. Yet, in the moments where death does lurch perilously close to home, grief and horror are felt as keenly and as brutally as ever.

* * *

Diarist 5399, F, Retired Nurse, Steyning, West Sussex, 01/01/44

I notice in the report on the training of nurses, given, I believe, by Lord Horder and others, it is suggested that the nurses PAY for their training. That is what the hospitals have always wanted, and did enforce as far as they could. Many of the biggest hosps. in London demanded a premium from the probationers. Yet the service the women give from the first day they enter the hospital to train, far outweighs the cost of their upkeep including the miserable wages they have received. For instance, I was told in 1905, when I tried to enter the 'London', I should have about 5/0 a week after the first three months for the first year, increasing a little the second and third years. Now, they could not have got a ward-maid to do the cleaning and scrubbing that probationers had to do, for that pay, nor to work the hours they had to work. I say that the whole of the hospital service in this country depends on the, almost, unpaid work of the nurses in training. And now they have the impertinence to suggest that they PAY for their training.

Diarist 5078, M, Royal Army Pay Corps, Bournemouth, Hampshire, 02/01/44

At training film show today talked to young lad. 18 ¾ late G.S.C. Teaching himself at night school 2 evenings a week.

Myself. 'I often wonder if these chaps ever think of their prospects after the war.'

Him 'Most of them, I think, think they will go back to the same jobs they had. They don't worry.'

Myself 'What about your prospects?'

Him 'Very few, I'm afraid. It'll be a big scramble. A lot of people will probably change their jobs after the war.'

Myself 'Yes. Perhaps the army has given them a new confidence making themselves more sure – broadened their outlook?'

Him 'I don't know, I think it's that they had a latent dislike for their jobs in peacetime and this army life has provided the break for them. Also I don't think the chaps who have lived an open air life will want to go back to their indoor jobs.'

Diarist 5240, F, Teacher, Watford, Hertfordshire, 08/01/44

Two young women & a man got out of a train behind me this evening. One woman had a big grievance which she voiced in a grumbling tone. 'We have been out all day & haven't seen anybody smile,' she said. 'People might try to look a bit more cheerful.'

Diarist 5256, F, Teacher, Thornaby-on-Tees, North Yorkshire, 09/01/44

Meeting at the Town Hall, Sir William Beveridge, 'Can we afford Poverty?'

2/6 reserved seats & 1/- unreserved, I think there were a few free. It was like a fashion parade. All the élite of the town was present. Ground floor was completely packed half an hour before time with middle class people. I wondered how many were apprehensive about what they might lose, & thought it was best to keep abreast of events.

Diarist 5401, F, Technical Journalist for Aircraft Factory, Slough, Berkshire, 15/01/44

What enrages me is that I have not had flu for years. I used to be the sort of person that very seldom had even a bad cold during the winter, but general war conditions have obviously been weakening my resistance . . . It enrages me because people like poor Julia who live by being ill seize on the news of other people's illnesses like a ghoul. Her eyes will brighten and she will blame the Government and the Germans and say how awful everything is and that we shall all in time die of undernourishment and war-strain . . . 'even the toughest people are feeling it now!' she will gloat, 'And then we are told that the nation's health has never been better . . .'

<u>Diarist 5443, F, Office Worker and Volunteer Mobile Canteen</u>
<u>Driver, London, 19/01/44</u>
We saw the film of the return of the repatriated prisoners, which
is being shown as part of a Red Cross appeal in all cinemas this
week. It is most moving, unbearably so some of it, but it does
seem disgraceful that these men have to appeal to charity. The
government should provide adequately for every man injured in
the service of his country.

<u>Diarist 5004, M, ARP Worker and Food Packing Manager,</u>
<u>Belmont, Surrey, 24/01/44</u>
I feel very cross this evening because I hear the President of the
Board of Trade has announced the austerity restrictions on men's
suits and overcoats are to be relaxed. I am annoyed as it was only
on Saturday last I received delivery of a new suit made by austerity standards. Not enough pockets and no turn-up. This latter
restriction is particularly annoying, as the trousers will only the
quicker wear out.

<u>Diarist 5402, F, Retired Teacher, Great Missenden,</u>
<u>Buckinghamshire, 25/01/44</u>
My hairdresser says he thinks this really will be the end of war,
so many people have experienced its horrors. I replied – thinking
of the Prime Minister's rejoicing that he's alive in this period –
that I feared that many of those in authority are having the time
of their lives, and that started him recalling his own experiences
– of the head of the local firefighting service, who rings up to say
'Mr. S will be round in 20 minutes: kindly have someone ready to
attend to him.' 'Mr S. is out of brilliantine: kindly send him a
bottle': of the chief warden, who thought it his duty to bully the

volunteers under him, until he was put into his place: and so on. It's a tragedy for the human race that power nearly always corrupts.

Diarist 5447, F, Clerk and Housewife, Sheffield, 31/01/44

I suddenly realised last night that, barring following my stepmothers' funeral just on 2 years ago, I haven't been in a motor car for 3 years. Never before since I became adult could I have said that.

Diarist 5289, F, Teacher, Skipton, North Yorkshire, 08/02/44

Had lunch at station – quite good sardine sandwiches & they let me take the teacup with me in the train because I hadn't time to drink it. Is the easing-up of this restriction a sign of general optimistic attitude?

Diarist 5349, F, Journalist, London, 11/02/44

Very entertaining, the present temper shown to Churchill's dictatorship in re the by-elections by electors and press. He of course is an autocratic old devil, ruling a turbulent people – no doubt he appreciates the historical continuity of the whole position as much as anyone does. But he continues to bring his best broadsides to bear on local issues – it is rather like trying to crush a nit with a steam-hammer.

Diarist 5399, F, Retired Nurse, Steyning, West Sussex, 11/02/44

It is strange how we ordinary people sense the war situation, no matter how careful the press is not to alarm us. A dressmaker (widow) in this road told me yesterday that the rag and bone man said to her that he thought things were going badly for us in Italy, and he felt very depressed about it all. She said, she felt the same and rarely listened to the news, because she felt she couldn't bear it. I feel the same, and said so. I rarely listen to the end of the news these days – just now I listened and the first words were to the effect that Pres. Roosevelt said that the situation in Italy was tense. I felt like saying 'You're telling us.' And shut off.

Diarist 5157, M, Retired Policeman, Wallasey, Merseyside, 19/02/44

That the German raiders have not finished with us yet was brought home to me – my nephew's wife and his two children (4yrs & 20 months) who had been stopping here for a month left early this week but they are back again tonight. They had a raid in this district Friday–Saturday night and her husband decided they had better come back and here they are. Of course with two young children if you have a safer place to go it only seems natural to do so.

Diarist 5205, M, Laboratory Technician, Potters Bar, Hertfordshire, 20/02/44

Have spent several evenings recently making a fair copy of my diary, though this will be a long job, as it now covers four and a half years. The entries for the first few months of the war make interesting reading. What silly things people, including myself, said and thought!

Diarist 5233, M, Radio Operator, Newport, Wales, 20/02/44

The Labour Candidate is in in West Derbyshire. I am profoundly glad; so is my wife. I will attempt to give my reasons; they are by no means all purely rational; in fact, I feel pleased deep down within me in a way that can only mean that something in my subconscious has been touched. Well, I have always been a bit of a rebel. I resent dictation, I both think & feel that the Government has had everything its own way far too long. And the Government means, to a great extent, the Tory Party. Though I approve of Churchill as war-leader, I disagree with his politics & do not want to see him Prime Minister after the War. I hope that if the Coalition breaks up a Tory victory is not inevitable, & am glad of any evidence to this effect.

In addition I feel that the adoption as official candidate of the heir to a duke, aged 25, with no other qualifications is an insult to the electorate. It is, in effect, putting them on a level with 18th & early 19th century potwallopers, who were expected to vote for the local squire or, by gad sir, he'd know the reason why.

Diarist 5349, F, Journalist, London, 21/02/44
B. also remarked during the height of the raid, that the Germans were getting it far worse, and that flesh and blood ought not to be asked to endure such things: such seems to be the general verdict, and a woman at the office just now discussed with me the fact that Europe is just being smashed to nothing, and we agreed that the coming business wd. carry on the good work, and what wd. be left of civilisation – day by day everything gets more tough and brutal. Was v. upset by the terrific loss of bombers over Leipzig, and thought of the air-crew boy I talked to the other night who was probably in it: he was nothing then but a walking mass of nerves, a shadow man.

<u>Diarist 5447, F, Clerk and Housewife, Sheffield, 29/02/44</u>

My hairdresser today told me of a case she knows personally – two women they know went to a wedding where there were lovely eats, got in Black Market. Next day they went to Food Office and reported it.

<u>Diarist 5443, F, Office Worker and Volunteer Mobile Canteen Driver, London, 03/03/44</u>

We are hearing more about the damage in Well Hall, and Joyce went round this evening with a man in her office who has lost his home. She says it is absolutely ghastly, about 40 or so houses laid completely flat, and hundreds damaged terribly – all from one bomb, it seems incredible. Apparently as the 'all-clear' sounded, they used a mobile searchlight to floodlight the area, and this enabled rescue work to be carried on more easily. A couple we know, garage proprietors, were left in their night clothes only, and there are dozens of cases where families were in their houses and the shelters were smashed, and dozens of examples of the opposite, families in shelters and houses down to the ground. Mrs. L. and Pauline next door are going away on Monday for a fortnight, as Mr. L., when he saw little children being brought out of the wreckages with legs and arms smashed and all manner of dreadful injuries, said that Pauline should be out of it. I think this is alright for them, but there are thousands of people in London who can't go back and forth as the raids get bad.

<u>Diarist 5331, F, Shop Assistant, Dewsbury, West Yorkshire, 09/03/44</u>

Rumours & hints & whispers of the invasion increase. One customer said that the 18th was definitely fixed for the great move and another just afterwards told me that there would be no invasion, the Germans had had enough with the bombing and would soon be calling for a halt. But one and all they say fervently 'I wish it were over.'

Diarist 5349, F, Journalist, London, 15/03/44

Is there any worse daily journalism at present than The Times' leaders in lighter vein? It is at once smug and facetious and dreary. It drags in allusions without gusto, and lives forever in a world of buttered toast, maids with hot water and so on.

Diarist 5324, F, Hostel Worker, Gloucester, Gloucestershire, 25/03/44

A glorious day and all seemed right with our world (unfortunately the thought of the rest of the world being right too was out of the question and seemed to hang in the background however happy we feel in one another's company.)

Diarist 5349, F, Journalist, London, 29/03/44

Odd to think that, e.g., one couple I know – he is a captain in the Army, high in his own profession, intelligent, university graduate, and she a professional woman, one son of 6 between them – should have no direct influence whatever on the present Government of the country because they are only 30 and have never voted in a Party election. In fact the Govt. is sitting on nothing but its own self-esteem and a dwindling sense of public gratitude. It is rushing through its 4-yr plans, etc., etc., and Churchill seems to think that we ought to be extremely grateful for this blue-printing of our future.

<u>Diarist 5349, F, Journalist, London, 30/03/44</u>

I wonder how long it is before we have a strike of women workers – striking as a body of women, I mean? The trouble is, that this is not a war merely of armies and fronts, but a gigantic convulsion, going down to the bowels of things. And guts are not pretty!

<u>Diarist 5314, F, Housewife and Farmworker, Tayvallich, Argyll, 01/04/44</u>

L. got a good April Fool off on us. It was really directed at the Land Girl but caught us all. He sent her over saying I wanted to see her before post time to fill up some forms. While she, N, J & I were discussing what he could possibly mean, the date dawned on us. It was one of the better jokes.

<u>Diarist 5261, F, Factory Clerk, Manchester, 03/04/44</u>

Mrs. R. made us laugh today. Her husband works at the local aircraft factory & when the lunchtime buzzer went, he opened his office door to go for lunch when 'something' whizzed past along the passage. When he collected his wits he was amused to see a lad <u>on roller skates</u> making his way – ahead of all others – to the canteen.

<u>Diarist 5076, M, Accountant and Volunteer Police Constable, Sheffield, 05/04/44</u>

My annual inspection of pawnbrokers shops in the Yorkshire coalfield. There were plenty of idle miners about on strike. In one shop a customer was complaining that these bloody miners were 'making us do without coal' (deliveries of coal in that area are prohibited) and that they would soon make 'us do without food'. A miner's wife replied 'It's alright for thee, thou't not a

245

collier. If they doan't stick up for their own rights now, they'll never get them.'

Diarist 5429, F, Secretary, London, 07/04/44

I find with the Jewish question, as with others, such as the Indian problem, that I experience a sense of impatience and exaspera-tion – that it is all a jolly old nuisance and I don't want to be bothered to think about it. This is probably because there is so much going on, and so many demands on one's sympathies and emotions, due to the war, that a point comes when one feels used up and cannot take a keen interest in anything more; whereas each of these problems deserves close study and interest on its own merits.

Diarist 5402, Retired Teacher, F, Great Missenden, Buckinghamshire, 10/04/44

Persistent pain is a terrible thing to bear: I don't think that men like Churchill, who find war so elating, have any real conception of the price that our wounded have to pay. In the [hospital] bed next to me was a little W.A.A.F, who said that she loved her work (servicing a 'Mosquito') & spoke of the thrill of seeing it return safely from a flight. She said that she was more conscientious than the men – they did the work all right but didn't check up on it twice, as she did. She says there is tension between the 'Battledress' & the uniformed W.A.A.Fs – those who sit in offices & sign forms considering themselves superior to those who do the real work. My other neighbour was a woman who seems to have had a terrible time with a shell-shocked husband ever since the last war. The people who bear most during a war, are just those who have least chance of happiness after it.

Diarist 5349, F, Journalist, London, 12/04/44

Saturday's shopping was a fearful and wonderful business – perhaps 50 or more in the bread queue, many in the fish queue, the scene in the grocer's being one long queue involuted on itself within the shop until it reached the bacon counter. Biscuits of a kind were available. Came through King's Cross on Monday evening, and the tube exchange station was a seething mass – everyone good-tempered.

Diarist 5399, F, Retired Nurse, Steyning, West Sussex, 16/04/44

I have had some wonderful white broccoli this week, and could spare some to give away to a neighbour who gave me some last year. Another neighbour gave me some onions, she had so many they were all sprouting. I gave her some of my potatoes, as all hers were finished and I have plenty. That is how we manage. Another neighbour gave me last year a lot of leek seeds, and I was glad to be able to spare her a broccoli this year in return. Lettuce are late. I grew a lot indoors in the warm, and thought I had hardened them enough to set out. But came a hard frost the night after and they have all died.

Diarist 5444, F, Housewife, London, 18/04/44

Lovely day. Went to town to attend annual Siamese Cat Club meeting. Very entertaining. Notice many really elderly members have aged considerably. Two appeared very opulent but most looked tired & work worn hands were conspicuous, most told same story; more work to do than they could manage, no help, but kittens selling well & all determined to carry on as best possible.

<u>Diarist 5428, F, Clerk, London, 20/04/44</u>

Miss F., who feels the cold and loves warmth like a cat, was a little plaintive on the subject [of heating restrictions]; a little surprised that <u>we</u> need be so law-abiding and careful. Miss B., who does <u>not</u> feel the cold, was instantly up in arms, drawing horrid pictures of the workers of Moscow who had no heating at all throughout one winter. She was very indignant about 'people who never expect to have to put up with any difficulties themselves.'

<u>Diarist 5289, F, Teacher, Skipton, North Yorkshire, 27/04/44</u>

Aberystwyth University was in mourning for a young lecturer who committed suicide a day or two before the beginning of term – a brilliant & inspiring scholar, a scientist, heavily involved with extramural & Home Guard Duties – no known troubles, the only son of his mother, etc.

I turned this over in my mind & thought it might well be a war-casualty, though not in battle, except that to borrow a phrase, it's all a battlefield.

<u>Diarist 5399, F, Retired Nurse, Steyning, West Sussex, 30/04/44</u>

All friends who write to me speak of the strain of waiting [for the invasion]. My sister wrote from Sidmouth, 'It is fear, fear all the time, as to what is coming.' It was the same in Gloucestershire, and as for Sussex, even the M.P., Lord Winterton, spoke of the strain under which we were living, not only from enemy action but from the 'vast propaganda' as to imminent invasion of the French coast. And it has been going on for months. [. . .] To me here, almost untouched by what will happen (as far as anyone I know is concerned) the strain is almost intolerable, so I know what it must be to others more directly implicated in it all.

Diarist 5045, M, Nurseryman, Newick, East Sussex, 01/05/44

An interesting sidelight on how rumours spread. My Co-Platoon officer in H.Gs some while back lost his only son in the blowing up of a transport in the Mediterranean. A few days ago a rumour went all round the village and even to the next one that he was saved and a Prisoner of War. There was no truth in it whatever. It was very distressing for the parents. I helped him trace the origin of the rumour and we found it had originated with a daily worker in the house next door who saw the poor lad's trunks etc returned to his parents' house and drew her own conclusions.

Diarist 5428, F, Clerk, London, 05/05/44

I came home by bus again today, but this time the journey was not so pleasant, for in the seat behind were two Communists. In theory I have nothing against Communists, I do not particularly like or dislike them; but I do dislike fanatics, whatever form their fanaticism takes. These two talked all the way from Victoria to Aldgate, and I could not help but listen, half amused and half-irritated. I have never heard such wholesale debunking before. I gathered that children are not taught any single thing that is true: that if the truth of England's history were put before them, they would be ashamed of her. I know that the educational system is far from perfect, and that there are many things in our history we cannot be proud of (of what country cannot this be said?) but at the same time, they did exaggerate, and these ideas were obviously not their own. I cannot stand people with spoon-fed minds.

Diarist 5004, M, ARP Worker and Food Packing Manager, Belmont, Surrey, 06/05/44

It is a terrible thing to find that our road casualties have exceeded the number of men killed on active service. Road traffic even taking into account military vehicles is much less than before the war, but still the road slaughter continues. There does not seem to be much which can be done about it – propaganda has been tried with apparent small effect.

Diarist 5401, F, Technical Journalist for Aircraft Factory, Slough, Berkshire, 08/05/44

Mrs. M told me today at lunch about the husband of a friend of hers. He had a good position in a Building Society in the North of England and was deferred until about a year ago when he went into the Navy as an A.B. Went through the training but would not try for a Commission much to the disappointment of his wife – he said that at 38 he was too old to work for exams and was not interested. He then went in for a very hush hush radio course in which they were not allowed even to take notes and passed with flying colours. His wife heard from him last week that he has now volunteered for the mines! His explanation is that he has been in the Navy for 10 months, 'loafed' for 8, spent 7000 miles travelling in trains and feels that he can be of more use to the war effort in the pits. His wife and all his friends are amazed and can not understand the change at all. 'Such a quiet, steady sort of man,' said Mrs. M., 'Catching the 8.10 every morning and returning by the 5.40 every day of his life for years . . .'

Diarist 5389, F, Housewife, Sutton Coldfield, Warwickshire, 08/05/44

Wish sale of other house completed, then should have capital to augment Army pay. Have decided to use pay for cash expenses, & pay Gas & electricity & 'phone from capital. This should keep me going till Evan goes to school then I can get a job. Often feel am shirking by staying home with him, but really difficulties of scrimping & scraping quite as formidable as hard work, & do feel I ought to be with Evan in these formative years.

Diarist 5110, M, Vicar, Boston, Lincolnshire, 09/05/44

Sat in a garden this evening & drank gin & discussed equal pay for equal work, am surprised to find married women greatly against unmarried women having it.

Diarist 5378, F, Writer, Farmer and Housewife, Campbeltown, Argyll, 23/05/44

Lois turned up just before lunch, told me a lot more, about her rather tough and unwashed platoon: 50% lousy and a lot of scabies. But she is very keen on the whole thing for 'the girls', one of whom for instance had worked in an underground shop and never seen as much of the light, another was married at sixteen, had no children, had been told there was something wrong, but hadn't ever seen a doctor till now. A lot were having teeth seen to, some spent all the first mornings with the dentist, Lois was the only one who had perfect teeth. The medical must have been funny, all stripped and after waiting for some time they were merely asked if they bit their nails! She says there is a general belief in the ranks that the officers buy their commission which is odd. I asked her if the NCOs ever swore at them, she said of course not, the platoon would burst into tears! I gather they are very well looked after, even fussed over. But tremendous class distinctions between privates.

Diarist 5460, F, Railway Clerk, Newport, Wales, 25/05/44

I woke up this morning with a feeling of anxiety and distress. I could not think why until I remembered Churchill and France. It is too much. After all these years of worry and bitterness to go back to where it all started – buttering up that Christian gutter-snipe, that stab-in-the-back two-faced Franco. I now prepare myself for the next war and for wars and revolutions all my life. What does he think we are?

Diarist 5240, F, Teacher, Watford, Hertfordshire, 31/05/44

I was told of a woman today who does not have her cheese ration wrapped – she eats it in the shop!

Diarist 5261, F, Factory Clerk, Manchester, 01/06/44

She told me a story supposed to be quite true about an American Negro soldier & a girl from the local High School. It was funny, then, when I got home & found Mary F & Betty there, to hear them recount exactly the same scandalous story, only the High School was situated on the opposite side of the town to the one in the first story. It is a real lesson to me never to repeat these stories.

Diarist 5402, F, Retired Teacher, Great Missenden, Buckinghamshire, 06/06/44

Although I knew, theoretically, that it must come, I had almost given up on expecting news of the invasion. When I heard it at 8 o'clock this morning my heart sank: the terror & suffering that must engulf so many had begun. Then I felt most irritated that the news was from German sources. Why couldn't we have been told by our own Government first?

Poor France, to be again devastated by war! I'm quite sure that if I were the mother of a French family I would rather live under Vichy than have my children under the guns & bombs of two opposing armies & I find it very difficult to believe that the ordinary people of Europe are really anxious to pay the terrible price of 'liberation'.

Diarist 5444, F, Housewife, London, 07/06/44

All gradually settling down & hanging on news, some seems awful, eye witness accounts from correspondents etc wonder if it's really necessary to give so many details, such as English & German dead laying along the roads & stories of individuals suffering & death, everyone with a husband or son over there wonders if it might be he.

Diarist 5399, F, Retired Nurse, Steyning, West Sussex, 08/06/44

They are telling us a lot of first-hand news about the invasion. It will keep some people glued to the radio, but I can't listen as some do. If I did I should never live to see the end of it all. I told that to my sister in 1940, when I found she was listening all day long. In America they interrupt any programs to tell any new item of news, and she kept her radio going all day in case she should miss anything. She even bought a second radio to have in her bedroom, for after they went to bed. I begged her not to listen so much. She died suddenly Sept 1940. I know it sends the blood pressure up, and hers was very high already. I dare not let my B.P. go higher.

<u>Diarist 5271, F, Local Government Clerk, Bury St Edmunds,</u>
<u>Suffolk, 10/06/44</u>

We had amusing visitors in that shelter & outside a woman was
going to have a baby & there was neither doctor nor midwife to
be got, though one arrived in the nick of time. My warden
brother-in-law was more scared over that woman than over
anything else that night. Bombs & fires were ordinary things but
a confinement was something unknown.

<u>Diarist 5199, M, Retired Railway Draughtsman, Paignton,</u>
<u>Devon, 15/06/44</u>

We are wanting rain very badly indeed. We are asked not to
'waste water'. All water from washing, washing-up, etc., I store
for watering the garden, and also use some from the tap, but not
much. I have not used a single clothing coupon! I think I ought to
be awarded the O.M. or something like that! Also I have depended
upon the garden for all vegetables since January, except that I
spent 8d. for lettuce and cress when my daughter-in-law visited
me: this is excepting potatoes, which we were advised NOT to
grow. This means I abstain from what I have not in the garden,
and of course the diet is more monotonous than most people
would like. I gathered stinging nettles as a vegetable, for weeks,
to give variety! I have not tasted rhubarb. But I keep very well.

<u>Diarist 5402, F, Retired Teacher, Great Missenden,</u>
<u>Buckinghamshire, 17/06/44</u>

I felt a bit scared in the night when during an alert, a plane –
probably a succession of planes, for it seemed as though the
noise would never stop – making a most peculiar sound, passed
over. There's one comfort, in this wooden bungalow one place is

as unsafe as another, so there's no point in getting up. During the day, I wanted to look up almost every time a plane passed over: I hope that no winged bombs will come our way, but I should hate to miss one if it did!

Diarist 5256, F, Teacher, Thornaby-on-Tees, North Yorkshire, 20/06/44

Teacher in Infant School says babies' drawings always end in aeroplanes, & cowboys, no matter what she starts them off with.

Diarist 5110, M, Vicar, Boston, Lincolnshire, 21/06/44

A unit of local boys seems to have been badly knocked about in France, but only one from this parish, so far. The wife, I married them last Jan., heard that he had been wounded in the head and was in hospital in Oxford, that was late this afternoon, she, her mother, his mother, and two aunts started off to Oxford at once, although they hadn't been asked to go, heaven alone knows how they will get through to Oxford, and I expect that they will have to stay in London the night. I tried to get them to wait for more news, but they wouldn't do so. How the hospital will hate them, as they were not told to go to the hospital, just the ordinary announcement.

Diarist 5045, M, Nurseryman, Newick, East Sussex, 30/06/44

Death has shaken hands with us this month in more ways than one. He has come in one of his most peaceable moods to carry away my old father peacefully in his sleep barely two months short of his ninetieth birthday. Well, he for one is well out of a nightmare world. As I type this I leave off to go out and listen to the big barrage some miles north of us and to check up on the buzznbuzzbbuzz of the Robot's engines and then the glad sound of their ceasing and the big thump that follows. Thank God that hasn't got to London though some poor country folk may have suffered, but the odds are so much more in our favour better here and hereabouts than in poor old London. Yes June 1944 I am unlikely ever to forget you.

11. IT WILL NOT BE LIGHTS UP, BANANAS FOR ALL

July to December 1944

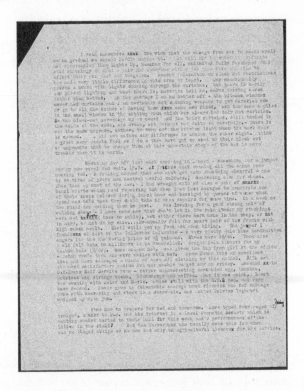

'I read somewhere the view that the change from war to peace would be so gradual we should hardly notice it. It will not be something definite and spectacular like Lights Up, Bananas for all . . .'

Here, in the final furlong of the war, victory has never looked closer. In Europe, Allied troops of all nationalities are slowly converging on Germany, liberating the towns and cities of the occupied countries as they go. Their success is replicated throughout the world and, by the end of the year, the Japanese armies are suffering defeats throughout Asia and the Pacific. However, at home the V1s are joined by V2s, rockets that fall at the speed of sound and cause massive destruction without warning.

Although these new weapons statistically cause less damage than the air raids of the early war, people are unable to build up resilience as they did in nightly blitzes. They have let their emotional guard down, removed their mental armour and assumed that, with the Axis forces in retreat, there was no longer any threat to life at home. For many, whether cowering in the target areas or watching in disbelief from another part of the country, this 'second wave' of destruction feels like history repeating itself. New hordes of evacuees flee the south-east and deposit themselves elsewhere, bringing many of the sensations of the early war – upheaval, displacement and, for some, adventure – out of storage. However, with peace so clearly on the horizon, even these old feelings are laced with a new anticipation.

*   *   *

<u>Diarist 5399, F, Retired Nurse, Steyning, West Sussex, 02/07/44</u>
A neighbour told us that her sister wrote from N London that she was to be sent home from a Holloway hospital with a baby only 8 days old, in order to empty beds for casualties. That there were 1500 a day coming in. I said I didn't believe it; that someone was exaggerating. (But that is the kind of stories being put about.)

Diarist 5444, F, Housewife, London, 17/07/44

Still suffering from an acute depression mental & physical. How wrong all this is, little homes & hospitals smashed up, personal possessions scattered, children sleeping on Tube platforms, cats & dogs being put to sleep as fast as possible or left to roam the streets homeless.

How can any good come out of this chaos? Man's inhumanity to man in this age of so called civilisation!!!

Diarist 5199, M, Retired Railway Draughtsman, Paignton, Devon, 21/07/44

I am an amateur printer, and occasionally am 'moved' to print slips. One I printed some weeks ago, on THE RESPONSIBILITY OF WOMEN, led to the Women For Westminster Movement being mentioned to me. Now I have set up type for a slip PACIFISTS SHOULD REPENT. I sent this to the Ministry of Information to be censored, and the approval came very quickly, and I shall now go ahead and print a few – on second-hand paper (postal wrappings, etc.)

Diarist 5444, F, Housewife, London, 21/07/44

Heated some milk & sat sipping it in dining room & trying to read paper, heard another bomb coming in on a queer note, it sounded heavy & grinding its way along; decided to go under stairs & had no sooner sat down that [sic] I heard thing overhead & engine cut out, now I thought, this is it, pray God it's not a direct hit. Bomb suddenly dropped with a noise like a rushing express train & I waited, for a few minutes, all was noise, glass breaking, wood splintering, tiles falling & heavy thuds all around, I covered my ears & waited until all seemed quiet &

carefully tried to peer out, very surprised at finding myself intact: could not move door so yelled at top of voice as could now hear voices, a boy ran in & moved something a little so that I could squeeze out & I saw that front door had blown off, sailed down hall & hemmed me in under stairs.

Diarist 5306, F, Housewife and Volunteer Teacher, Burnley, Lancashire, 25/07/44

Evacuees arrived here recently and are noticed about the town. We have not had many in previous evacuations. The problem of placing mothers and babies is very difficult. A baby is a very destructive element even in its own home, where things have been modified and its habits arranged for. Bedding, carpets & table-cloths are very scarce things and may suffer when young children are about. Wireless sets, china, and ornaments are also liable to rough treatment. It is the fashion to flatter and admire other people's babies, so the mother is very sensitive to an atmosphere of coolness when she is billeted on strangers.

Diarist 5450, F, Trainee Probation Officer, Welwyn Garden City, Hertfordshire, 26/07/44

It was pleasant to walk over to the film at Welwyn this evening, and good to see a worthwhile film. 'Now, Voyager' – I like the title and the film is I think one of the most 'real' I have ever seen. I wonder why it is that during wartime we seem to get down to the essentials of life. Good music has certainly come to the fore-front, and people are getting to understand one another a little better, possibly because as Lawrence James says, because their aggression can go out to the 'enemy', and vent itself there.

<u>Diarist 5068, M, Cost Clerk and Special Constable, Beverley,</u>
<u>East Riding of Yorkshire, 28/07/44</u>

Somewhat eccentric chap at our place has got one of the typists to do him a letter to the military authorities with regard to the behaviour of an Anti-Aircraft unit in the field next to his house. He said discipline was slack and the unit had been there too long. He wrote once before & got a sharp reply. Girls were discussing him & some tho't he was jealous of the nice little garden the A/A men had got; he is a keen gardener. I suggested someone wrote to our Sec'y saying that he (author of letter) had been *here* too long.

<u>Diarist 5261, F, Factory Clerk, Manchester, 02/08/44</u>

On the way back a London woman, supposedly an evacuee, asked me to direct her to a certain fishmongers, which I didn't know, but I pointed out one on the other side of the road. She said she had been there but they hadn't the kind she wanted. Perhaps she hadn't yet learnt that one can't be 'choosey' about fish in Manchester. Usually we are thankful to take what is offered.

<u>Diarist 5303, F, ATS Typist (hospitalised), Stanmore,</u>
<u>Middlesex, 02/08/44</u>

Visiting day, but no visitors as Mother is too frightened of buzz-bombs, so mentally damn the Jerries even more. My bedmate up to show her parents she <u>can</u> walk – wonder when my turn will come? Hope buzz-bombs finish before I go home, as I don't intend spending my days or nights in shelter.

<u>Diarist 5402, F, Retired Teacher, Great Missenden,</u>
<u>Buckinghamshire, 03/08/44</u>

When I was hearing & sympathising with complaints of the nuisance of evacuees, it struck me for the first time that I'm one myself. Having been one for four years makes the offence worse rather than less.

<u>Diarist 5358, F, ATS Clerk, Grays, Essex, 05/08/44</u>

Mother and I join a queue at the greengrocers stall for tomatoes and green stuff. Two grubby little boys, in disreputable clothes, are hanging about the stall, eying a pile of glistening red and yellow tomatoes, overflowing into a neighbouring pile of muddy carrots. Stuck into the latter is one of the old greengrocer's price-signs – 'EAT MORE FRUIT// per 3d. LB.' As the assistant moves down to our end, one of the boys says 'Miss, what fruit is that?' The poor urchins were clutching a few coppers, and their fruit-hungry eyes were taken by the colourful tomatoes, which they probably took to be some exotic fruit, all at the magical price within their reach!

What a reflection on our present mode of life it is that children have hardly known what it is to be able to spend their few pennies on ices and sweets. They can only remember queues and crowds, sirens and shelters, and have never eaten a toffee-apple! These children have lost five years of their life, and we must try to make it up to them.

<u>Diarist 5274, F, Unstated, Eastham, Merseyside, 06/08/44</u>

Walked 20 miles – it seemed a long way. We asked at a cottage for a drink of water, and a cup of tea was pressed on me by an old woman who told me about the awful pains she has in her legs, due to electricity sent over on purpose by Dr. Goebbels. I told her to think as little as she could about it.

Diarist 5004, M, ARP Worker and Food Packing Manager, Belmont, Surrey, 16/08/44

A Day of Prayer, September 3rd – what on earth is the value of this sort of thing? I am not a particularly religious man, but neither am I the complete unbeliever, but how a Christian can justify this sort of concentrated prayer passeth my understanding.

Diarist 5179, M, Retired Chemist, Tring, Hertfordshire, 18/08/44

I have removed the bottles, tins, and broken china and glass from the bin provided for such waste. I put it piece by piece into the wheelbarrow and dumped it on the refuse tip. I recognised broken pieces representing 11 cups, three plates, one dish, 5 saucers, 1 egg cup, a glass fly trap, two basins, and a large mixing bowl. These things alone represent probably between 35/- and 40/-. The bulk have been broken by the evacuees or their children, and no offer of recompense.

Diarist 5289, F, Teacher, Skipton, North Yorkshire, 23/08/44

On a journey from Skipton to Cardiff during the height of the pre-Bank-Holiday rush, I was horrified to see a gravely wounded soldier. He had lost either one or both of his legs, merely wrapped in a blanket & carried by two soldiers, being crowded into an ordinary compartment of a train. At Derby and Gloucester he was transported from one platform to another by means of luggage lifts – No sign of a stretcher. The soldiers with him didn't appear to be particularly skilful at their task & by the time he reached Cardiff the unfortunate hero was a dreadful grey in the face.

Diarist 5045, M, Nurseryman, Newick, East Sussex, 30/08/44
We went to a larger neighbouring seaside resort and 'gate-crashed' a lovely bathe. There was a beach marked for troops only but the few troops bathing there more or less invited us to join in and so we did and managed to get in a bathe before the police came and turned us off. Well why not, I myself as a Home Guard, my wife as a Red Cross worker, my son as a cadet, my eldest daughter a Red Cross nurse and my second daughter braving the 'doodlebugs' in London making munitions six months before she was obliged to, all felt we were really entitled to one.

Diarist 5403, F, News Office Worker, Evesham, Worcestershire, 01/09/44
Also, working in a news office as I do, I get rather out of touch with what the so-called 'man in the street' is thinking, and I am rather inclined to imagine people are apathetic and ignorant about the news, when I compare their outlook with that of highly specialised and experienced journalists. I do find, though, that I can divide people into two types; on one hand there are people who read the papers very little, know not more than the bare headlines of what is going on, and care even less; on the other hand there are people who read the papers quite religiously, who believe everything they see in print and who have a great knack for getting hold of false information. The first class of people are usually those who have some other, greater interest, and just have not time to bother about the intricacies of a world

war – which is a pretty full time job in itself – while the second class do not know anything of what goes on behind the scenes of the newspaper racket, however interested they may be in world affairs.

Diarist 5068, M, Cost Clerk and Special Constable, Beverley, East Riding of Yorkshire, 02/09/44

I keep thinking about the question of remaining in the Specials after the war.

Pros: (1) Being among the first to be ready for duty in the event of emergency; I rather regret not having joined up at the first appeal for volunteers at the time of Munich; actually I joined on the outbreak of war. (2) General sense of public duty; civil disturbances such as strikes etc. are more likely to call for the help of the Specials than the war did in this quiet area. (3) Keeping in contact with friends made during the war. (4) Possibility of being a useful key man in some future emergency.

Cons: (1) Lack of physical & temperamental qualifications for 'rough stuff' in the event of civil disturbance. (2) Other demands on my time; family matters & so on; (3) Freedom of thought & decision on political matters; in the event of a strike my sympathies might conceivably be with the strikers.

Diarist 5205, M, Laboratory Technician, Potters Bar, Hertfordshire, 03/09/44

The fifth anniversary of the outbreak of war. Looking back, my main feeling is one of awe at the huge panorama of events which we have lived through. What a lot of things have happened, to me personally and to people in general. In the comparative safety of what I feel to be the last weeks of the war I can say that I wouldn't have missed it for anything. (No doubt, if I had been in the battle-line, I wouldn't say that.) During these five years, we have run the whole gamut of emotions, seen human nature at its most naked. We have had to put up with many unpleasant things and now we feel that our patience has been rewarded.

Diarist 5443, F, Office Worker and Volunteer Mobile Canteen Driver, London, 03/09/44

Our thoughts have been going back a long way today, and although it is such a long time since Sept. 3rd 1939, I can remember very clearly what we did on that hot day, and I still remember running down the garden to our shelter when the siren went clutching a chair to sit on. These years have passed very quickly, but nonetheless they have been a fifth of my life and of course for many of my friends a larger proportion than that. I couldn't help thinking too of what the boys out in Japanese prison camps are thinking today – wondering no doubt how we have managed to stick out these years, because things were in a bad way when they left, and when I think seriously about it, I often wonder <u>why</u> we have managed to stay the course, because on Sept. 7th 1940 I really thought the war would be over the following day, so little faith had I in the power of the people to 'take it'.

Diarist 5039.2, M, Factory Worker and Volunteer Fireman, Mansfield, Nottinghamshire, 06/09/44

Peace is in the air. Everywhere one goes, there is one idea, peace before Xmas. A new kind of spirit is in the air. A kind of relief or buoyancy, call it what you will. The War is nearly over! Mr. A thinks it will be over before the end of October.

Diarist 5198, M, Woodworking Machinist, Enfield, Middlesex, 07/09/44

Rather thoughtful today. Feel fear at approaching end to war. Will industry be in turmoil. Will there be jobs. Will it be worth-while carrying on active participation in class struggle. Dare I. If so, dare I get married as I hope to do. A married man must fear his boss, whereas a single man may have independence of spirit selfishly and almost unconsciously. I do not desire end of war. Rationally, I do. War is HELL. I feel that many others must also fear end of war for same reason . . . dread of unemployment.

Diarist 5256, F, Teacher, Thornaby-on-Tees, North Yorkshire, 07/09/44

Relaxation of fire-watching duties, lifting of blackout, abolition of compulsion for the Home Guard, has more effect on morale than the news of military victories. Everyone remarks on it. To us the fire-watching looms the most important. Lately we had all got very fed up because it seemed so pointless.

Diarist 5380, F, Voluntary Worker and Clerk, St Albans, Hertfordshire, 12/09/44

I am reading 'A Leaf in the Storm' just now & that & the accounts of our Polish friends make me realise just what a sheltered life we lead in Britain; the evacuation & bombing are very minor upheavals compared with those most nations have gone through. Even the new, more settled countries like America, Australia, South Africa, have a recent memory of trekking, lawlessness & hardship. Sometimes I think our stability must give us a balance & sanity of outlook, certainly more civilised, than others & sometimes I wonder if we aren't too narrowly reasonable,

& utterly lacking in understanding of the reactions of those that have gone through so much – probably both these aspects are true.

<u>Diarist 5399, F, Retired Nurse, Steyning, West Sussex, 13/09/44</u>
Unless I can keep away from the radio news, I am afraid I shall die from listening to the news of victory. My heart is stirred, so that I am almost in tears as I listen to the incidents, like the pipers band playing through the streets of St Valery, and the French people making flags of the Allies out of old pieces of stuff, all put together wrongly. Oh, but I am thankful to God or some Power, that I have lived to see these days. And I know how our hard-fighting men feel, and Montgomery and CHURCHILL.

<u>Diarist 5390, F, Secretary, United States War Shipping Administration, Glasgow, 18/09/44</u>
Thousands of Glaswegians must have gone into the city to see the lights on last night. In fact the word 'illuminations' has been used seriously and without consciousness of exaggeration. At 8 o'clock we had looked out of the window at the standard lamps in Hyndland Road, and Mother with disgust had declared that they were the same as last year. They looked the same, perhaps they were. It has been said that the dim out is to raise morale. There is no doubt that the black out was the wartime inconvenience most disliked.

<u>Diarist 5110, M, Vicar, Boston, Lincolnshire, 04/10/44</u>
I have been trying to get people to talk about the White Paper, but they all seem to find it too complicated to understand. This is a very different attitude to the time that the Beveridge Report

came out nearly 2 years ago, then all kinds of surprising people bought it & read it. I think most likely the reason is that we are becoming a very, very tired people. This is shown I think by another thing, & that is the way the Arnhem affair has been taken. Sentiment & mass 'tears' please I do not want to be nasty, but the Borough is simply wallowing in it. Want of proper perspective. I look on it as <u>very serious.</u>

Diarist 5331, F, Shop Assistant, Dewsbury, West Yorkshire, 04/10/44

Some wool from the W.V.A. to knit garments for the 'occupied' children. My hairdresser was rather sarcastic when I told her of this & said were there no British children who needed to be knitted for. I said, well, didn't she think it was partly propaganda, a sort of bribery of the continental countries. She said, yes, America & Britain would now be sort of rivals for the admiration of these foreigners.

Diarist 5399, F, Retired Nurse, Steyning, West Sussex, 05/10/44

The weeks fly by so quickly I don't know where they go. There is a woman living opposite who came here with one child in 1941 to escape London bombing. The first time I spoke to her she told me she would never have come to a place like this from LONDON, if it hadn't been to escape the danger. SHE had lived in London. She has had a second child, but as a local married man was seen to go in and out of her house at all times of the day and night, there is some question as to who is the father. Her husband is in the army and away most of the time. I have never talked to her, because I couldn't stand her pretentiousness. Today, for some reason I went across and spoke. I said, I supposed she would be thinking of getting back to London. Oh yes indeed, as soon as she could. I said, it seemed wrong for anyone who could stay where they were to try to return until things were in better shape. Oh yes, but when one had lived in London, you couldn't be happy in a place like this. I said, Don't be silly. I was born in London, and lived there all my young life, and had lived in Paris, New York, Belgrade, and I was satisfied. She said, (and she would have said worse if she had dared, I could see it in her eye) 'You are old, I am young (and she puffed out her chest and swung her arms) and full of life. I want life, and then I have children to think of and to find good schools for.' I said I thought we here ought to be very thankful. Bombs had dropped all around us, but we had escaped. But she wouldn't have that. SHE had had bombs before she came down, enough for a lifetime. She quite agreed that those who had been here all the time ought to be thankful. THEY did not know what bombing was.

Diarist 5401, F, Technical Journalist for Aircraft Factory, Slough, Berkshire, 11/10/44

I read somewhere the view that the change from war to peace would be so gradual we should hardly notice it. It will not be something definite and spectacular like Lights Up, Bananas for all, unlimited fully fashioned real silk stockings at 2/6d a pair and everyone with a job they like and able to afford their own plot and bungalow. Recent relaxation on Black Out restrictions has made very little difference in this area at least. One occasionally passes a house with lights showing through the curtains, but there is hardly any street lighting and what there is, motorists tell me, makes driving worse rather than better.

<u>Diarist 5181, M, Secretary, New Malden, Surrey, 15/10/44</u>
Yesterday I spent mainly in the garden, putting grass seed back in what used to be vegetable plots. I am getting the garden into its pre-war shape, so is the man next door.

<u>Diarist 5306, F, Housewife and Volunteer Teacher, Burnley, Lancashire, 23/10/44</u>
Two men are loudly complaining about the greengrocers in town. One could not get eating apples as he is not a regular customer. The other advises him to remember that after the war he will be at liberty to turn on the greengrocer and say 'I am <u>not</u> one of your regular customers.' So it is spreading to the men now, and <u>they</u> don't like it either!! That is why most people dislike all talk of continuing controls. It all depends on who is controlled – the people who submit or are patriotic enough, are controlled. Others are not.

<u>Diarist 5240, F, Teacher, Watford, Hertfordshire, 01/11/44</u>
At 8.30 p.m. there was an unearthly bang outside, with a slight rattling of the windows. There had been no warning. For the first time during this war I felt scared, & for 1½ hours I was trembling. It was probably a rocket bomb falling miles away but it is a most unpleasant thought that one has no chance of sheltering from such a bomb.

<u>Diarist 5004, M, ARP Worker and Food Packing Manager, Belmont, Surrey, 02/11/44</u>
It is a very shaken Mass-Observer who writes today: With my wife we were exercising the dog on the Downs in the late afternoon, and whilst I was telling her of my impressions about an

'unknown missile' which fell near me in London today, there was suddenly a terrific flash and an explosion which is indescribable. It was the loudest bang I have ever heard. In a second we were bowled over, and I suppose we stayed on our backs for about a minute. We were not conscious of any blast, nor did we notice debris flying over us. Rather shaken we got up, and the sky overhead was covered by black smoke reaching up to about 2,000 feet. Yes, of course it was a V2, and having collected ourselves together, we found ourselves to be extremely fortunate because the bomb had fallen about 200/300 yards away. Several people have told me that the fall is preceded by a terrific rush of air and a swishing sound. Actually we heard nothing – one minute was all silence – next a terrific crump.

Diarist 5296, F, Housewife, Gateshead, Tyne and Wear, 06/11/44

Americans abound around Mansfield. – Elsie & co play hockey with them & say it's the A's who provide the food good & plenty of it . . . Say Americans:– 'What is the matter with you English? You let your govt. put upon you right & left. You suffer more than any country & you just go patiently on letting them ground you down to shameful rations. You're amazing. Why, there's more food in France than you get here. What will you do in peace you amazing folks! I bet you go on like this & let them keep you down because you have become accustomed to being imposed upon.'

And all this makes us wonder if it is true, for we know that all the country aren't getting the same poor food. It annoys us to hear radio doctors praising our physique etc when we know most folks are tired & weary & sick unto death.

Diarist 5376, F, Teacher, Burwash Weald, East Sussex, 07/11/44

I am making up a few oddments into garments, hoping to see some address to which garments can be sent en route to the people of Holland or Greece or Yugoslavia – a pair of boys pants from old corduroy breeches, baby's shoes from an old felt hat etc.

Diarist 5358, F, ATS Clerk, Grays, Essex, 08/11/44

In the bus today, I noticed a woman with a brown paper carrier bag on her knee. It bore the name of a fruiterer, with the address 'Cape Town', followed by the words: 'Crystallised fruits a Speciality. Parcels for friends overseas.' What a vision this conjures up – a warm-hearted South African, walking into a Cape Town store, its shelves laden with the tempting fruits of that part of the globe, and placing his or her order; a choice selection of preserved fruits tenderly packed and despatched to the sister or mother in chilly, bomb-racked London. The gasp of pleasure when the parcel is unwrapped over here, and the joy of sampling the half-forgotten flavour of its precious contents – I wish I had a relative in South Africa!

Diarist 5198, M, Woodworking Machinist, Enfield, Middlesex, 19/11/44

More rockets, not that I hear them, I sleep. More rain. Which is the greater nuisance? I've heard more rain moans than rocket ones. Everybody seems to be having a dose of fed-upness.

<u>Diarist 5443, F, Office Worker and Volunteer Mobile Canteen Driver, London, 21/11/44</u>

Major Lewis Hastings broadcast this evening on his return from the continent, and paid tribute most movingly to the ordinary British soldier who is doing such great deeds out there and as usual made one feel ashamed at the petty grumbles we are so often indulging in – certainly we oughtn't to make such a fuss about rockets and doodles (I soon forget this resolution when I hear one).

<u>Diarist 5358, F, ATS Clerk, Grays, Essex, 22/11/44</u>

The stretch of pavement from the corner to the door of our billet is shining bright – and completely deserted. Ever since the ATS descended upon this quiet Kensington backwater, at the beginning of the war, countless swains, of all nationalities, have bidden a fond farewell to their khaki-clad Juliets of the evening, on this slip of pavement. Now the lights have gone up on this paradise, and the couples will be forced to seek some less public rendezvous for the goodnight kiss. Among many of the girls of my Unit, the lifting of the blackout at this particular spot is most unpopular, and they say so, with feeling!

<u>Diarist 5261, F, Factory Clerk, Manchester, 23/11/44</u>

Talk in the office about men coming back to their old jobs after the war, & the problems they would create. A lot of them would go out as youths earning a youth's wage & would come back as men, expecting an adult wage, yet only possessing as much knowledge of the job as they did when they went.

Diarist 5303, F, ATS Typist (hospitalised), Stanmore, Middlesex, 25/11/44

Terrific discussion about some scandal in the 'Daily Mirror'. If only people would get as het-up over the things that really concern us, we might get somewhere. But of course if it's only a case of losing some right, or accepting some more control, or being swindled out of something, why should they worry – when there's a nice, juicy scandal or murder? It makes me sick!

Diarist 5402, F, Retired Teacher, Great Missenden, Buckinghamshire, 02/12/44

Today I heard that my furniture has been absolutely ruined by rain. I do wish it had been directly by a bomb instead, as I feel that I'm partly to blame – though exactly what I could have done to save it I don't know. It's very sad to lose treasures that have been lovingly cared for by one's forebears for years, as a result of negligence. In my own case, this loss of what is left to me of my Home, seems to have cut me adrift from the future as well as the past: I just don't belong anywhere.

Diarist 5403, F, News Office Worker, Evesham, Worcestershire, 03/12/44

Home Guard Stand-down parade today: I didn't see anything of the parade, but from what I hear it was impressive. Everyone is rather sad; the Home Guard was an almost domestic institution; the older men loved it for the comradeship and for the happy memories it brought back of last war days – and despite the horrors of war, men will often look back on it with nostalgia.

<u>Diarist 5233, M, Radio Operator, Newport, Wales, 08/12/44</u>
My wife was very nervous about me going, though she admitted that, with 8 million people constantly living in London, the mathematical chances of my getting hurt were not very great. She could not repress her fears however, & she worked on my own so much that, not only might I have called the thing off if it hadn't been my last chance to go in 1944, but when I got there I was so V2-conscious that a backfiring car would make me start violently & only felt really comfortable when in the Underground. As a matter of fact I did not hear a single explosion while I was there.

<u>Diarist 5337, F, Housewife, Fritwell, Oxfordshire, 08/12/44</u>
Had a pathetic letter from Peggy T. whose elder splendid boy was killed in Sept to tell me the second Boy who is a great friend of Bay's is home badly wounded in the head, they hope they will save his sight. Oh, the sadness everywhere, it all seems like a hideous nightmare sometimes, and now they seem to think the War will continue till next summer, who will be left?

<u>Diarist 5324, F, Hostel Worker, Gloucester, Gloucestershire, 09/12/44</u>
We have raised our blackout here and funnily enough we are not sure whether we like it or not. The police said we could have the curtains undrawn to guide people outside. It is alright outside, but inside it seemed uncosy. In the foyer and dining hall the uncovered windows seemed to play on our unconscious mind as we found ourselves constantly looking towards them with the sort of feeling that we were being naughty.

Diarist 5186, M, Shorthand Typist, Woking, Surrey, 13/12/44

In this part of the country, as I expect in many rural districts letters to be posted are often left tucked in the letter box or in some other convenient place for the postman or postgirl to collect. My Aunt wrote in a note to me 'The birds have begun to chew the letters put out for posting. Miss Cartwright rang today and shewed me two nearly opened and a bit of a 2½d. stamp gone.' I suppose there is far less put out for them than heretofore and the cold weather finds them without sufficient provisions. Unfortunately they are not the only ones in that predicament.

Diarist 5284, F, Nurse, Leeds, 18/12/44

June & Margaret went to town to see father Xmas at Lewisses. Pity that mean old devil couldn't have found something in the way of presents for children. When he does give them presents after the war, they'll die of shock, all these 3 year olds!

Diarist 5331, F, Shop Assistant, Dewsbury, West Yorkshire, 23/12/44

Bread came at half past nine last night so got up early to get off orders. (400 teacakes.) Then we cleared a space for if oranges <u>did</u> come. Unusually slack until nearly twelve. Everyone off into Dewsbury seeking oranges. There were ugly scenes. Not enough to go round. Only getting two per customer & then had to buy a basketful of vegetables. A pound of nuts if you spent 10/6, at one place. At one shop there was a free-for-all fight & the police had to be fetched. Our own customers drifted in after dinner, chastened & orangeless, resigned to waiting until after Xmas when there will be plenty.

<u>Diarist 5110, M, Vicar, Boston, Lincolnshire, 24/12/44</u>
Awakened by an alert at 5.50. Almost at once flying bombs started to come over. I said to myself: 'Arthur Leslie I would rather be blown up in comfort than die of a chill,' & so I turned over & went to sleep. Awakened just after 6.0am by the all clear, & I said 'Arthur Leslie, you've been wise,' & turned over to sleep again.

12. PLANS ARE BEING MADE AND SHELVED CONTINUALLY

January to August 1945

'It is a breathless time; news of normally worldwide importance causes barely a headline, and is soon forgotten in later happenings. There is suppressed excitement everywhere. Plans are being made and shelved continually, nothing seems stable.'

Victory! Or, rather, two brief moments of victory surrounded by months of exertion, trepidation and complication. From January to May the British public witness military success after military success, and by March the last doodlebugs have fallen and the home front is no longer a war zone. 'Victory in Europe' (VE Day) is declared by a tipsy, bunting-clad nation on the eighth of May but it takes three more months and two atomic bombs before 'Victory over Japan' (VJ Day) on the fifteenth of August. In the interim, a general election sees a shock result, with Churchill and the Conservatives voted out in favour of Clement Attlee's Labour party.

For those on the home front it has been six long years. Some fall prey to exhaustion and apathy but many others are directing new energy to thoughts of Life After the War. Across the nation they're preoccupied with big questions: who will govern them? How should Germany be punished? How will Europe be rebuilt, and who will pay for it? Many crave recompense for what they've been through – some want revenge, some want reform, but most just want easy access to plentiful food and to quietly pursue a life of their own. Behind these practical questions sit nebulous monsters (the horrors of Auschwitz and Belsen and the existence of weapons of mass destruction) and great hopes (the welfare state and burgeoning NHS, the United Nations). They punctuate a great mass of tangled feelings – joy, relief, anger, apprehension, sadness, resolve, fear, faith – all inextricable, and utterly human.

* * *

Diarist 5331, F, Shop Assistant, Dewsbury, West Yorkshire, 08/01/45
To W.V.S. Arrangements made to take evacuees to panto. Surprised to learn there are still 95 in our district. 15 out of the

25 rest centres are to be closed in Dewsbury. Ours – one of the 'stars' is to remain open. We have been warned to turn up immediately after any local blitz there may be.

Diarist 5216, M, Research Chemist, Broxbourne, Hertfordshire, 08/01/45
One of the V2s was within a mile of the works, and there were at least six more today, making me rather uneasy. Being under fire may be a stimulant to a soldier, but even in this diffuse way it is a bad influence rather than an ennobling one on an ordinary civilian.

Diarist 5240, F, Teacher, Watford, Hertfordshire, 09/01/45
On my way home at teatime, the snow was dry & crisp & very pleasant to walk on. In this road, twenty people at least were out, sweeping & shovelling the snow from the pavement. One neighbour said to me: 'I've been saying I wish it were sugar.'

Diarist 5403, F, News Office Worker, Evesham, Worcestershire, 17/01/45
Correspondents are now using superlatives about the Russian offensive – 'the greatest in this war' and even 'the greatest in the history of modern warfare'. They are so sure and so unanimous about it that there can be little doubt that this really is the Big Push of all Big Pushes. It's taken everyone so completely by surprise that they hardly express any opinion, but some people are beginning to talk about the end of the war being a good deal nearer that we thought in the gloomy days at Christmas.

Diarist 5205, M, Laboratory Technician, Potters Bar, Hertfordshire, 26/01/45

Weather colder still, colder than I ever remember, I think. It is an unfortunate coincidence that this cold spell has come when the fuel shortage is most acute. We had our electricity cut off for about twenty minutes the other morning. I feel especially sorry for the bombed-out, or rather, for those who are not quite bombed-out, but have to live in houses with windows or doors missing and with cracks in the walls and holes in the roof and sometimes without coal for the fire.

Diarist 5401, F, PR in Aircraft Factory, Slough, Berkshire, 03/02/45

Washed my hair tonight. Don't remember doing this for at least 2 years and maybe 3 – (I don't mean that my hair hasn't been washed for 3 years!) S. had embarkation leave last weekend, I had to cancel my appointment. Impossible to get another fitted in during the week & my next one booked 3 weeks ahead so I decided I must do something about it myself. Found a 'Camilatone' shampoo & Golden Rinse stored away with astonishing & heart-lifting assortment of five hairpins, Kirby grips, setting combs & curlers & what not and remains of Amami setting lotion. All real treasure. Took me over an hour to wash & set hair – Am now sitting in front of kitchen fire listening to late dance music – Also turned out my soap & toilet roll store (Toilet rolls & sanitary towels now very difficult to buy I am told – I always keep a store of both but will have to see about replenishing.) Soap I have in quantity.

Diarist 5198, M, Woodworking Machinist, Enfield, Middlesex, 06/02/45

Bombs! Bombs!! Bombs!!!

The news headlines sicken me. It is revolting to think of hideous position in Berlin now. After all, they are human beings.

Diarist 5358, F, ATS Clerk, Grays, Essex, 06/02/45

The gratuities to be awarded to the forces on demobilisation have been announced. They are quite generous, and added to the post-war credits and the leave pay, will comprise a respectable sum, even for the lowly private. Once again, however, the old distinction creeps in – A.T.S. are to receive two-thirds as much as the men. I am not a feminist, but I do like to see equal pay for equal work. At the Headquarters where I work in London, A.T.S. work side by side with soldiers unfit for overseas service, doing exactly the same work and duties. Why should these men receive half as much again as the girls?

Diarist 5068, M, Cost Clerk and Special Constable, Beverley, East Riding of Yorkshire, 11/02/45

Mr. M. [the refugee] is no further on with his arrangements to return to France. The passport people are apparently not satisfied with his proof of British nationality & are requiring him to produce his birth certificate. He has written to Somerset House & they can't find it, so his next move will be to write to the police at South Shields (where he first came to live on his arrival in 1940) & ask if they can tell him on what evidence they accepted him as British. He has never held a British passport. I suppose it is possible that he is British by French law and French by British. If so he is in a jam. Of course, if he has not accepted the responsibilities of any nationality he can't claim the benefits!

Diarist 5303, F, ATS Typist (hospitalised), Stanmore, Middlesex, 11/02/45

Spent the afternoon thinking in the canteen about going home. If only my mother would, or could stand the rockets – everything would be simple. Oh, isn't everything a bloody mess!! I know plenty are far worse off than me, but I get so cheesed! The absolute futility of living seems to grow on me. My trouble is that I don't <u>want</u> anything very badly – I don't particularly want a husband – I haven't any ambition – and I haven't a belief in anything – I shall probably come to a sticky end!!

Diarist 5402, F, Retired Teacher, Great Missenden, Buckinghamshire, 12/02/45

An Xmas Cake arrived from a cousin in Australia: even the lettering on the icing is practically intact. It's very nice to have it, but I think that shipping space should not be allowed for private parcels.

Diarist 5004, M, ARP Worker and Food Packing Manager, Belmont, Surrey, 18/02/45

I was interested to read in the 'Observer' that France's zeal for immediate reforms is waning – the French people have got tired of trying French collaborators, and in politics are moving from the Left to 'mid-Right'. In the first flush of victory England and other countries are likely to do just the same. 'Reform, reform' will be the cry to echo through the land, but as the people settle down to earning a living, all the driving forces which initiated reforms under the stress of war will be lost, and we will be more concerned with work, and our surplus leisure will be devoted to pleasure.

<u>Diarist 5039.2, M, Factory Worker and Volunteer Fireman,</u>
<u>Mansfield, Nottinghamshire, 27/02/45</u>
Heard P.M's speech on wireless. Disliked his reference to armed League of Nations. Mentally, the nations of the world are not ready for a League of Nations, however desirable that may be, and a League made up of strongly armed nations, will be a menace to the peace of the world. <u>Let everyone disarm completely.</u>

<u>Diarist 5443, F, Office Worker and Volunteer Mobile Canteen</u>
<u>Driver, London, 06/03/45</u>
This evening we went to see 'Meet the Navy', and although I don't care for revue, I thought this absolutely first-class, it reminded me of a slick Hollywood musical film, so grand were the costumes, scenery and effects. The comedians were funny, the chorus attractive, altho' I couldn't get used to seeing so many men dancing on the stage – we have seen our rather elderly choruses, menless, for nearly 6 years and have got used to them.

<u>Diarist 5261, F, Factory Clerk, Manchester, 08/03/45</u>
The Rhine has been crossed! This amazing news was given out at 9-o-clock. It is a surprise to me & to Dad also. It's not often Dad gets excited over news, but he said this called for a celebration & I think that if it wasn't that he hated the stuff he would have gone out & celebrated in beer. I should love to see Hitler at this moment.

<u>Diarist 5296, F, Housewife, Gateshead, Tyne and Wear, 11/03/45</u>

<u>Old people</u> – poor, poor souls! – Euthanasia? Both Tom & I & many more 'hope' 'twill be in force when we grow infirm. – For all my children's 4 grandparents (strong) have had long hard 'dyings'.

<u>Diarist 5447, F, Clerk and Housewife, Sheffield, 12/03/45</u>

Husband's 2 aged aunts both dead. Were taken to hospital last week, both over 80. One died Sat. afternoon, other Sunday morn (yesterday), so a joint funeral is being had tomorrow, which is a blessing. [. . .] Now someone will have a job clearing up their house, bung full of Victorian furniture. Wonder to whom they have left everything. Poor old dears, present furniture shortage will make their stuff more valuable than it wd have been otherwise.

<u>Diarist 5110, M, Vicar, Boston, Lincolnshire, 17/03/45</u>

Today has been CUT RATION day. Some of the daily papers have hinted that our rations have got to be cut again, and this is not popular with anyone, men and women alike. The line that is being taken is that we have put up with so much, isn't it time for someone else to put up with something. Troops coming home on leave are not telling the story of real shortages in the occupied countries that people had expected, and they bring home such wonderful presents that people are saying, why cannot the people in such countries spend more time growing food instead of being able to sell our men such goods at fancy prices. There may be a perfectly good answer to these points, but the government ought to give them to us, as otherwise I can see a nasty situation arising. There is a strong feeling that the foreign countries expect to be fed by us, while they make money out of us by selling luxury goods to our men.

Diarist 5331, F, Shop Assistant, Dewsbury, West Yorkshire, 27/03/45

What if there is no end to the war? If it just peters out? What about flag waving then? I can see it's going to be different to last time when everyone went mad. I do believe we've learned a bit of sense since then. Anyway, there are no flags to buy.

Diarist 5186, M, Shorthand Typist, Woking, Surrey, 30/03/45

I consider it a fallacy that a country can spend its way back to prosperity. Certainly spending money does help to cause employment, but is the community any better off, I very much doubt it.

Diarist 5378, F, Writer, Farmer and Housewife, Campbeltown, Argyll, 05/04/45

Stormy weather. I met horrible Ian S. who said something about Lois and the ATS to which I replied about the good thing it was for girls to leave home and be on their own a little. After a few remarks of, I suppose, a prickly kind, he said 'We men like our women to be a little effeminate.' It was in a way a merely comic remark, but annoyed me so much that I said to him that this was only true of remote and ignorant places such as Carradale and that he could no more speak of 'we men' than I could of 'we women. I do dislike him acutely and obviously he thinks of himself as a dominant male; he dances roughly even if one is dancing with him in a reel, which spoils a dance completely for me, he hauls everyone round.

<u>Diarist 5358, F, ATS Clerk, Grays, Essex, 17/04/45</u>

Events are moving at an astonishing rate. I feel as if I am poised on a precipice, waiting for the signal to start off on the giddy plunge into 'after the war'. It is a breathless time; news of normally worldwide importance causes barely a headline, and is soon forgotten in later happenings. There is suppressed excitement everywhere. Plans are being made and shelved continually, nothing seems stable. I find myself thinking of inconsequential things – for instance, I have an insane desire to buy a new swimsuit, the first for six years; I want a two-piece, in a vivid colour, and hang the waste of coupons! I also have a fervent wish that this will be my last summer in uniform. The sudden heatwave revives the old discomfort of serge skirt, thick stockings and heavy shoes, not noticed in cooler weather.

These trivial thoughts, when such big issues are at stake!

<u>Diarist 5399, F, Retired Nurse, Steyning, West Sussex, 19/04/45</u>

This morning I saw the sun which had just risen, and it was shining direct into my kitchen. I had looked at it through the window and noted it would be a fine day, when, as I turned to go out of the room, I passed right across the rays, level as they were with the room. I turned instinctively to do what I always do when I leave a room – turn off the light. Imagine it. I had got so used to the blackout and turning off the lights that I, for a moment, went to turn off the sun.

<u>Diarist 5233, M, Radio Operator, Newport, Wales, 20/04/45</u>

All the newspapers emphasise the horror disclosed in the captured German concentration camps at Buchenwald, Belsen & elsewhere. They all say that public opinion has been profoundly shocked, but the News Chronicle points out that it knew these things & reported them long before the war & reprints a selection of headlines. It says that the public was wilfully blind & just refused to believe these things because it did not want to. I suppose this is largely true.

Diarist 5270, F, Office Worker, Heswall, Merseyside, 21/04/45

Mrs. V., middle-aged typist, with children at school remarks slowly: 'There's only one thing to do with the German people. Our men should use flame-throwers on every town and village they come to, and wipe them all out. Show no mercy.'

Mrs. G., about 24 yrs old, married, one child, husband fighting in Germany: 'Yes, but they won't do that. Our fellows fraternise with the Germans and feel sorry for them, because they're women and kids without homes. They won't see that it's those people who are responsible for such awful things.' (Incidentally, Mrs. G's husband smuggled home a pile of looted articles from Germany, including leather gloves, mirror, knitted wear, child's doll, etc. and a very lovely tablecloth. 'He said there was glassware and sewing machines and all sorts, lying about the streets, all the men were picking up what they could carry, to send home. There were no Germans left to claim the stuff.')

Diarist 5307, F, Stenographer, Birmingham, 29/04/45

I still can't grasp or believe that the actual war itself is nearly over – I suppose few people with the ordinary size of imagination or 'soul' can rise to an occasion of this size so as to experience it fully.

<u>Diarist 5331, F, Shop Assistant, Dewsbury, West Yorkshire,</u>
<u>01/05/45</u>

B.H. came in this morning in a bad temper because her husband, H.H (bus inspector) supposedly enjoying his weekly 'day off' was sitting glued to the wireless waiting for peace to be declared. He had, upon hearing that, to rush down to the bus station to make arrangements for taking the work people home (drivers & conductors to be bribed with extra pay to do this) then the buses to cease – anyone not a worker who happens to be from home will be stranded. Never heard anything so daft. It's going to be as bad as the general strike.

<u>Diarist 5240, F, Teacher, Watford, Hertfordshire, 02/05/45</u>

I noticed the 11.30 a.m. siren test bell, although it is almost a habit not to notice. Then the 11 a.m. news said that no more sirens were to be sounded, & we wondered if we should ever hear the tests again. We shall miss them.

<u>Diarist 5205, M, Laboratory Technician, Potters Bar,</u>
<u>Hertfordshire, 03/05/45</u>

I asked Mrs. H. what she would do when peace was declared. She said, 'I shan't do anything. Some'll go mad. Others will just heave a sigh of relief, like myself. I don't think there's much sense in celebrating while we're still at war with Japan. There's been too much tragedy in this war, for civilians as well; there's not much to celebrate . . . I might have a drink.'

<u>Diarist 5324, F, Hostel Worker, Gloucester, Gloucestershire, 04/05/45</u>

Tonight B, A & E (my workmates) & myself discussed whether we should get drunk on V-day. As none of us have ever done so we thought it was a suitable opportunity to 'try anything once'. We have decided we shan't worry a snap of the fingers as to what our bosses & the residents think then and we have as much right on that day to be uncivilised as anyone else.

<u>Diarist 5307, F, Stenographer, Birmingham, 07/05/45</u>

The room we were in began to get very noisy and smoky – the people were singing songs of the last war, mostly, but in rather a laboured and not very spontaneous way – so we moved into a quieter one at the back and had another round. The last comers told us the Nine o'clock news, which confirmed what we already knew. Mrs. D., who had won the post sweep by drawing the nearest date to the actual date of announcement, was handed her winnings, and bought another round with it. Our eyes got pricky and our heads just a shade muzzy. [. . .] The head warden, I might add, read us the last Divisional Order, which told us we were all released [from the ARP] as from that date and mentioned Victory Parades. 'But they can't COMPEL us to attend them' said the Junior Man Warden happily.

<u>Diarist 5443, F, Office Worker and Volunteer Mobile Canteen Driver, 08/05/45</u>

This evening Pop, Joyce, and I went up to town about 8 o'clock, arriving at Charing Cross just before 9, where we heard the King's speech, watched the seething, pushing crowds in Trafalgar Square, with Pop saying the whole time 'My this is nothing like the crowd on Armistice night 1918,' the whole trying to get through the vast mob of people. Then we went on down to Woolwich, where on the parade ground, the R.A. band gave a concert, and the barracks and academy were floodlit and we had a searchlight display which was quite thrilling, in a peacetime way. The band played until 11.45 and the vast crowd sang last-war songs and hymns and danced then the soldiers from the garrison put on a firework display which was reminiscent of the Blitz, with hand-grenades and verey lights [flares] going off and rockets and various other noisy fireworks adding to the din. Several children around were frightened, thinking no doubt it was a raid, but the men loved it.

Diarist 5076, M, Accountant and Volunteer Police Constable, Sheffield, 08/05/45

In January 1941 we purchased some tinned chicken, and as we have never been called upon to use it, we promised ourselves a treat on Peace Day, and we did open it today. As with many things, it proved somewhat of a disappointment, for although it is genuine chicken; – bones, skin and meat – it is spoilt by aspic jelly. Another long-cherished tin, of sausages purchased in November 1940, proved much more acceptable for lunch.

Diarist 5110, M, Vicar, Boston, Lincolnshire, 08/05/45

I was entranced looking out of the window at the Countryside. There was hardly a house without some kind of flag or decoration. I saw several old German Imperial Flags, & wondered if the owners knew what they had put up. Reached London too late for me to catch the 10.10 from Kings Cross as I was hoping to do. So I walked from Waterloo to Kings Cross. Crowds, plenty of them.

Happy contented crowds. Crowds out to see as much as they could; but how different they were from the crowds that I saw when I was on leave on Nov 11th, 1918. They were enjoying themselves just as much, perhaps more. They were crowds who had tasted the horrors of war, & knew that they had been delivered from a great peril.

<u>Diarist 5378, F, Writer, Farmer and Housewife, Campbeltown, Argyll, 08/05/45</u>

Then we went off to Piccadilly Circus, where we met Av looking as untidy as ever. I bought a small USSR flag for Val she was wearing a blue skirt, light blue blouse and red silk scarf and looked beautiful. I didn't get any myself but wore my croix de Lorraine. She put hers in her hair. We had lunch at the Cafe at 12.45. It wasn't very full or decorated, nor did the people look special in any way. But when we got out there was quite a crowd. The children had wanted to go to the Zoo but Pic Circ seemed better, so we wandered along slowly, looking on. A number of other people were doing the same thing, in fact almost everyone was tired and wanting to look rather than do.

<u>Diarist 5390, F, Secretary, United States War Shipping Administration, Glasgow, 09/05/45</u>

I feel like writing 'absolutely nothing happened' and 'I am too tired to write about it in any case,' Anti-climax I suppose. Miss S. over her evening paper at 5 'How dull the papers are today' (and remember we have had no papers since yesterday morning). That too would be anti-climax I suppose. The terrific tension that preceded VE Day has obviously left us limp. I feel that nothing that ever happens in my life to come can mean so much as the victory over Germany. Surely this is the highest spot in our nation's history. I used to think the defeat of the Spanish Armada was high spot No. 1, and I dare say the defeat of Napoleon was high spot no. 2. But this triumph! Oh I am proud, but I am tired too.

Diarist 5243, F, Clerk, Blackpool, Lancashire, 19/05/45
The Saturday before Whitsun – and an influx of visitors into the town (Blackpool), but not the number expected. Can it be that the Blackpool 'boom' is over? It's been a lovely war for the hotels and boarding houses here, in addition to the masses of Lancashire folk for whom 'Blackpool' and 'holiday' are synonymous, many others who would normally go to the East coast or the South have had to come to Blackpool. In the main Blackpool has used her monopoly in a way which does her no credit and I hope they will 'feel the draught' this season.

Diarist 5393, F, Music Teacher, Boscastle, Cornwall, 24/05/45
The Coalition was formed when the country was in danger when we needed to sink all party differences & pull together for the common cause. It seems to us strange that only a _war_ should necessitate this 'pulling together' & sinking of party differences & that the coming years are going to be every bit as dangerous in some ways & the need is every bit as great as during the war.

Diarist 5447, F, Clerk and Housewife, Sheffield, 03/06/45
A thing and a thing, TWO ugly things, – who will tell us where to dump civilian gas masks and fireguard tin hats? They just take up room now. I'll be glad of the space in this flat.

<u>Diarist 5270, F, Office Worker, Heswall, Merseyside, 05/06/45</u>
Conversation turned to pre-war summer holidays by the sea, 'when the weather used to be lovely'. (The War seems to be blamed even for the disgusting weather we are getting this year!)

<u>Diarist 5401, F, Technical Journalist for Aircraft Factory, Slough, Berkshire, 18/06/45</u>
This woman was hot on the subject of our feeding Europe, 'We are having to do it because the Americans won't. Why should we? We've gone without willingly all through the war because we've known it's been going to Our Boys. But <u>why</u> should we feed Europe. I resent the idea of helping the Germans or the French ... Though the Dutch I do think have done a good job ... But I have a family of young children to feed & I think the essential foods should at least go to them first.'

But we have not starved during the war, as Aunt Aggie says, we have never gone <u>hungry</u> – There are some people who in all seriousness thought that as soon as the war ended the shops would be filled with pre-war goods & we should be free to buy what we liked.

<u>Diarist 5110, M, Vicar, Boston, Lincolnshire, 04/07/45</u>
I mentioned to a Dr. today what a lot of illness there seems to be about, & he says that since VE Day there has been a very great amount of work for Drs, he puts it down to the sudden relaxation of tension. It is mostly tummy troubles.

Diarist 5076, M, Accountant and Volunteer Police Constable, Sheffield, 15/07/45

Both my wife and I disliked putting the clock back by an hour so early in the summer. Double Summer Time has been one of the two blessings of the war in our opinion, the other being the disappearance of private motoring.

Diarist 5243, F, Clerk, Blackpool, Lancashire, 16/07/45

This is the first day of the meeting of the Big Three at Potsdam. President Truman's first attempt and I feel he has America behind him.

The decisions taken at this meeting will be of paramount importance and yet not one person has mentioned the meeting to me today – people seem more interested in home affairs. What government are we going to have and when will things begin to get going here.

Diarist 5303, F, ATS Typist (hospitalised), Stanmore, Middlesex, 17/07/45

Treatment this morning. Had a discussion with my masseuse. She said that it didn't matter about improving conditions of people, because if they were used to them, they wouldn't realise, and wouldn't be unhappy – a lot of rot! She's the most negative person I have met. Like a lot of people, she reads about previous centuries, but as <u>all</u> books appear to have been written from the aristocracy's point of view, life appears good. I told her if I had to go back a hundred years and be an aristocrat I wouldn't mind, but if I had to go back as the working class – would I like it hell?!! One of the so-called 'lower orders'.

Diarist 5216, M, Research Chemist, Broxbourne, Hertfordshire, 06/08/45

Announcement of the atomic bomb has caused a lot of talk, I do not think it more immoral to kill lots of civilians with one bomb than with a thousand, so it seems to me to make only a lesser difference to the wrongness of all war.

Diarist 5240, F, Teacher, Watford, Hertfordshire, 08/08/45

At the chiropodist's, the talk turned upon mankind in general, & though the atom bomb was not mentioned, I am sure that it was in his mind when he said, 'I do not think we shall ever be free from wars. Man is such a fool he will never learn to control himself & the forces he uses.'

Diarist 5447, F, Clerk and Housewife, Sheffield, 08/08/45

Papers and BBC say grapefruit has arrived for Scotland – why not say where from? A little thing, but all helps to waken folk to the world beyond these borders. I see that my country [South Africa] has offered this country some thousands of tons of meat, cheese, fruit, jam and sugar. Let us hope the new Food Minister will get the ships for transporting it, as it is no use us howling for food if ships are not available.

Diarist 5372, F, Housewife, Sevenoaks, Kent, 09/08/45

Atomic bomb. Well, if scientists are not drowned at birth, suppose the sooner we polish ourselves off the better. Preferable to days, months & years of nagging air-attack anyway. Don't feel shall ever get over that.

<u>Diarist 5403, F, News Office Worker, Evesham, Worcestershire,</u>
<u>10/08/45</u>

First news of the Japanese surrender rocked London today. The reaction was immediate – cheering crowds at lunchtime; storms of paper floating down from windows; in the evening VE-night scenes in Piccadilly Circus. Rumours that surrender was 'unconditional' spread like wildfire. No one knew exactly what the position was, but the amount of spontaneous enthusiasm was amazing. On the other hand, many people treated the reports with reserve and refused to get excited until they heard more definite news. I did not feel any of the VE-day enthusiasm myself. The atmosphere was totally different and I have never been able to feel that the Pacific war touched me nearly.

<u>Diarist 5399, F, Retired Nurse, Steyning, West Sussex, 12/08/45</u>

I feel rather happy today, because I have been able to do an act of justice to someone who has served this little community through the war. The milkman who brings milk to this estate, which is ten minutes' walk from the High St and rest of the town, has pushed a heavy milk-cart up the hill seven days a week throughout the war. Not a day off till the last week or two, and never missed a day, seven days a week. I have helped him push the truck some days, when coming up at the same time. He came through the heavy rain or deep snow, and he looks bowed and thin almost as if in the last stage of TB. I spoke to one or two women up here, and they agreed it would be a nice thing if we collected a small subscription for him. I went to everyone here (that is, every HOUSE – some were not in –) and asked them. Mentioned anything from 3d to a shilling, and have got one pound sixteen shillings.

Diarist 5076, M, Accountant and Volunteer Police Constable, Sheffield, 15/08/45

The sound of fireworks woke me from a deep sleep early in the morning, but I was merely annoyed at them, thinking they were a continuance of those I had heard last night. I got up as usual, prepared for the office, and over breakfast switched on the 8.0 a.m. news. I was quite surprised to hear that the Jap offer had been accepted, and still more astonished to learn that today and tomorrow were to be general holidays. This latter news was of more practical importance to us at the moment than the end of the war, and both my wife and I suffered from an illogical sense of annoyance about the shortness of the notice.

Diarist 5243, F, Clerk, Blackpool, Lancashire, 15/08/45

Travelling from Blackpool to Wolverhampton wasn't too bad – it was good to be home and to know that the War is really over now. But what would bring it home to me more than anything else would be if I could return to London or definitely be told where our final location will be. Then I could arrange to move my family there and I could live in a home (and not a billet) again. Then I really should believe the war was over.

Diarist 5270, F, Office Worker, Merseyside, Cheshire, 25/08/45

The chief troublemaker in the office – a married woman whose husband is a surveyor – told us this morning that she was not going to apply for her release (none of the married women, here, have done so) – as she felt that her job 'couldn't be taken over by anyone inexperienced'. Having delivered that howler, she then told us that she had been 'discussing things' with the manager yesterday. 'We had quite a nice little chat about the work, and the future of this place' she smiled. I thought that one of the girls was going to throw something at the woman, she looked angry. We knew what that 'cosy little chat' had been about.

Diarist 5045, M, Retired Nurseryman, Brighton, East Sussex, 30/08/45

I was never of the pessimistic school who held that the Jap war would go on for years after the German one, but I did give it another year to run. One can hardly believe that the years of war are indeed over. For my own part it really makes little difference. It may speed up my prospects for emigrating to Canada eventually, but I still find the subject of emigration one that is not given much prominence anywhere. First it was the end of War in Europe, then the election, next the end of Jap war and now the sudden termination of Lease Lend that seems uppermost in everyone's mind and therefore the subject of comment in all the press. Demobilisation, housing, exports and food all crowd up for examination and so I look like yet having a long period of possessing my soul in patience until the all-important question as far as I and my family is concerned gains the attention of the Powers that be.

EPILOGUE – SEPTEMBER 1945

<u>Diarist 5460, F, Railway Clerk, Newport, Wales, 18/09/45</u>
Katherine is nine months old today. The war is over. It is difficult
to believe it. The celebrations here for VJ day were the same as
for VE day – bonfires, flags, and green bowers built around the
doors of the houses in the poorer districts – but the war had
become both remote and in other ways unending. I did not expect
life to be different but I cannot feel the war really over until it is.
If it ever is.

FURTHER READING

A selection of anthologies

Wartime Women: A Mass-Observation Anthology – Dorothy
    Sheridan (1990)
* Diarist 5284, 'Amy Briggs'
* Diarist 5324, 'Muriel Green'
* Diarist 5353, Nella Last
* Diarist 5390, 'Pam Ashford'/'Miss French'
* Diarist 5423, 'Mrs Trowbridge'

*Our Hidden Lives: The Remarkable Diaries of Post-War
    Britain, 1945–1948* – Simon Garfield (2004)
* Diarist 5076, 'Cyril Gardner'
* Diarist 5401, 'Maggie Joy Blunt'/Jean Lucey Pratt
* Diarist 5447, 'Edie Rutherford'

*We Are At War: The Diaries of Five Ordinary People in
    Extraordinary Times* – Simon Garfield (2005)
* Diarist 5212, 'Christopher Tomlin'
* Diarist 5390, 'Pam Ashford'/'Miss French'
* Diarist 5396, 'Tilly Rice'
* Diarist 5401, 'Maggie Joy Blunt'/Jean Lucey Pratt

Private Battles, How the War Almost Defeated Us: Our Intimate Diaries – Simon Garfield (2006)
* Diarist 5205, Edward Stebbing
* Diarist 5216, Ernest van Someren
* Diarist 5390, 'Pam Ashford'/'Miss French'
* Diarist 5401, 'Maggie Joy Blunt'/Jean Lucey Pratt

Our Longest Days: A People's History of the Second World War – Sandra Koa Wing (2008)
* Diarist 5165, Henry Novy
* Diarist 5210, 'Peter Baxter'
* Diarist 5212, 'Christopher Tomlin'
* Diarist 5324, 'Muriel Green'
* Diarist 5341, 'Doris Melling'
* Diarist 5353, Nella Last
* Diarist 5401, 'Maggie Joy Blunt'/Jean Lucey Pratt
* Diarist 5447, 'Edie Rutherford'

A selection of standalone diaries

Among You Taking Notes: The Wartime Diary of Naomi Mitchison, 1939–1945 – ed. Dorothy Sheridan (1985)
* Diarist 5378, Naomi Mitchison

Nella Last's War: The Second World War Diaries of 'Housewife, 49' – ed. Richard Broad and Suzy Fleming (2006)
* Diarist 5353, Nella Last

Nella Last's Peace: The Post-War Diaries Of 'Housewife, 49' – ed. Patricia and Robert Malcolmson (2008)
* Diarist 5353, Nella Last

Nella Last in the 1950s: The Further Diaries of 'Housewife, 49'
   – ed. Patricia and Robert Malcolmson (2010)
* Diarist 5353, Nella Last

A Notable Woman: The Romantic Journals of Jean Lucey Pratt
   – ed. Simon Garfield (2015)
* Diarist 5401, 'Maggie Joy Blunt'/Jean Lucey Pratt

The View from the Corner Shop: The Diary of a Yorkshire Shop Assistant in Wartime – Kathleen Hey, ed. Patricia and Robert Malcolmson (2016)
* Diarist 5331, Kathleen Hey

ACKNOWLEDGEMENTS

The hours I spent in the written company of MO's Observers were a pleasure and a privilege; their honesty, foresight and equanimity will always seem extraordinary to me. I am grateful to the University of Sussex for making their writings, and the rest of the Archive, available for research. I owe an enormous debt of gratitude to Tom Hockenhull, who faithfully transcribed all the extracts in this book. His unwavering support, fearsome intellect and bad jokes were essential, as indeed they always are. I am thankful too for the creative counsel and general brilliance of my friends and colleagues at Curtis Brown – Lisa Babalis, Niall Harman, Lucy Morris and Norah Perkins – and for the wisdom of the aptly-named Gordon Wise. I would also like to thank my editor Rupert Lancaster, Cameron Myers and all the team at Hodder, and am indebted to Jacqui Lewis for her meticulous copyediting. Finally, I am unendingly grateful for my family; Kate Brown, for always understanding; my parents, Steve and Vanessa, for a formative diet of *Dad's Army* and Judith Kerr; and my grandparents, Gifford and Jennifer Brown, whose childhood memories of the war filled me with wonder when I was very small.

PICTURE ACKNOWLEDGEMENTS

Chapter 1: © Evening Standard/Getty Images

Chapter 2: © Northcliffe Collection/ANL/Shutterstock

Chapter 3: © Hulton-Deutsch Collection/CORBIS/Corbis via Getty Images

Chapter 4: © Hulton-Deutsch Collection/CORBIS/Corbis via Getty Images

Chapter 5: © Hulton-Deutsch Collection/CORBIS/Corbis via Getty Images

Chapter 6: © George W. Hales/Fox Photos/Getty Images

Chapter 7: © Hulton Archive/Getty Images

Chapter 8: © AP/Shutterstock

Chapter 9: © Keystone/Getty Images

Chapter 10: © Hans Wild/The LIFE Picture Collection via Getty Images

Chapter 11: © Popperfoto via Getty Images/Getty Images

Chapter 12: © TopFoto